The Early Black History Movement, Carter G. Woodson, and Lorenzo Johnston Greene

Pero Gaglo Dagbovie

UNIVERSITY OF ILLINOIS PRESS

URBANA AND CHICAGO

∞ This book is printed on acid-free paper.

Library of Congress Cataloging-in-Publication Data
Dagbovie, Pero Gaglo.
The early Black history movement, Carter G. Woodson, and Lorenzo Johnston Greene / Pero Gaglo Dagbovie.
p. cm. — (The new Black studies series)
Includes bibliographical references and index.
ISBN-13 978-0-252-03190-8 (cloth : alk. paper)
ISBN-10 0-252-03190-3 (cloth : alk. paper)
ISBN-13 978-0-252-07435-6 (pbk. : alk. paper)
ISBN-10 0-252-07435-1 (pbk. : alk. paper)
1. Woodson, Carter Godwin, 1875–1950.
2. Greene, Lorenzo Johnston, 1899–
3. African American historians—Biography.
4. Historians—United States—Biography.
5. African Americans—Historiography.
6. Historiography—United States—History—20th century.
I. Title.
E185.97.W65D34 2007
973'.049607307202—dc22 2007005065

The Early Black History Movement, Carter G. Woodson, and Lorenzo Johnston Greene

THE NEW BLACK STUDIES SERIES

Edited by Darlene Clark Hine and Dwight A. McBride

A list of books in the series appears at the end of this book.

For my parents (Prospero Y. Dagbovie and Frances R. Dagbovie), ancestors, and teachers, and for the generations of African American historians, scholars, and freedom fighters who laid the foundations for me.

To you, then, comes the challenge as to what you will do in building upon the foundation which they have laid. These people whose civilization was marked by the kerosene lamp, the wash tub, the hoe, and the ox-cart disappointed the prophets who said they would be exterminated; and on the contrary they enrolled themselves among the great. What will you do in the day of the moving picture, the radio, and the aeroplane? If we do not take hold where they left off and advance further in the service of truth and justice, we are unworthy to claim descent from such a noble people.

—CARTER G. WOODSON, "THE HERITAGE OF THE NEGRO"

If you ever feel discouraged
Success striving to attain,
If you feel that toil is useless
That the sacrifice in vain—
Contemplate the rare old masters,
Men who writ their names on high,
Learn their rise to heights was not like
Meteors flashing cross the sky.
But from humble, mean beginnings,
And through years of toil they came,
Climbing, day by day, life's ladder,
Rung, by rung, to lasting fame.
From their lives, faint heart, take courage,
Fame is not won overnight;
Grit your teeth and keep on plodding,
You will win, if you but fight.

—LORENZO JOHNSTON GREENE, "EXHORTATION"

Every generation has the opportunity to write its own history, and indeed it is obliged to do so. Only in that way can it provide its contemporaries with the materials vital to understanding the present and to planning strategies for coping with the future. Only in that way can it fulfill its obligation to pass on to posterity the accumulated knowledge and wisdom of the past, which, after all, give substance and direction for the continuity of civilization.

—JOHN HOPE FRANKLIN, "ON THE EVOLUTION OF SCHOLARSHIP ON AFRO-AMERICAN HISTORY"

CONTENTS

PREFACE

This book is about Carter G. Woodson (1875–1950), "The Father of Black History," and Lorenzo Johnston Greene (1899–1988), longtime history professor at Lincoln University, Lincoln, Missouri—two of the most important figures in the early black history movement. They were "willing to sacrifice" for the study and promotion of black history as if it were a "life-and-death struggle," as Woodson often described their work. Both Woodson and Greene published seminal monographs, played vital roles in the professionalization of the black historical enterprise, democratized the study of black history, and successfully balanced their professional scholarly careers with a commitment to social activism, educational reform, and racial justice. The black historical profession has undergone at least five significant stages of development from the antebellum era until the present. Its formative years coincided with the early black history movement from the founding of the Association for the Study of Negro Life and History (ASNLH) in 1915 until Woodson's death in 1950. During an era of overt Jim Crow segregation and antiblack behavior in all sectors of U.S. society, Woodson, Greene, and their colleagues produced the first significant body of scientific historical scholarship on African American history. They vindicated "the race" in academe, laid the foundations for the rigorous study of African American history, and, equally important, were committed to teaching and popularizing black history.

Two major biographies have been published on Woodson, and many articles and chapters in books have explored aspects of his program. Despite Woodson's legendary position in the evolution of African American history and historiography, there have been relatively few scholarly monographs devoted to his life and career. Many important issues concerning his life, work, and thought deserve further consideration, however. Greene repeatedly noted that Woodson had an "intricate" personality. In his mid-eighties, he commented that the "real," intimate biography on Woodson had not been written. Responding to Greene's observations, this book seeks to reveal Woodson's personality by examining previously overlooked and underacknowledged dimensions of his life and work. I probe into his "intricate" personality and contributions to the black historical enterprise by looking closely at the historiography on Woodson, the annual ASNLH meetings and proceedings, the *Journal of Negro History,* the *Negro History Bulletin,* a wide variety of Woodson's publications, as well as what Woodson's disciples, contemporaries, and colleagues wrote about him.

Arvarh Strickland was the first scholar to write about Greene in any significant way. In 1989 and 1996, he edited and published diaries that Greene wrote during the Great Depression while working for Woodson and the ASNLH. These sources are invaluable, and Strickland contextualizes them well. Beyond Strickland's scholarship, no full-length biography or detailed analysis of Greene's life and work has been published. This book critically explores dimensions of Greene's life from his birth until the end of the early black history movement. I draw extensively from the Papers of Lorenzo Johnston Greene, located in the Manuscript Division at the Library of Congress. This repository of primary sources is a documentary trove containing more than 44,000 items.

My study contributes to many subjects and subfields within the growing field of twentieth-century African American studies and history, including black intellectual history, the history of the proto–civil rights movement, black professional-class history, black women's history, and, most important, the history of black historians. My study moves beyond the traditional biographical approach to analyzing black historians. A group of noteworthy studies, including Linda O. McMurry's *Recorder of the Black Experience: A Biography of Monroe Nathan Work* (1984), John Hope Franklin's *George Washington Williams: A Biography* (1985), Elinor Des Verney Sinnette's *Arthur Alfonso Schomburg: Black Bibliophile and Collector, A Biography* (1989), Jacqueline Goggin's *Carter G. Woodson: A Life in Black History* (1993), Kenneth Robert Janken's *Rayford Logan and the Dilemma of the African American Intellectual* (1993), and Michael Dennis's *Luther Porter Jackson and a Life for Civil Rights* (2004) have focused on the lives of influential black historians as solitary figures. Important books like Earl E. Thorpe's *Black Historians* (1971), August Meier and Elliott Rudwick's *Black History and the Historical*

Profession, 1915–1980 (1986), Wilson Jeremiah Moses's *Afrotopia: The Roots of African American Popular History* (1998), Julie Des Jardin's *Women and the Historical Enterprise in America: Gender, Race, and the Politics of Memory, 1880–1945* (2003), and John Ernest's *Liberation Historiography: African American Writers and the Challenge of History, 1794–1861* have acknowledged communities of black historians and considered various intriguing subjects within the African American historical profession.

I focus on two forerunners of the early black history movement who had a close yet tenuous relationship. While part of the African American biographical tradition, my study demonstrates the advantages in viewing Woodson together with one of his most dedicated disciples. The book's comparative approach helps us to better understand the complexity, inner workings, and collective identity of the early black history movement. It is the first study to provide a comparative analysis of two seminal figures in that movement.

Rather than attempt an overarching theoretical formulation, as a historian I have scrutinized the evidence to see what it unveils. The Papers of Lorenzo Johnston Greene, Woodson's writings and various papers, as well as primary sources pertaining to the ASNLH are revealing. One important theme Woodson's and Greene's careers and accomplishments do speak to is the responsibility and function of the relatively privileged, middle-class, black-professional, intellectual historian and scholar. Though they were different in some key facets, Woodson and Greene agreed that black historians and other black professionals should be committed to social reform efforts and, in simple terms, should help exploited, oppressed, and vulnerable African Americans. Both men made monumental sacrifices for black history and for disempowered African Americans, especially the working class and the youth. The lives of Woodson and Greene demonstrate how much individuals can accomplish when they are committed to a cause and "willing to sacrifice." Equally important, their experiences serve as useful case studies for better understanding the realities of black scholars active during the essential proto–civil rights movement and era of Jim Crow segregation.

ACKNOWLEDGMENTS

The various debts incurred during the process of writing this book cannot possibly be repaid, only recognized and greatly appreciated. My first thanks must go to those professors who helped me grow as a historian and realize my intellectual potential. Their moral support was vital. David Bailey, Wilma King, and Harry Reed were especially supportive and helpful. Their various suggestions were invaluable. This book had its origins a decade ago in my research for a paper in Harry Reed's graduate seminar in African American historiography. Participants in the seminar were challenged to choose one historian of the black past and research his or her life, scholarship, and contributions. He encouraged me to explore Greene's contributions, almost guaranteeing me that I could add something of value to the field. Little did I know then that a decade later I would complete a study on Greene and Woodson. Over the past fifteen years, Harry Reed has been a great friend. I must also acknowledge those teachers over the years who have influenced me: C. B. Martin, Frederick Roth, Jojo Macy, Sharon Minor-King, and Norman Pollack.

The bulk of the revision for this book was completed while I taught in the Interdisciplinary Studies Program, College of Lifelong Learning, at Wayne State University, Detroit, Michigan, and in the Department of History at Michigan State University, East Lansing, Michigan. At Wayne State, Stuart Henry, Fred Wacker, Percy Moore, and the supportive staff welcomed me and my scholarship with open arms. Many dynamic Wayne State students directly challenged me to reevaluate and develop my teaching strategies, in turn making me a more solid historian. Daphne Ntiri went to great lengths to make my transition into professorship a pleasurable experience. My new colleagues in African American and African Studies and History at Michigan State University have proved to be kind and supportive. Daina Ramey Berry offered useful suggestions as I made my revisions.

I must single out Darlene Clark Hine. A Woodson scholar herself, she has consistently encouraged my interest, research, and scholarship in African American historiography, challenged me to explore the deeper meanings of African American history, especially in black women's history, and provided me with invaluable insight, advice, and support. Professor Hine has supported this book from its earliest stages, routinely reminding me that the historical profession is not for the faint of heart. I am grateful for her insightful comments on various incarnations of this book. I am also grateful to V. P. Franklin for sharing his vast knowledge of African American history with me. He has played a significant role in my development as a historian and rigorous scholar.

I thank my close friends and extended family for their unwavering encouragement and support. Unknown to them, our numerous informal talks helped me unpack important ideas and concepts included in this book. While conducting research at the Library of Congress, Washington, D.C., the Otubanjo family provided me with a home away from home. I am grateful for their generosity.

My immediate family is a constant source of inspiration, love, and stability. Since I first met her fifteen years ago, my wife, TShaka, contributed enormously to my growth. Her devotion to our family, motherhood, African cultural consciousness, and the teaching profession has helped me redefine my purpose in life. She has also been my greatest cheerleader. May she rest in peace. My three young boys, Pervoi, Kokou, and Agbelé, have forced me to balance the duties of fatherhood with academic responsibilities. They have kept me grounded and honest. I share with my sister Sika a passion for studying and teaching African American studies. Our relationship has given me great strength. Though four years my junior, she has in many ways helped signal important transitions in my life. My Togolese family's commitment to education, hard work, and a strong spiritual faith has helped me maintain my focus.

My parents and ancestors, especially my great-grandfather Adjinyo, are the ones who fundamentally prepared me to complete this book. Coming of age during the 1960s and 1970s, my mother, Frances R. Dagbovie, nurtured my passion and commitment to the study of African and African American history and culture. She continues to keep me updated on the latest happenings in African and African American culture as portrayed in popular media. She has always encouraged me to be an individual and to pursue my passions. She also spent hours proofreading. My father, Prospero Y. Dagbovie, is my primary role model. Much of his personality resembles Woodson's and Greene's. He is a master teacher, a man of high standards, and a critical thinker. I now understand why he had me till the soil and plant and harvest vegetables as if my life depended upon it during my early years. This book is evidence of the hard-work ethic that he and my mother have passed onto me. I am humbled by my parents' unwavering support.

Finally, for inspiring me to make the study of African American history, life, and culture my life's commitment, I must give thanks and praises to Carter G. Woodson and Lorenzo Johnston Greene. Whenever I faced obstacles during the course of writing this study, I humbled myself by reflecting upon their abilities to persevere and succeed in extremely trying times for African Americans.

Any faults that remain in the text are my responsibility.

Introduction

THIS STUDY EXAMINES THE LIVES, WORKS, and contributions of Carter G. Woodson (1875–1950) and Lorenzo Johnston Greene (1899–1988), two of the most important figures in the early black history movement. Coinciding with what John Hope Franklin termed the second and third "generations of scholarship in Afro-American history," the early black history movement lasted from the founding of the Association for the Study of Negro Life and History in 1915 until Woodson's death in 1950.[1] During this crucial thirty-five-year period, Woodson and his co-workers engaged in a collaborative struggle to legitimize, publicize, and popularize the study of black history as well as the history of other African descendants. Though there was a noteworthy generation gap separating Woodson from Greene—and they certainly had their ideological differences—they were similar in significant ways.

Woodson and Greene came of age as historians during an era of overt Jim Crow segregation, facing similar obstacles and sharing common philosophies.[2] They each belonged to a group of black scholars who received their post-bachelor's degrees from major, predominantly white universities, yet they were systematically excluded from teaching at such mainstream institutions. Both men insisted that black history could serve the dual function of instilling cultural pride and self-esteem in African Americans while combating racial prejudice by exposing white society to Africans' and African Americans' monumental contributions to American and world culture. They were preservers of the nineteenth-century credo of social uplift, a philosophy that was eroding during the first half of the twentieth century.[3] They were sympathetic to the needs of the black working class and the poor, yet they believed that certain features of black folk and urban culture needed to be altered so that blacks could be integrated into American society as equals.

Like many Harlem Renaissance intellectuals, Woodson and Greene grappled with W. E. B. Du Bois's notion of blacks' "double-consciousness" and "two-ness."[4] They acknowledged and celebrated African history and blacks' vital contributions to America's cultural identity. At the same time, they often had great trouble accepting many of the mores of the largely agricultural, working-class black people who Africanized American culture. They maintained part of the "Old Negroes'" personality in an era when, as Alain Locke posited, "It is the rank and file who are leading, and the leaders who are following."[5] Woodson and Greene shared a social vision that dictated they make their craft relevant and practical by working closely with and for the rank and file of their people. They were scholar-activists, "intellectual-activists," or "liberated intellectuals" who made "a career of uplifting the African-American race" and viewed the "liberation of their people as a priority," seeking to "utilize most of their talents and resources in this mission."[6] Building upon an established post-emancipation scholar-activist tradition that included influential nineteenth- and early twentieth-century figures such as Alexander Crummell, Edward W. Blyden, George Washington Williams, Richard Robert Wright Sr., Anna Julia Cooper, Ida B. Wells, W. E. B. Du Bois, members of the American Negro Academy, and others, Woodson and Greene, like many of their colleagues during the interwar era, adjusted "their careers by being critically and actively engaged in the social worlds of their time" and "stood on the outer shells of many different spheres—political, academic, and racial—at a time when these spheres were shifting and intersecting in new ways."[7]

As members of the early mid-twentieth-century black professional class, these men embraced a "service ethic" that "emphasized extraordinary work for the community far beyond the narrow scope of their training and occupations," "service to people whom the larger American society perceived to be marginal and peripheral by virtue of their race and subordination in socioeconomic and political status." For Woodson and Greene, this translated into taking black history to the black masses, the working class, and the youth throughout the nation. Darlene Clark Hine has further posited that "individual accomplishment, in order to render service, became the guiding credo of the black professional class and the meaning of a worthwhile life."[8] Woodson, Greene, and other twentieth-century black professionals faced myriad challenges while serving a clientele on whom they depended at many levels for their livelihood. Their interactions and relationships with many, often competing groups influenced them to develop nuanced strategies for black advancement. Above all, Woodson and Greene were committed to a common cause, the promotion of black history. As underacknowledged contributors to the interwar Intercultural Education Movement, they wholeheartedly believed that black history was a vital medium of social reform and cross-cultural understanding within American society. They demonstrated and demanded that practical, effective black leadership could emanate from the ranks of professional historians, a concept that declined following the end of the classic civil rights movement.

This examination of Woodson and Greene provides a window into the struggles, sacrifices, and achievements of black historians, scholars, intellectuals, and professionals during the first half of the twentieth century. Using these two historians and the early black history movement as points of reference, this work is also relevant to helping us to better understand the various challenges black historians have faced since the modern civil rights movement.

❖ ❖ ❖

Nearly a century ago, Carter Woodson began laying the foundations for the current advanced state of African American history and Black studies. He was the only individual of slave parentage to earn a doctorate in history from Harvard University, and though W. E. B. Du Bois had earned the same degree from Harvard about two decades earlier, Woodson was the first professionally trained historian to devote his scholarly career to advancing black history as if he were involved in what he routinely called a "life-and-death struggle." In 1930, Lorenzo Greene "marveled" at Woodson's endless devotion to "the cause." "His [Woodson's] capacity for work is certainly outstanding. Eighteen hours a day seems to be routine for him," Greene noted in his diary. "He does everything from writing books, editing the *Journal,* wrapping books, mailing letters and parcels. Nor is he above acting as a janitor and sometimes his own cook. Truly a remarkable man." Many of Woodson's other disciples and co-workers shared and reiterated Greene's sentiments.[9] To date, with few possible exceptions, no individual has contributed as much as Woodson did to the evolution of African American history.

After earning his doctorate in 1912, Woodson published his first book, *The Education of the Negro Prior to 1861* (1915), and established the Association for the Study of Negro Life and History (ASNLH), which he co-founded in Chicago on September 9, 1915, with George Cleveland Hall, James E. Stamps, and Alexander L. Jackson. They resolved that they would collect records pertaining to black America's past and disseminate the truth regarding African American history. During Woodson's lifetime, the ASNLH served as the center for the advancement of black history, an essential "parallel institution" for a diversified community of black scholars, historians, and educators united by their common interest in their peoples' past and present conditions. Like other black professionals active during the era of segregation, Woodson "identified the Achilles' heel of white supremacy" and transformed the oppressive conditions of his times into a motivating force for the intense study and promotion of black history. "Segregation provided blacks the chance—indeed, the imperative—to develop a range of distinct institutions that they controlled." The ASNLH, "a separate alternative institutional structure," was one of the many black organizations of this tradition during the proto–civil rights period.[10] More important, Woodson democratized his "parallel institution" by welcoming a broad cross section of the black community into the Association's ranks, including professionally trained scholars, school teachers, members of the black bourgeoisie and working class, and the youth.

Woodson's the *Journal of Negro History,* inaugurated in January 1916, became the first scholarly journal devoted to the study of the black past. Today, the volumes published under Woodson's editorship still function as starting points and essential references for researchers in the field of black history. In 1922, Woodson founded Associated Publishers in Washington, D.C., and published the first major textbook on black history, *The Negro in Our History.* This book was not replaced as the standard black history text until John Hope Franklin published his enduring classic, *From Slavery to Freedom* (1947). In 1926, Woodson received the NAACP's Spingarn Medal and launched his most famous program, Negro History Week, today recognized in American popular culture as Black History Month during February. During the peak of the Great Depression, Woodson published *The Mis-Education of the Negro* (1933); his most famous and durable book, it remains required reading for many Afrocentric thinkers and has sold millions of copies. In 1937, Woodson published the first volume of the *Negro History Bulletin,* a basic, easy-to-read black history magazine through which Woodson and his mainly female editorial staff sought to introduce black history to an audience beyond the *Journal of Negro History* readership, especially to schoolteachers and the black working class and youth.

Woodson was a remarkably prolific scholar. During his lifetime, he wrote, co-authored, and/or edited more than twenty books, more than a dozen major articles, and countless widely read newspaper columns and book reviews.

Though considered by some to be static and cantankerous in his approach and demeanor, between 1915 and 1950 Woodson adjusted his strategies to suit the broader transformations in American society and the black community, responding creatively to the Progressive Era, the Harlem Renaissance, the Great Depression and the New Deal, and World War II and its aftermath.

In 1945, Rayford W. Logan criticized Woodson for his "failure to attach himself to a young scholar." Likewise, historians have underappreciated Woodson's role as a mentor and promoter of intellectual talent. However, Woodson was the principal mentor and promoter for the early black history movement; he did for this movement what Alain Locke, Charles Johnson, and James Weldon Johnson did for the Harlem Renaissance,[11] facilitating productive, cross-generational dialogues and relationships. "The majority of serious students of the Negro in American history have become indebted to Dr. Woodson for inspiration, encouragement, and, in some cases, more tangible assistance," Alrutheus A. Taylor testified in 1950. "Indeed, several competent students of other phases of Negro life have become similarly, to a degree at least, obligated to him."[12]

Throughout his career, Woodson maintained a tight circle of seven younger black historians—Alrutheus A. Taylor, Charles H. Wesley, Luther Porter Jackson, Lorenzo Johnston Greene, Rayford W. Logan, William Sherman Savage, and James Hugo Johnston—who served as his apprentices for varying periods.[13] These scholars, born mainly during what Logan termed the "nadir," often possessed ideals that differed from Woodson's, but they usually put these differences aside in order to work with Woodson to establish the foundations for black history as a legitimate field of study and source of pride for African Americans. The dialogues, interactions, and relationships between Woodson and his disciples contributed significantly to the evolution of the black historical enterprise during a fundamental period in its maturation. Among Woodson's most dedicated disciples was Connecticut native Lorenzo Johnston Greene.

Charles H. Wesley introduced Greene to Woodson in 1925. Three years later, Greene began actively working with the ASNLH. He worked very closely with Woodson from 1928 until 1933. From the Depression years until 1950, Greene was one of Woodson's most important supporters and colleagues. He conducted and published historical and sociological research under the auspices of the ASNLH; Greene even helped Woodson with many of the books for which Woodson took credit. Not only did he regularly attend and participate in the Association's annual meetings, but Greene also substituted for Woodson as a lecturer on the low-paying but burgeoning black history speaking circuit. After white philanthropists withdrew their significant support from Woodson in the early 1930s, Greene contributed to the Association out of his own pocket. In 1945, Woodson assured Greene that he was "one of the few who appreciate the objectives of this undertaking and are willing to sacrifice something to attain these ends."[14] Under Woodson's guidance, Greene emerged as an important figurehead in the early black history movement.

Though Greene remained committed to Woodson and the ASNLH throughout his lifetime, by the 1930s and 1940s he was busy establishing himself as a historian, social activist, reformer, and teacher. From 1933 until 1972, Greene devoted his life to teaching young black adults at Missouri's Lincoln University. He thrived in this environment, challenging his students and the university administrators in intellectual and civic matters. In 1939 and 1940, he led a campaign among Lincoln students and faculty to help exploited sharecroppers in southeast Missouri. In 1942, he earned a doctorate in history from Columbia University and published his magnum opus, *The Negro in Colonial New England, 1620–1776.* To date, Greene's groundbreaking study has arguably not been superseded.[15]

During the pivotal 1940s, while mobilizing blacks to support the "Double V" campaign, editing a controversial and multidisciplinary scholarly journal, and working hard to complete a trilogy on blacks in New England, Greene struggled to earn respect at Lincoln. Though he did not publish as much as Woodson, Greene produced a significant body of scholarship. By 1950, he had produced three major articles, three sociological studies, one major monograph, a substantial body of unpublished scholarship, and an unpublished book of poetry. At age fifty-one, Greene—one of the most learned black historians—was, in the tradition of Woodson, committed to all three aspects of academe: teaching, research and publication, and service. Equally important, he was a committed social activist and educational reformer who, like a significant group of other outspoken black scholars since the 1920s, attracted the FBI's attention.

❖ ❖ ❖

Drawing upon the Papers of Lorenzo Johnston Greene (a repository that contains approximately 44,100 items) in the collections of the Manuscript Division at the Library of Congress, along with the recently released Papers of Carter G. Woodson and the Association for the Study of Negro Life and History, 1915–1950, the *Journal of Negro History* and the *Negro History Bulletin,* as well as popular and scholarly materials on black historians, I critically examine the lives, works, and struggles of Woodson and Greene side by side. This study is divided into two parts. In reconsidering Woodson, the first part of this book explores issues that scholars have either discussed briefly or ignored, such as Woodson's image in popular and scholarly writings and memory, the practical, democratic approach of the ASNLH, Woodson's role and position as a forerunner in an "iconoclastic tradition" of black thought, and the pivotal role of African American women in the Association during Woodson's lifetime. The second part represents the first major examination of Greene's life, focusing on the first half of his life, coinciding with the early black history movement, 1899–1950. As has been the fate of many of Woodson's protégés, Greene's contributions have not historically been adequately addressed: no full-length biography of Lorenzo Johnston Greene has ever been published.[16] I trace why and how Greene decided to use history as a tool for generating social change, highlighting his unpublished book of one hundred poems, his working relationship with Woodson, his historical scholarship, and his career as a scholar, teacher, and social activist at Lincoln University.

What were the fundamental ideologies and tactics Woodson and Greene employed, and how were these men molded by the times in which they lived? How have historians, scholars, popular culture, and collective memory shaped our views of Woodson and the early black history movement? While it is widely known that Woodson created the infrastructure for the modern study of African American history, in what ways was he ahead of his times, farseeing, and progressive? How did women contribute to the success of the ASNLH under Woodson's reign as Association director? Though Greene has been recognized for *The Negro in Colonial New England, 1620–1776,* what were his lesser-known contributions to the early black history movement? How did he interact with Woodson, and how were they similar and different? What cross-generational bonds and dialogues existed between the two? What were the obstacles Greene overcame in order to gain respect within the American historical profession during the crucial World War II era? In what ways are the ideologies, strategies, and approaches of Woodson, Greene, and other representatives of the early black history movement related to the broader development of the black historical enterprise? These are the questions this book seeks to answer.

Chapter 1 explores the variety of significant writings on Woodson. These include articles in the *Journal of Negro History* and the *Negro History Bulletin,* as well as articles in scholarly and popular journals, chapters or sections in books, relevant unpublished scholarship, and full-length biographies. Since Woodson's sudden death in 1950, Woodson scholarship has undergone various transformations. Throughout the 1950s and well into the 1960s, Woodson was most often remembered fondly in published and unpublished tributes by his protégés and contemporaries. By the Black Power era, a new generation of black historians found him to be a source of inspiration and pride. Since the late 1970s and the early 1980s, Woodson has attracted the attention of a more diverse cross section of scholars. While it appears that the more critical assessments of Woodson did not surface until the late 1980s and 1990s, in each decade after his death there have been a few scholars who challenged their counterparts to be more critical of Woodson. In a handful of cases, certain scholars, especially Woodson's disciples, evaluated Woodson more than once in their lives. Greene, for example, reflected critically upon Woodson's "intricate" personality from the late 1920s through the mid-1980s.[17] In a 1984 letter to a friend, Greene commented that "the real biography of Woodson remains to be written and, unfortunately, those who held the key to Woodson's real personality, the forces that drove him, and the psychic factors that made him Woodson, have passed, or are rapidly passing, from the scene."[18] The diverse body of writings on Woodson, especially those by his close coworkers, disciples, friends, and contemporaries, are essential sources in helping us better understand and reconstruct his dynamic personality.

Chapter 2 highlights how, after founding the ASNLH, Woodson democratized, legitimized, and popularized the study of black history using many different strategies. He liberally extended his services as a lecturer and researcher to black communities throughout the country. He opened the Association's doors to lay historians, secondary and elementary schoolteachers, working-class blacks, and black youth. He founded Negro History Week and other extension services, and he published the *Negro History Bulletin.* The chapter pays special attention to the nature of Woodson's messages to various sectors within black communities, including the middle class and professional class, the youth, and the working class.

Chapter 3 considers Woodson as an important figurehead in a twentieth-century African American "iconoclastic tradition." In addition to Woodson, this group includes E. Franklin Frazier and the recently deceased Harold Cruse. Though they came of age in different eras, these scholars directly challenged their black bourgeoisie colleagues for similar reasons and in many of the same ways. They indicted their colleagues in an outspoken, audacious manner, but their commentaries also served as public confessions and affirmations of their own personal growth in consciousness. By initiating and publicizing controversial debates within their communities of scholars, they shared the ultimate goal of persuading blacks of their class to more actively join the struggle for black liberation. They believed that certain black professionals sought to separate themselves from black culture and the dilemmas faced by the masses of their people. Though their associates often received their writings negatively, these iconoclasts' ideas are in many regards still relevant, speaking to the issues and audiences of today "with the same acuity" that they showed for "earlier readers."[19] Woodson was one of the first twentieth-century black scholars and one of the only black historians to outline the dilemmas endured by black college graduates, critiquing them in bold, often uncompromising terms and establishing what he perceived their responsibilities to be. He was one of the first black intellectuals to publicly critique historically black colleges and universities as well as the caste of educated leaders whom Du Bois so adamantly praised in the early 1900s. Unlike Woodson, most black spokespersons during the first half of the twentieth century did not challenge Du Bois's theory that "exceptional men," "distinguished Negroes," and "college-bred Negroes" were the best equipped group to save the race, to "guide the Mass away from contamination and death of the Worst," bringing them "in contact with modern civilization" and "broad culture."[20]

Chapter 4 responds to a host of questions regarding the place of women in Woodson's scholarship, mind, and overall program. How did Woodson portray black women in his scholarship? How were black women discussed in the pages of the *Journal of Negro History* from 1916 until 1950? Did Woodson conform to the gender conventions of his times? How did his writings respond to the derogatory myths and stereotypes about black women? What were the various roles black women played in the ASNLH during Woodson's reign as director? I argue that Woodson's views and treatment of black women may appear to have been at times ambiguous, yet he was quite progressive when compared to other black male scholars and historians of his time. In many ways Woodson challenged the masculinist ideologies prevalent during the first half of the twentieth century.

Chapter 5 traces Greene's early life and scholarship by focusing on the crucial period from his birth in 1899 until 1928, when he began working for Woodson. These years significantly affected Greene's development into a professional historian. His youth and early adult years in Ansonia, Connecticut, his frugal undergraduate years at Howard University, and his graduate studies at Columbia University played vital roles in molding Greene's worldview and his decision to join the early black history movement. I analyze Greene's largely unknown adroitness as a creative writer during the Harlem Renaissance era, during which he wrote several dozen poems, sharing his work mainly with his close friends, including poet Georgia Douglas Johnson and artist Louis Mailou Jones. Greene eventually authored more than one hundred unpublished poems.

Chapter 6 looks at a brief yet vital phase of Greene's career as a salaried ASNLH researcher. Greene's decision to work for Woodson was a major turning point in his life. He turned down better-paying job offers from West Virginia Institute, Fisk University, Howard University, and North Carolina Agricultural and Technical College at Greensboro in order to work for the Association. After several years of working for Woodson, Greene confided in his diary, "Negro History shall be my life's work . . . I know that I had found my life's vocation and that Dr. Woodson was my historical idol."[21] From the winter of 1928 until the fall of 1933, Greene was initiated into the early black history movement. He worked closely with Charles H. Wesley on a study of the black church in Maryland, New York, and Virginia, became Woodson's primary assistant, and spearheaded a nationwide bookselling campaign for the Association. He also produced one article in the *Journal of Negro History*, wrote two books, and penned an unpublished essay on blacks in the South during the Great Depression. These eye-opening experiences helped Greene further develop his philosophy of history, strategies for black cultural reform, and his life's purpose.

Chapters 7 and 8 focus on Greene's life at Missouri's Lincoln University from 1933 until the 1950s. Chapter 7 chronicles Greene's life from 1933 until 1944, when Greene embraced many civic causes. I analyze his commitment to teaching, his role in the ASNLH, and his increasing social and political activism, including his support of exploited southeast Missouri sharecroppers and his involvement in World War II. I also probe deeply into the publication and legitimization processes of *The Negro in Colonial New England, 1620–1776*. Chapter 8 explores Greene's challenging experiences at Lincoln University from 1944 until 1950. Researching, teaching, and family life must have helped Greene survive emotionally during these trying years. I delve into his battles with Lincoln over a salary increase, his activities within the Association, and his role as editor of the *Midwest Journal*. Though beyond this study's historical scope, I also briefly explore the significance of his *Desegregation of Schools in Missouri, 1954–1959* (1959).

In the conclusion, I compare and contrast the lives, approaches, and philosophies of Woodson and Greene, and I also briefly consider their approaches and contributions within the broader context of the black historical enterprise since the modern civil rights movement. During the last several decades, African American history has enjoyed a seemingly secure status in the mainstream American academy, and its historiography is today sophisticated, expansive, and multidimensional. In terms of popularizing and democratizing the study of the black past, making black history genuinely pragmatic and functional, and linking the black historical profession to social activism, we still have much to learn from Woodson and Greene. They made great sacrifices and developed innovative tactics to advance black history; their contributions deserve to be revisited.

PART ONE

Carter G. Woodson Reconsidered

1 Representations of "The Father of Negro History"

HOW WE CURRENTLY VIEW CARTER G. WOODSON in the black historical profession, American academe, and popular culture has been shaped by more than fifty years of historical scholarship, scholarly discourse, and popular writings. Though he has not received nearly as much scholarly or popular attention as many more famous black leaders and intellectuals such as Frederick Douglass, Booker T. Washington, W. E. B. Du Bois, Marcus Garvey, Martin Luther King Jr., or Malcolm X, a significant body of literature on Woodson exists. Since the 1920s, scholarly research, thought, and discourse on Woodson has evolved and matured, mirroring in some regards the broader transformations in the black historical profession, American academe, and U.S. race relations. Between 1926 and 1993, several dozen articles, tributes, and biographical sketches, as well as three major studies, have been published on Woodson. Many manuscript collections also contain correspondences to and from Woodson and important unpublished papers relating to him. In 1998, the collection entitled The Papers of Carter G. Woodson and the Association for the Study of Negro Life and History [ASNLH], 1915–1950 was processed and made available to scholars. Taken together, these various resources help us reconstruct, decipher, and explain Woodson's philosophy, program, and complex personality, the inner workings of the ASNLH, as well as the experiences of black scholars who came of age during an era of Jim Crow segregation.

While Sister Anthony Scally's volumes of the 1980s (notably *Carter G. Woodson: A Bio-Bibliography*) were informative and refreshing, only Jacqueline Goggin's 1993 biography of Woodson, *Carter G. Woodson: A Life in*

Black History, has received extensive, noteworthy attention from members of the American historical profession. Considering the magnitude of his accomplishments as a historian, institution builder, political activist, and race leader, Woodson and his contributions have been slighted to some degree. In response to this marginalization, the Association for the Study of Afro-American Life and History (ASALH) (the name the Association adopted in 1972) has recently proposed a two-part documentary project that "hopes to pull Dr. Carter G. Woodson's American experience from the cracks of history and expose the world to its importance."[1] Nevertheless, when viewed within the broader context of African American intellectual history, the historical scholarship on Woodson is provocative, promising, and developed in significant ways. Many African American scholars and intellectuals who came of age during the era of segregation have received much less scholarly attention than "The Father of Negro History." With the possible exceptions of W. E. B. Du Bois, who is known more for his multidisciplinary approach, and John Hope Franklin, no black historian is more widely known in popular culture than Woodson.

In the late 1970s, Woodson's Negro History Week became Black History Month; every February since then, millions of Americans, especially black and white elementary schoolchildren and African American college students, participate in this celebration. In 1984, in commemoration of Woodson, the U.S. Postal Service issued a stamp of the ASNLH founder as a part of its Black Heritage Series. In 2001, the Carter G. Woodson House was placed on the National Trust for Historic Preservation's list of "11 Most Endangered Places in the U.S." Most Americans who have heard of Woodson still know very little about his life, work, and contributions. The history and evolution of the historiography, popular scholarship, and media coverage on Woodson is provocative and informative. It helps explain the current state of Woodsonian scholarship while providing scholars with ideas for future research.

❖ ❖ ❖

Woodson's impact on American and African American academic culture is in part evidenced by the fact that a small yet significant group of scholars highlighted his accomplishments before his death. In 1926, the year Negro History Week was founded, Kelly Miller published a pamphlet on Woodson under the auspices of the ASNLH in which he analyzed Woodson's philosophy and rationalized his sacrifices. Whether Woodson encouraged or commissioned Miller, a Howard University intellectual, to write this piece is unknown, but it is highly unlikely given Woodson's response to his "Boys," who sought to honor him more than a decade later.[2] In the late 1920s, Woodson was included in the pages of *Who's Who in Colored America: A Biographical Dictionary.* During the era of segregation, Woodson was among the few blacks included in white-authored reference books. The editors of such texts were probably very impressed with his receiving the NAACP's Spingarn Medal in 1926.[3] Before his death, Woodson was profiled in more widely circulated reference books, including *Who's Who in America* (1926–1950), *Current Biographical Dictionary of Notable Living Men and Women in the United States,* and *Who's Who and Why.* With the possible exception of Miller's piece, these brief sketches were most likely furnished by Woodson himself.

In 1935, Joseph Grimes, a master's degree candidate at the University of Iowa, wrote a thesis on black historians and briefly mentioned Woodson's contributions,[4] but the inclusion went largely unnoticed until several decades after Woodson's death. In his 1940 autobiography, Harlem Renaissance figurehead Langston Hughes briefly recounted his experiences working as Woodson's personal assistant in the ASNLH Washington, D.C., office during the 1920s. Hughes described his work as being very difficult, "much harder than the laundry" work he had previously done. "Although I realized what a fine contribution Dr. Woodson was making to the Negro people and to America, publishing his histories, his studies, and his *Journal of Negro History,*" Hughes remembered, "I personally did not like the work I had to do."[5] Though his comments were terse, Hughes preceded many of his contemporaries who waited until the commemorative May 1950 or the 1965 Special Summer issue of the *Negro History Bulletin* to share their personal experiences of Woodson.

The lack of analytical writings about Woodson by his protégés before his death, as well as their reservations to publish about him after his death, can largely be explained by their mentor's well-known "peculiarities." Woodson's personality was very strong and at times hard to decipher. In late February 1940, L. D. Reddick, Schomburg Collection curator, wrote to Lorenzo Johnston Greene and proposed that along with Luther Porter Jackson, James Hugo Johnston, Charles H. Wesley, Sherman Savage, A. A. Taylor, Rayford Logan, and a few others, they publish a tribute to their elder: "It has occurred to me several times and I am sure to many others that it is about time we got together a volume of essays in honor of Dr. Woodson. . . . The old boy is getting along and though he might last longer than any of us, I am sure that it would gladden his heart for 'his boys' to do just such a thing. Of course, it is necessary for me to say how significant his work has been, despite his peculiarities."[6]

According to Reddick's plan, the essays would need to be collected by July 1940 so that they could surprise their "teacher" with the volume at the September annual meeting, the ASNLH's silver anniversary in Chicago. Coincidentally, on March 1, 1940, Greene sent a similar yet more detailed letter to Reddick and about a dozen other people "who have either been associated directly with Dr. Woodson or who have sought their inspiration from him." Greene suggested that for the silver anniversary "some tangible expression of appreciation should be extended to Dr. Carter G. Woodson," a small volume of essays totaling about two hundred pages, covering "a cross section of relatively unexplored areas dealing with the Negro." Greene, who first began thinking about such a project with Luther Porter Jackson, William Sherman Savage, and David Jackson in New Orleans in October 1939, proposed that the book be sold for one dollar, capitalizing on the "enthusiasm generated by the meeting." Greene suggested that the essays be submitted by June 1, 1940.[7]

Practically every leading scholar of the time to whom Greene wrote, including Rayford W. Logan, whom Woodson publicly attacked in a circular four years earlier, responded enthusiastically in support of the project. By mid-March, Greene and Reddick had agreed to serve as joint editors, though Greene took the lead in organizing the volume. By March 16, 1940, Greene had received tentative paper titles from L. P. Jackson, Clarence Baycote, Rayford W. Logan, Horace Mann Bond, A. A. Taylor, William Sherman Savage, Mercer Cook, Charles H. Wesley, Ralphe Bunche, James Hugo Johnston, James Browning, and David Jackson. Reddick agreed with Greene to write the volume's opening piece, an essay tracing the contributions of black historians from William Cooper Nell to Woodson. The contributors worked seriously on this project during March, April, and May. Then, a month before the deadline, the fruits of Greene's labors were dealt a great blow from the very person to whom it was to be dedicated. On the first day of May 1940, Woodson wrote a demeaning and belittling letter to Greene. Woodson stated:

> The purpose of this letter, however, is to write you about the book of essays which you outlined for me sometime ago. I have never taken the matter very seriously because some of the persons called upon to contribute know very little about history and cannot write correctly in the English language. I would seriously object to a volume dedicated to the undersigned, unless he has a chance to see that the work be published in proper style and conforming with the rules of modern historiography. I do not care to be put to shame on the occasion of our twenty-fifth anniversary.[8]

Greene waited for nearly a month before he shared Woodson's sentiments his colleagues. In late May 1940, he informed Reddick, "Since I last heard from you, I received a letter from Dr. Woodson which I regard as a deliberate and unwarranted insult to us who are attempting to honor him. It made me so angry that I have virtually decided to drop the entire project." Greene continued, "Savage has already stopped writing. Many of the fellows, I believe, would assume a like stand." Greene concluded that they should publish the essays "at a later date when the gentleman might not be so publicly 'humiliated.'" The particular tribute organized by Greene was never completed or published. Nearly a year after Woodson's death, Reddick wrote a letter to Woodson's "Boys" seeking to reinaugurate the project as a "fitting memorial" for the Association's founder. "My notion," Reddick proposed, "is that it should contain a sketch of his life and work, and about a dozen or so essays on various aspects of Negro life and history." Though this particular proposal did not result in a published volume, many tributes to Woodson appeared after his death, months before Reddick's letter was circulated.[9]

Woodson's disciples' serious attempts to honor him in 1940 demonstrate Woodson's widespread impact on the black historical profession and illustrate the admiration the younger generation of black scholars held for its elder. This 1940 incident also gives more credence to those who described Woodson as being cantankerous and hard to get along with. It helps explain perhaps why Woodson's protégés did not often publish their personal thoughts about the Association's founder before his death and perhaps why none of them decided to write a comprehensive biography of him in the decades immediately following his passing. Had Woodson been less hard to please and more supportive of these efforts, it is possible that scholarship on Woodson and black historiography could have been further enhanced.

The exact motivations behind Woodson's response to Greene in May 1940 will never be known. While he may have meant what he said to Greene, Woodson's humility and dedication to "the cause" may have influenced his behavior. It is possible that Woodson did not want to divert attention away from the more important aspects of the black history movement during a pivotal moment in its maturation. Throughout his scholarly career, Woodson promoted black history not for personal recognition or gain but for the overall advancement of African American culture. In their later years, other major black historians, including John Hope Franklin and Benjamin Quarles, also requested that their accomplishments not be celebrated by younger generations during their lifetimes. Woodson's, Franklin's, and Quarles's behavior can be explained by the times in which their ideologies were molded.

Despite Woodson's wishes, several black historians independently profiled his life and work in the mid- to late 1940s. In 1945, Rayford W. Logan published a brief article on Woodson in Du Bois's *Phylon.* This was the first of several important articles in which Woodson's immediate successor as ASNLH director commented on Woodson's life and work. Logan called upon the public to recognize Woodson's contributions, which had been overlooked by Edwin Embree's *Thirteen Against the Odds.* "For by any criterion of solid achievement Dr. Woodson should rank among the first five contemporary Negroes," Logan declared. Yet Logan decided to critique his mentor's leadership skills and personality traits: "Dr. Woodson's refusal to join this rival project illustrates what even some of his friends term his great weakness, that is," Logan recounted concerning their intense conflict over the Phelps-Stokes Project's *Encyclopedia Africana,* "his devotion to his own cause which makes him suspicious of any one else engaged in the same work." Logan also responded to Woodson's attack on him during the early 1930s and criticized the Association's founder for not paying his employees enough and for supposedly not taking anyone directly under his wing. "Perhaps the one quality lacking in Dr. Woodson to make him great," Logan concluded, "is his failure to attach himself to a young scholar who loves the work as much as Dr. Woodson does and who would dedicate himself to perpetuating it as the greatest monument to his magnificent achievements." According to one of Woodson's close friends, William M. Brewer, "Rayford's profile in *Phylon* . . . made Dr. Woodson furious."[10]

Logan publicized his criticisms of Woodson for several reasons. Foremost, Logan's wide range of experiences before joining the Association affected his approach to Woodson. By the early 1930s, he had graduated from Washington's most prestigious secondary school for African Americans, attended Williams College, participated in World War I, traveled throughout France and Europe, assumed a high position in the post 1919 Pan-African Conferences, taught at Virginia Union University, and established himself as a leading African American political activist, intellectual, and polemicist. Logan was unlike Woodson's less experienced protégés. Early on, he was an outspoken critical thinker who did not feel obligated to work with Woodson in a common cause at the expense of masking his true feelings. He was especially offended over how Woodson publicly dismissed him before the black scholarly community, black college presidents, and the *Journal of Negro History* readership in the 1930s. The outspoken Logan was unwilling to allow his character to be defamed as such.[11]

In the remainder of the 1940s, Woodson's achievements were noted in a handful of other publications. Self-taught, Jamaican-born historian J. A. Rogers (1883–1966) included an essay on Woodson in the second volume of his *World's Great Men of Color.* Rogers was most impressed by Woodson's outspokenness on the black bourgeoisie's failure to alleviate the problems facing the black masses. It appears that Rogers included excerpts from their conversations in his essay. Rogers did not publish in the *Journal of Negro History* or the *Negro History Bulletin* during Woodson's lifetime. Woodson did, however, objectively review Rogers's *Sex and Race.* While he observed that Rogers was not a "scientifically trained historian" and that he made several small errors, Woodson commended the Jamaican immigrant for his tenacity and thoroughness in collecting and publishing data "at his own expense."[12] A year before his death, Woodson was possibly becoming more receptive to those who sought to write tributes to him. In 1949, he welcomed Georgia Douglas Johnson's brief tribute for the short-lived *Midwest Journal.* Johnson told Greene that Woodson was "real pleased" with her sketch.[13]

The first distinct scholarly body of writings on Woodson flowered immediately following his death. Those who undertook the task of seriously chronicling Woodson's life, however, faced major dilemmas with regard to sources. Patricia Romero, who in 1971 completed the first major doctoral dissertation on Woodson, explained the problems that scholars researching Woodson faced. According to Romero, when she first arrived in Washington, D.C., in 1965, the ASNLH headquarters possessed various file cases containing manuscripts for the *Journal of Negro History,* materials dealing with *The Encyclopedia Africana,* various pamphlets and journals, and a handful of correspondences between Woodson and Victor Daly. Within the first few months after her arrival, Romero recounted, a woman named Willie Miles had once "intimated" to her "that she had burned a lot of the junk in the files." Romero told Lorenzo J. Greene roughly a decade later that "what happened to the Woodson correspondence between the founding of the organization and his death is a complete mystery." Sometime in the mid- to late 1970s, Romero herself was accused of stealing Woodson's personal papers; she defended herself, concluding that the Association was "using that accusation as a mechanism for keeping researchers out of what they did have."[14] Before 1978, we can assume that researchers interested in Woodson's life and work encountered challenges in securing large amounts of primary sources which could have revealed significant information about Woodson's character, personal life, and thought.

After Woodson died, the white American scholarly community, in a few cases, remembered this pioneering intellectual in the back pages of their journals. In June 1950, the *American Sociological Review* noted his death and provided a brief biographical sketch resembling those found in the *Washington Post* and *New York Times.*[15] Woodson received even less attention in American historical journals: under the editorship of Wendell H. Stephenson and Fred C. Cole, the *Mississippi Valley Historical Review* ignored his death, and the *American Historical Review* did not mention his passing either, although both editors knew Woodson, who had reviewed three books in the *Mississippi Valley Historical Review* (1918–1920) and had written one review for the *American Historical Review* (1927). The *Journal of Southern History* mentioned Woodson's death in passing in its "Historical News and Notices" section of the August 1950 issue when it noted the April 12, 1950, death of Luther Porter Jackson, one of their members, and mentioned Woodson by association: "Shortly before his own death, Professor Jackson had returned from the funeral of Carter G. Woodson, founder and editor of the *Journal of Negro History* and author and editor of many volumes on the American Negro."[16]

Many black scholars and leaders remembered Woodson. In the dawning of the 1950s, Rayford W. Logan, Mary McLeod Bethune, and Charles H. Wesley published brief accounts of their deceased friend and mentor in the *Journal of Negro History.* Wesley's article was the most in-depth. He laid out the five major characteristics that made Woodson a scholar to emulate. He was, in Wesley's estimation, "a Discoverer of the Truth," who "did not want the Negro people to meet 'the awful fate of becoming a negligible factor in the thought of the world'" and who "never hesitated to abandon the false for the true, whatever the cost to him or the cause"; "a Contributor to Truth" by publishing and editing extensively; "an Organizer of Truth" who left behind a movement; "a Disseminator of Truth" to scholarly and unscholarly audiences; and "a Fighter for Truth" who fought all "traducers" of the race, regardless of race or class.[17]

While the *Journal of Negro History* touched upon Woodson in the decade following his death, the *Bulletin,* more widely read by the rank-and-file, celebrated him. The May 1950 edition featured a photo of a characteristically confident Woodson on the cover, included several photos and memorabilia, and devoted every article to him. The "Biographical Sketch" in this volume was reprinted from *Current Biography—Who's News and Why* (1944). It highlighted his major achievements and reprinted direct quotations from "The Father of Negro History." Mary McLeod Bethune, ASNLH president at the time, recounted how Woodson had helped her develop. "He helped me to maintain faith in myself," she recounted. "He gave me renewed confidence in the capacity of my race for development, and in the capacity of my country for justice for her own people and for all peoples." John Hope Franklin placed Woodson within the context of American historiography and measured his "far-reaching" contributions in terms of his diverse scholarship and his editing skills of rare primary sources and journals. L. D. Reddick, the "youngest member of the Woodson circle" who "early on advocated an avante guard approach to black history," applauded Woodson's "most characteristic creation," Negro History Week. Others, including Arnett G. Lindsay, Alrutheus A. Taylor, and Langston Hughes, remembered Woodson for his seriousness, mentoring abilities, ethic of hard work, and high expectations.[18]

The *Bulletin's* "Children's Page" paid special tribute to Woodson. Above a reprinted copy of Woodson's Teacher's High School Certificate, a motivational device for the magazine's young readers, is a brief sketch of his life and work. "But Dr. Woodson was not always a writer, lecturer, and a teacher," the female authors of the "Children's Page" pointed out in encouragement, "He was once a little boy, with all the love of fun and mischief which other boys have." Following these words is a set of fill-in-the-blank questions quizzing the young readers' knowledge of Woodson. An eight-year-old Washington, D.C., student's poem simply entitled "Dr. Woodson" illustrates the understanding that many children had of Woodson:

> Dr. Woodson, all of his days
> Improved his mind, improved his ways.
> He wrote history for school,
> And never broke the golden rule.
> He wrote history for our race
> And never made himself a disgrace.
> Now Dr. Woodson was a kind man;
> His death left heavy hearts.
> I don't think that anyone else
> Could step in and take his part.[19]

But Woodson was not eulogized so uncritically by all of his associates. In 1950, W. E. B. Du Bois wrote a scathing critique of Woodson in *Masses and Mainstream.* Though he praised Woodson for his "crowning achievement," Negro History Week, Du Bois devoted his brief article to critiquing his contemporary. According to Du Bois, Woodson had "a good mind, but was by no means brilliant"; he "lacked background for broad historical writing" (for he had "never read Marx"); he overate; he was stubborn; he had "no ties, family or social." He was a loner with a "rather narrow outlook. . . . He was, and had to be, a cramped soul. There was in him no geniality and very little humor. To him life was hard and cynically logical; his writing was mechanical and unemotional. He never had the opportunity to develop warm sympathy with other human beings; and he did develop a deep-seated dislike, if not hatred, of white people of the United States and of the world," Du Bois asserted. "In his death he does not leave many very warm friends; there were few tears shed at his grave." Du Bois's article vexed at least one of Woodson's close friends: as William Brewer told Lorenzo J. Greene, "Dr. Du Bois has a nasty article on Dr. Woodson in *Masses and Mainstream* for June 1950 which does Du Bois no credit."[20]

Why was Du Bois so critical of Woodson after he died? For one, Du Bois was one of black America's leading social critics and intellectuals. By 1950, he had established a tradition of openly criticizing black American leadership, as was the case with Booker T. Washington, Marcus Garvey, and Walter White. It was also easier for Du Bois to openly critique Woodson because they did not have a very close relationship. One of Woodson's closest co-workers commented that he could not recall ever seeing Du Bois in Woodson's office. On top of this, Du Bois and Woodson had a topsy-turvy professional relationship. The long-lasting debate between the two began in about 1918, when the NAACP received some philanthropists' money to do a project on black participation during World War I. During the same time, Woodson was denied funding for a similar project. This did not totally destroy their relationship. In the 1920s, upon Woodson's invitation, Du Bois participated in various ASNLH annual meetings. In 1925, Du Bois nominated Woodson for the NAACP's Spingarn Medal. "Woodson is not a popular man," Du Bois wrote to John Hope, "He is, to put it mildly, cantankerous. But he has done the most striking piece of scientific work for the Negro race in the last ten years of any man that I know. He has maintained his integrity, his absolute thought and action, and has been absolutely oblivious to either popular applause or bread and butter."[21] By the early 1930s, their working relationship was damaged by the Phelps-Stokes Project's *Encyclopedia Africana*. Woodson, who refused to work with the interracial organization, labeled Du Bois a traitor in a 1936 edition of the *Afro-American* (Baltimore) for serving on the editorial board, which, at first, had excluded both men. When the preliminary volume to Du Bois's encyclopedia was published in the mid-1940s, Woodson wrote a scathing critique of it in the *Journal of Negro History*.[22]

Throughout the 1950s, Woodson's characteristically serious picture and prophetic words graced the pages of the *Bulletin*. Most of these brief articles praised his achievements. In one sense, L. D. Reddick challenged his colleagues by publishing one of the first articles in the *Negro History Bulletin* after 1950 that portrayed Woodson as more than a fallen hero. He revised his own obituary for Woodson appearing in *Phylon* three years earlier.[23] Like Logan and Du Bois, he discussed Woodson's seriousness and authoritative nature. "If anything, Woodson was forthright. Much of his stimulation to others came by way of challenge. He had little more than contempt for pretense or excuses," Reddick asserted. "Those who did not know him too well considered him to be a 'hard' man—and, upon occasion, he could be as cantankerous and as irascible as they came." Yet Reddick remembered how much he profited from "the good Doctor" in their long and "engaging" discussions when Reddick visited the Washington, D.C., area from his former residence in New York. Like John Hope Franklin, he placed Woodson within the proper context of his time. In Reddick's estimation, Woodson mirrored his predecessors in realizing that racial stereotypes were facilitated by institutional racism and that these antiblack images simultaneously facilitated institutionalized oppression. Woodson was a pioneer because he initiated and sustained, "as almost nobody before him had done," the black history movement to combat this. Reddick speculated that his mentor was naturally driven to such accomplishments by his childhood, adolescence, and early adulthood experiences, his "rugged" health, and his commitment to a solid set of principles. Reddick concluded by calling upon young scholars to join the ASNLH in modernizing the black history movement, in continuing the work of a "truly great man!"[24]

During the remainder of the 1950s, Woodson received little scholarly attention. The *Negro History Bulletin* routinely saluted its founder, but between the magazine's May 1950 edition and Earl E. Thorpe's pioneering 1958 publication on black historians, only a handful of scholars commented on Woodson's contributions. One of these assessments was John Hope Franklin's "The New Negro History," published first in *The Crisis,* fittingly during February 1957. Franklin, who at this time one of the most respected and established authorities on African American history, emphasized that "the changes that have occurred in the writing of the history of the Negro race are as significant and, in many ways, even more dramatic than the very events themselves that the writers have sought to describe." Franklin underscored that the power derived from so-called scholarly misrepresentations of black people "provided the historical justification for the whole complex of mischievous and pernicious laws designed to create and maintain an unbridgeable gulf between Negroes and whites." He acknowledged the pioneering efforts of John Russworm, William Cooper Nell, and George Washington Williams, and he credited Woodson for "launching the era of 'The New Negro History.'"

He noted that the new movement sprung from a combination of factors in American life, but he underscored Woodson's and the Association's work:

> This [Woodson's effort] was, perhaps, the most far-reaching and ambitious effort to rewrite history that has ever been attempted in this country. But it was more than an attempt to rewrite history. It was a remarkable attempt to rehabilitate a whole people—to explode racial myths, to establish a secure and respectable place for the Negro in the evolution of the American social order, to develop self-respect and self-esteem among those who had been subjected to the greatest indignities known in the Western world. Finally, it was a valiant attempt to force America to keep faith with herself, to remind her that truth is more praiseworthy than power, and that justice and equality, long the state policy of this nation, should apply to all its citizens and even to the writing of history.[25]

❖ ❖ ❖

The first extensive critical assessment of Woodson was authored by Earl E. Thorpe, a black historian who came of age in the years following Woodson's death. Influenced greatly by Helen Edmonds, who received her doctorate in history from Ohio State University (1946) and authored *The Negro and Fusion Politics in North Carolina, 1894–1901* (1951) and *Black Faces in High Places* (1971), Thorpe completed a pioneering dissertation on black historians in 1953 at Ohio State University. Five years later, he published the first monograph on black historians. The broad, inclusive nature of *Negro Historians in the United States* contextualizes the historical development of this vocation. At the same time, such broadness oversimplified the life and work of many. As a student of psychology, Thorpe also insightfully tried to explain the evolution of each of his four schools of scholars. But, in doing so, he applied mid-twentieth-century psychology to late nineteenth- and early twentieth-century case studies. He also often glossed over various scholars' development over time. In Thorpe's defense, he was writing during a period when such panoramic studies were needed in order to establish a foundational historiography on black historians. He was greatly instrumental in initiating a discourse that is still in an early stage. Transcending the vindicationist tendency of celebrating and romanticizing black history, Thorpe critically assessed a group of thinkers from whom he had obviously received a lot of spiritual strength.

For Thorpe, Du Bois and Woodson "stand above all other Negro historians."[26] But this designation did not excuse them, especially Woodson, from the scrutiny of Thorpe's critical eye. Thorpe outlined "Woodsonian convictions" as being threefold: a belief that race prejudice resulted from the failure to acknowledge black history; an unrelenting struggle to show blacks that they have a credible history; and a desire to educate whites about blacks' role in America's past and the growth of world civilizations. Based on a few short articles in the *Journal of Negro History,* Thorpe highlighted the popular appeal of Woodson's work. "Businessmen, ministers of the gospel, housewives, lawyers, doctors, school presidents or principals or grade school teachers," Thorpe asserted, "they came from all walks of life and made some aspects of the work of the Association a middle-class mass movement."[27] Thorpe then identified more than twenty of those laypersons who labored in the trenches for Woodson's cause.

Thorpe's analysis of Woodson's published scholarship was problematic in some aspects. From 1915 until 1942, Woodson published twenty-two books. It would be very hard—nearly impossible—to adequately explore these books in a study of fewer than two hundred pages; Thorpe reviewed them in fewer than ten, with all of the books receiving extremely shallow treatments. In a review of *The Mis-Education of the Negro,* which he misdated as being published in 1923, Thorpe failed to place this one-of-a-kind polemic in its proper context.[28] By 1958, the *Negro History Bulletin* had featured many important articles on Woodson. Thorpe ignored this magazine and used the *Journal of Negro History* sparingly. Thorpe also reiterated the concerns of many white critics. "A significant aspect of the historical writings of Woodson, as is the case with about every Negro historian," Thorpe contended, "is his failure to present the negative aspects of the black man's role in the U.S."[29]

Surely, Woodson did not dwell upon "bad features as high crime rates, slums, disease, and other undesirable phenomen[a]" in books like *The Negro in Our History.* But he did conduct sociological studies that addressed such problems; more important, in most of his publications he did look critically at the past record. Thorpe concluded that Woodson's writings represented no major contributions in scholarly terms and said that his style was "not very impressive." He contended that Woodson's major achievement was to be found in the launching and popularizing of a "successful movement." Thorpe's pioneering 1958 study, reprinted thirteen years later with very few changes, does not seem to have attracted the attention of any of Woodson's biographers. Nonetheless, his study is important because it constitutes the first major monograph on black historians and, to a lesser degree, because it challenged the 1950 recollections of many of Woodson's disciples. Thorpe drew great inspiration from his predecessors and went on to serve as the Association's president from 1980 until 1982. When criticizing Woodson and his co-workers, he probably saw himself as taking the profession to a new level. He may have been more comfortable offering such criticisms because he was not closely associated with Woodson.

A year before Thorpe's study appeared, the American Society of African Culture was founded by a group of leading African American scholars who attended the First International Congress of Negro Writers and Artists. In the fall, Alioune Diop asked the group if they would author two volumes of *Presence Africaine,* dealing with how African Americans viewed Africa and how they interpreted the problems facing them in the United States. As a result, *Africa as Seen by American Negroes* was published in 1958. Several articles in this volume surveyed Woodson's contributions. Ulysses Lee, an associate professor of English at Morgan State University, assistant editor of the *College Language Association Journal,* and member of the *Journal of Negro History's* editorial board at the time, wrote a detailed article on Woodson's interest in Africa as revealed by the contents of the *Journal of Negro History* and the ASNLH's activities from 1916 until the late 1950s. Lee highlighted how the journal served as a vital discursive arena in which leading scholars, black and white, reconstructed African history. According to Lee's findings, the journal's significant articles dealing with Africa concerned "broad aspects of African civilizations and cultures;" Africa's relationship with the New World, Europe, and the international community; Liberian political and social history; colonialism; and Africa as a subject for anthropologists.[30] The Association, Lee added, also "developed a number of other activities and projects which became vehicles for the expression of interest in Africa," including annual meetings addressing Africa's problems, *The Encyclopedia Africana, The Dictionary of Negro Biography,* and the *Bulletin.* Lee suggested that Woodson himself was very much responsible for black America's recasting of Africa in the first half of the twentieth century. Woodson wrote most of the book reviews on Africa; he traveled to Europe in the 1930s to collect primary documents dealing with African history and culture; in sum, he devoted the last several decades of his life to topics in African history, especially *The Encyclopedia Africana.* Lee's article stands out because he was one of the first scholars to comb carefully through articles in the *Journal* and to conduct a thematic study of Woodson's work.[31]

Ironically, during the 1960s, the second half of which is referred to as the period of black cultural awakening and militancy, there were no major studies written on Woodson.[32] In 1965, at the fiftieth-anniversary annual meeting of the ASNLH in Atlanta, there was a "Carter G. Woodson Memorial Session" with tributes presented by James E. Stamps, Willie Miles, William H.

Brewer, Louis R. Mehlinger, Lorenzo J. Greene, C. Walker Thomas, and Harry V. Richardson. Why nobody chose to write a serious biography on Woodson during this decade is somewhat baffling. Enough time had elapsed for his protégés to chronicle his life and work more objectively. Woodson would have been a prime candidate for serious study, considering the intensified interest in black history during that period. Historians interested in black America coming of age during this dynamic era appear to have been more concerned with the important task of revising and creating subfields such as slavery studies than with pioneering a discourse about African American intellectual history. The number of professional black historians at this juncture was also small. The decade of the 1960s was not, however, entirely unproductive in terms of Woodson scholarship.

Throughout the early 1960s, Woodson's contributions were recognized in a reappearing "About the Founder" sketch located on the *Bulletin's* back page. He was also featured on the cover page of the February 1962 volume. The mid-1960s witnessed a resurgence of writings on Woodson in the *Bulletin.* The 1965 special summer issue celebrated fifty years of the ASNLH. Charles H. Wesley introduced the golden-anniversary volume with a concise account of Woodson's work. The magazine's subscribers read firsthand accounts of the Association's early years. Wesley eloquently captured the disposition with which Woodson approached his mission:

> Despite the founding associates, Woodson, our Founder, belonged to the list of post-nineteenth-century pioneer personalities in the techniques of American life who believed that it was necessary to work one's plan alone. He had, in this respect, a type of intolerance and self-opinion, which some of us regarded with humor and indulgence because we looked upon the cause as well as the man as equally valuable. This was an aspect of rugged individualism, which has helped to create the greatness of our nation through individual initiative and energy. He belonged to the era, the earmarks of which we hope have not entirely disappeared, when the individual will endeavor to be creative in his contributions and not to act so as merely to imitate the work launched by another.[33]

Wesley, who had his fair share of serious conflicts with Woodson, contextualized and justified his elder's peculiar personality (deemed selfish and self-centered by others who did not know him too well), which Wesley interpreted as being a beneficial characteristic and a product of his age. He ended his assessment with a call to others to join the cause: "Let us take up the Torch, lighted up fifty years ago by Carter G. Woodson, our pioneer, our historian. . . . We follow in his footsteps with his Torch. . . . We shall not fail him or ourselves!"[34]

Included in this volume are other valuable insights into the impressions Woodson left on his co-workers. Jessie H. Roy told *Bulletin* readers how Woodson actively mentored her and other black women.[35] In the twenty-eighth volume of the *Bulletin,* Lorenzo Johnston Greene shared from his detailed journal some of his experiences with Woodson in 1930. In this particular entry, Greene "marveled" at Woodson's leadership and devotion to black history.[36] The remainder of Greene's journal was published in two volumes several decades later by Arvarh Strickland in 1989 and 1996. Greene was much more critical of Woodson in a paper entitled "Dr. Carter G. Woodson: The Man As I Knew Him," which he delivered at various venues from the mid-1960s until the early 1980s. Greene's unpublished essay went far beyond simply honoring Woodson. Greene's critique angered at least one of Woodson's contemporaries. William Brewer, longtime editor of the *Journal of Negro History* after Woodson's death and an outspoken Woodson advocate, "became irate" when Greene once read a "shorter version" of this paper in Atlanta. "He [Brewer] swore I had defamed Woodson; further that so long as he was editor, it would not be published either in the *Journal* or the *Bulletin,*" an eighty-five-year-old Greene recounted in a letter to one of his confidants.[37]

What was it that Greene had said that made Brewer so furious? Like Woodson's other "Boys," Greene shared many positive memories about "the master," such as his endless devotion to "the cause," his "forceful, sincere, clear, and convincing speaking abilities," his unmatched work ethic, his isolated acts of extreme kindness, his "phenomenal memory," his love of children, and his modesty. He also stressed that "Dr. Woodson was a complex, many-sided man." According to Greene, "many admired Woodson, but few could love him. It was certainly so with me . . . Woodson had little consideration for the feelings of his co-workers. On several occasions when he cruelly hurt me, I remained faithful to him but only because of the movement which he personified. He was egotistic, opinionated, truculent, sarcastic, vindictive and at times seemed to take a sadistic delight in offending or hurting persons. We used to say at the office when Woodson spoke, no dog barked." Greene underscored his point, noting that "Woodson often disparaged and derided his associates. He seemed to take pleasure in crushing any vestige of self-confidence in them."[38]

Greene shared many personal examples and several cases of other employees to validate his claims. He added that as an employer, Woodson paid his employees little, pressured and overworked them, and fired them suddenly, exemplified by Greene's own case and that of Charles H. Wesley. Attempting to explain the origins of his teacher's peculiar personality, Greene surmised: "Despite the obvious greatness of the man and the adulation heaped upon him, deep down within, I believe Dr. Woodson was obsessed by a feeling of insecurity. It may have stemmed from the deprivation of his childhood. At any rate, his seeming compulsion to disparage, humiliate, even hurt those who worked closely with him led some of us to wonder whether he feared lest some younger man might push him from his intellectual stool and usurp his position."[39] While Woodson's "Boys" often wrote to each other to share their intimate views of their elder, Greene appears to have been the most critical and detailed in striving to explain Woodson's personality. In mid-March 1984, Greene told Patricia Romero that he planned to publish the paper, but it never appeared in published form. Brewer may have objected to Greene's portrayal of Woodson, but a cousin of Woodson's, after hearing Greene deliver this paper at Washington University in February 1983, approached the emeritus professor and said, "That was Carter G. Woodson." Had Greene published his paper or had he written a biography of Woodson, the historiography and scholarship on Woodson and black historians would have certainly been different.[40]

A year following the golden anniversary of the *Bulletin,* while Greene was president of the ASNLH, the *Journal* featured many tributes to Woodson. Prominent white scholars and leading black historians commented on the *Journal*'s achievements. Wesley alone assessed Woodson as a person. He reiterated what he had written in earlier articles, highlighting that Woodson's "rugged individualism" set him apart from most of his co-workers and that it was also his greatest weakness and strength. He still perceived his elder as being a pioneer, "as the first of the organizers of modern research, writing, and publication in the history of the people with darker color in all parts of the world." Dr. Woodson, Wesley stated, "pioneered in the cause of uniting these processes and succeeded."[41]

❖ ❖ ❖

During the peak of the Black Power era in the late 1960s, a handful of young black scholars turned to history as an outlet for social activism. Along with Vincent Harding, John Blassingame, and John Bracey, Sterling Stuckey called for a new interpretation of black history. Around the same time that his groundbreaking article "Through the Prism of Folklore" appeared, Stuckey published a piece in *Negro Digest* in February 1967 that illuminated the meaning of Africa to Woodson and Du Bois, specifically how they affirmed their African heritage and adopted a "rhetoric of African recognition." For Stuckey, Woodson (and especially Du Bois) did the most work to "recover the African past and instill pride in Negroes."[42] Stuckey highlighted that Woodson devoted five chapters to Africa in his 1922 classic; challenged the widely accepted views of missionaries, travelers, and public functionaries; maintained that Egypt was a black civilization and thoroughly researched other early African empires; and, most important, popularized Africa within the African American community. Stuckey's article, featured in *Negro Digest*—the major source for the scholarly and popular expression of the leading voices of the Black Arts Movement of the late 1960s and early 1970s—complemented Ulysses Lee's piece published nearly a decade earlier. Stuckey's work indicates that Woodson influenced one of the most prolific historians and cultural nationalists coming of age in the 1960s.

At the end of the sixties, Noreen Hale, a graduate student at the University of San Francisco, wrote the first major intellectual biography on Woodson. Though she did not have access to the personal papers of Woodson, which were guarded closely by the ASNLH, she developed some original analyses about Woodson's place in African American thought and in the development of the American historical profession. In her estimation, Woodson's thought was "the fusion and vacillation between various tenets of both conservative and radical 'schools' of black thought, and the two major revolts among Black intellectuals from the 1890s to 1930 (i.e., the militant reaction led by Du Bois . . . and the second revolt, the racial discovery of the 1920s)." Hale detailed how Woodson's approach simultaneously fell into seven categories of early twentieth-century black thought. Another feature distinguishing this unnoticed master's thesis was its critique of Woodson. "Woodson's writing tended to be colorless, humorless, ponderous, and vague in exposition," Hale asserted in a tone that August Meier and Elliott Rudwick would echo nearly two decades later. Hale's comments differ from Meier and Rudwick's in that she paints a more balanced portrait.[43]

During the second half of the Black Power era (1970–1975), the writings on Woodson acquired a more scholarly flavor; 1971 appears to have been a landmark year. In this year, a master's thesis, a dissertation, and a large part of a monograph were devoted to Woodson.[44] These studies seem to have been generated independently and do not suggest a new, uniform wave of interest in Woodson. While Detroit historian Richard Thomas produced an exhaustive master's thesis at Michigan State University, Patricia Romero's 1971 manuscript represents the first detailed dissertation on Woodson. Romero, born in Columbus, Ohio, in late July 1935, began working with the ASNLH a year after she received her bachelor's degree from Central State University in Ohio. From 1965 until 1968, she served as a research associate and assistant editor for the *Bulletin.* Having some access to unpublished ASNLH papers and to people who worked closely with Woodson, she was able to "plough a new furrow" in black historiography. She conducted painstaking research. Charles Wesley loaned her his papers dealing with Woodson, and she obtained important, unpublished papers and advice from Greene. Romero also interviewed Woodson's family members, including Callie Barnett, Nelson Bickley, Belva Clark, and Nelson and Carl Barnett, and some of his co-workers such as Herbert Aptheker and the Association's co-founders, Victor R. Daly, Charles Wesley, Langston Hughes, and Louis R. Mehlinger. Just as John Hope Franklin had pursued George Washington Williams, Romero "stalked" Woodson. She even traveled to the Sorbonne in Paris, where she learned that all of the records concerning Woodson's brief stay there in the early 1900s had been destroyed during World War II.

While Romero's study is comprehensive, she only briefly touched upon Woodson's intellectual persona and personality. Like Noreen Hale, she suggested that Woodson was the "product of the thinking of both Washington and Du Bois." She posited that Woodson patterned the Association after the NAACP and the Urban League, stressing how much Woodson's work meant to him. "The birth of the *Journal* was to Woodson literally something more than a mere publishing event; throughout his life he devoted himself to the *Journal* as most men would to a family," Romero contended. "When he had conflicts with other men, or organizations, he would turn to the 'Notes' section of the *Journal* to unburden himself. A lonely man except for his work, he used the *Journal* as some men might a wife as an emotional outlet." Romero's point is well taken. A significant part of Woodson's personality can be reconstructed through an examination of the *Journal.* Romero clearly admired Woodson, but her biography is by no means uncritical or celebratory. She cited the criticisms of men like Victor Daly, who asserted that Woodson "was a hard man to get along with. He was not a lover of his fellow man." She herself critiqued Woodson for not opening the ASNLH to potential allies and for not being strategic enough in his dealings with others. Woodson, she noted, "wrote and said what he thought, even though it often hurt his cause." Though it was never published, Romero's 275-page study still stands as a solid exploratory analysis of Woodson.[45]

Several years after Romero's dissertation appeared, Woodson's immediate successor as ASNLH director published a thoughtful paper first delivered before the fifty-seventh annual meeting of the Association in Cincinnati on

October 21, 1972. "It is hoped," Rayford Logan humbly announced, "that this lecture will suggest the need for further investigation that will result in an authoritative biography. The address is not authoritative; indeed, it is not complete because I have not had time to finish my investigation of the Woodson Papers at the Association Headquarters, those in the Manuscript Division of the Library of Congress, and some materials in the National Archives."[46] Logan attempted to explain how Woodson's experiences before the founding of the ASNLH affected his unwavering character established thereafter. Assembling information from primary sources—articles from the *Journal,* Harvard University's archives, and his own memories—he wrote a concise history of Woodson's thought. Logan posited several original ideas that were later examined by various scholars.

He discussed the relationship between the ASNLH and the American Negro Academy, founded nearly two decades earlier; he revised the apolitical image of Woodson by suggesting that during the early years of Woodrow Wilson's presidency, Woodson joined the Epsilon Boule, Sigma Pi Phi fraternity, for its political flavor, and he analyzed the problems that Woodson had with philanthropists and large foundations. For the rest of the 1970s, Woodson received passing attention in the *Journal,* the *Bulletin,* and other scholarly journals; he was a centerpiece of at least one creative dissertation that compared Woodson's program and philosophy of education with Booker T. Washington's and Paulo Friere's.[47] In the late 1970s, several key microstudies were published on Woodson. In 1977, Sister Anthony Scally (who, by 1981, was the head of the Carter G. Woodson Library at the ASNLH's national headquarters),[48] published an essay in the *Bulletin* wherein she explored the Woodson–Jesse Moorland correspondence housed in the Moorland-Spingarn Research Center at Howard University. Scally's analysis of these letters revealed a Woodson who was "always sensitive to criticism" and "very touchy" during the Association's early years.[49] In the same year, Marcus Garvey's chief biographer published a refreshing article in the *Bulletin* drawing connections between these "two giants of the 1920s." Tony Martin found that John Edward Bruce first introduced Woodson to Garveyite circles; that the *Negro World* publicized the Association's work and at times published reviews by scholars who critiqued Woodson's books; and that Woodson had a weekly column for the Universal Negro Improvement Association (UNIA)'s paper in the 1930s. Woodson also gained popularity among the UNIA ranks by not siding with "Garvey Must Go" advocates during an era of significant West Indian–African American conflict.[50] In Martin's estimation, Woodson and Garvey shared other important philosophies, such as self-help, race pride, the fear of physical and/or ideological "extermination" and assimilation, as well as distrust of Du Bois. According to Martin, after Garvey's death Woodson also published "one of the few sensible assessments" on Garvey and the UNIA by an African American intellectual.[51]

❖ ❖ ❖

The most sophisticated scholarship on Woodson was produced during the 1980s and 1990s. In the 1980s, the *Journal, Bulletin,* and magazines like *The Crisis* continued to acknowledge Woodson's contributions, especially during February of every year. None of these articles added any real substance to what Logan had researched in the previous decade, except for a 1981 essay by Sister Anthony Scally concerning Woodson's experiences in the Philippines. Inspired by the lack of available scholarship on Woodson, Scally also published the first full-length biography on Woodson. In writing her brief study, Scally interviewed Woodson's relatives, combed through various archives, and corrected some the inconsistencies generated by previous scholarship. Scally's study was further authenticated by her experience as a librarian for the ASALH and as a regular contributor to the *Bulletin.* Jacqueline Goggin, Earl E. Thorpe, and Charles H. Wesley all praised Scally's *Walking Proud.*[52]

In the early 1980s under the presidency of Earl E. Thorpe, the Association further consolidated its efforts to honor and publicize its founder's life and work. On April 1, 1982, the executive director of the ASALH proposed that "a statue be erected to Dr. Woodson's memory in the mini-park bounded by 9th Street and Rhode Island Avenue N.W. and Q Street." In late May of the same year, the Association called for a national historical editing project which sought to "(1) identify those repositories throughout the nation which hold documents relating to the life and times of Carter G. Woodson; (2) process and select materials including those housed at the ASALH national headquarters; (3) publish the edited volumes; and (4) complete a definitive biography of Carter G. Woodson as well as an administrative history of the ASALH and the Associated Publishers."[53] The editor-in-chief was to be Charles H. Wesley and the managing editor was to be J. Rupert Picott. Other editors included Clement Price, Jacqueline Goggin, Robert Hill, Louis Harlan, Herbert Aptheker, and Daniel T. Williams. Though these projects did not materialize beyond the planning stages, they do demonstrate that there was a genuine interest in documenting Woodson's life and work and the Association's maturation.

In the mid-1980s, the ASNLH organized several panel discussions on its founder at various meetings. In December 1984, the Association had a "Day of Commemoration for Woodson" at its headquarters. The program for the event included six accounts of Woodson from those who knew him best, recognition of honorees, and various exhibits featuring Woodson artifacts, memorabilia, and books by and about him. Those who attended certainly heard more intimate stories about this man who kept largely to himself. About a year after this event, the Association had a seminar on Woodson at their annual meeting; it included as panelists L. D. Reddick, John Hope Franklin, Dorothy Porter Wesley, Arnett Lindsay, and Lorenzo J. Greene. In 1985, Scally also published her bio-bibliography of Woodson. While her brief biographical sketch sheds some light on many of the unknown facets of Woodson's life, Scally constructed an in-depth chronology of Woodson's experiences, highlighting the various endeavors he simultaneously undertook. Most important, Scally listed nearly all of Woodson's books, pamphlets, and articles (including book reviews and weekly columns in various black newspapers), as well as the theses, dissertations, books, book reviews, articles, and manuscript collections dealing with him in varying degrees. In many cases, she even provided succinct reviews of these sources. In total, she assembled more than eight hundred items, providing an indispensable study for Woodson scholars. Scally was certainly one of the individuals best qualified to write a critical, exhaustive study on Woodson, but she opted to leave that task to future generations.[54]

In the same year Scally's *Walking Proud* was published, Jacqueline Goggin completed her dissertation on Woodson at the University of Rochester under the guidance of American slavery historians Eugene Genovese and Stanley Engerman. In many respects, Goggin's dissertation is one of the most informative studies on Woodson. Meier and Rudwick relied heavily on her research in writing the first chapter of their *Black History and the Historical Profession, 1915–1980*. It equals her 1993 biography on Woodson in many regards.[55] Goggin sought to assess how and why Woodson used black history to uplift black America and how the American historical community responded to him. She described her dissertation as surpassing previous studies by incorporating the papers of Franz Boas, John Hope, James Weldon Johnson, Julius Rosenwald, the Terrells, Arthur Spingarn, James F. Jameson, Nannie Helen Burroughs, Luther Porter Jackson, James Hugo Johnston, Benjamin Brawley, Alain Locke, Kelly Miller, the Grimke brothers, and W. E. B. Du Bois. Goggin also interviewed and maintained fruitful correspondences with many of those historians who worked closely with Woodson.[56] She wrote to Lorenzo Greene as early as November 1980 to ask the former Woodson employee about the fate of Woodson's personal papers and the realities of being a black scholar during the era of segregation. Greene responded to Goggin's various inquiries, stating, foremost, that her theory that Woodson destroyed his own papers was without a doubt inconceivable.[57]

Goggin offered many insightful observations. "Without the *Journal,*" she pointed out, "it is doubtful that black scholars would have been able to publish their work." She argued that the *Journal* also pioneered in writing history "from the bottom up," especially in terms of slavery studies, and provided a medium for liberal and leftist white scholars. She explained how Woodson was a trailblazer in comparative history who cultivated a distinct interdisciplinary approach. The last three chapters of Goggin's study are exemplary, tracing how Woodson popularized black history, how he raised funds for the Association activities, and how his "cantankerousness" affected his work. She paid special attention to his rocky relationships with white philanthropists and his co-workers, including Du Bois, Jesse E. Moorland, Benjamin Brawley, Kelly Miller, and James Hugo Johnston. Goggin underscored that Woodson refused to join any project for which he was not the primary director. Woodson had, she surmised, an "intense personal independence."[58]

Since countless dissertations go widely unnoticed, it is hard to gauge their influence. In Goggin's case, this is partly possible. She sought advice from several of Woodson's protégés. Lorenzo Greene offered her some valuable constructive criticism. In March 1984, he commented that he was impressed by her "diligent" search for materials and the heavy documentation in her work. He challenged Goggin "to paint a more intimate picture of Woodson the man." Greene preceded some of Goggin's more recent critics. "Intensively as you have researched Woodson, your study is not a biography of the man. You have not drawn a flesh and blood picture of your subject," Greene continued, "We see him depicted as 'highly independent, principled, opinionated . . . moody . . . self assured', with a 'domineering personality.' The reader would like to know what made him so."[59] In a manner reminiscent of Woodson, Greene proceeded to pinpoint specific pages where Goggin committed some oversights, and he posed eight detailed questions for Goggin to grapple with. He also challenged her to extend Woodson's influence beyond the factors implicit in the title the "Father of Systematized Black History." In 1984, Greene lamented, "The real biography of Woodson remains to be written and, unfortunately, those who held the key to Woodson's real personality, the focus that drove him, and the psychic factors that made him Woodson, have passed, or are rapidly passing, from the scene."[60]

❖ ❖ ❖

In the early 1980s, a group of historians held a first-of-its-kind conference on the study and teaching of black history at Purdue University under the auspices of the American Historical Association. Woodson's contributions received little attention in the papers delivered and then published three years later in 1986. John Hope Franklin's paper represents the volume's sketch of the profession, and he located Woodson's chief function and contributions in the second generation of historians of the black past spanning from 1915 until the mid-1930s. Franklin, who spent "many hours with [Woodson] each year between 1940 and 1950," credited Woodson with providing "the intellectual and practical leadership" for his colleagues and protégés. In Franklin's estimation, Woodson did "everything possible to keep the history of Afro-Americans before them and before the larger community as well."[61]

In 1986, Darlene Clark Hine, editor of the important volume in which Franklin's essay appeared, published an informative essay documenting in great detail Woodson's "paradoxical and, at times, peculiar relationship" with "major white philanthropists and officers of the Carnegie Fund, the Julius Rosenwald Fund, and the three Rockefeller trusts." Hine dissected Woodson's philosophy and approach beyond his challenging quest for funding his movement. She proposed that Woodson's movement to promote black history was "a three-tiered operation composed of the rank-and-file Association members, professional historians, and Woodson himself."[62] In 1986, August Meier and Elliott Rudwick devoted one quarter of *Black History and the Historical Profession, 1915–1980* to detailing Woodson's struggles with various philanthropists and individuals. Though they acknowledged Woodson's central role in the black historical profession, they portrayed Woodson as being unfulfilled by his work, ideologically confused, and contradictory in his convictions. "While Woodson thus laid the foundations, he did not live to see Afro-American history either recognized by the mainstream of white historians or anything more than a marginal specialty or to be embraced by Negroes themselves with the enthusiasm that he had envisioned," Meier and Rudwick contended in the first paragraph of their study. "These things did not come pass until two decades after his death."[63]

Meier and Rudwick appear to have overlooked Woodson's annual reports in the *Journal* and his various polemic pieces in which he constantly celebrated the rank-and-file's enthusiasm and the general evolution of the study of black history. Meier and Rudwick accurately observed that part of Woodson's goal was to publish the records of black America so that "the race," as he repeatedly proclaimed, "may not become a negligible part of the world." They had trouble in pinpointing Woodson's thought and program because they sketched a picture of Woodson's personality based almost entirely upon personal papers that focus on his conflicts with certain individuals; because Woodson did not fit into their preconceived dichotomy of black thought; and because they did not appreciate the value of popularizing the study of black history. Holding tightly to their archaic protest-accommodation dichotomy, Meier and Rudwick employed a flawless, saintly image of Du Bois as a yardstick for measuring Woodson. Woodson, they argued, possessed an "essentially conservative nature."[64] They said, "Woodson did not function as an influential historian through his monographs; outside the group of historians he gathered about him in the 1920s and 1930s he has not functioned as an inspirational figure in the profession. . . . Woodson, unlike Du Bois, did not produce monographs that are read and admired to this day."[65] Meier and Rudwick oversimplified Woodson's character, suggesting that "unlike Du Bois he [Woodson] lacked a broad strategy of reform and, as we have seen, consciously and pointedly avoided ideological controversy." Major reviews of Meier and Rudwick's work ignored their misinterpretations of Woodson.[66]

During the remainder of the 1980s, no major study on Woodson appeared. By the early 1990s, Jacqueline Goggin emerged as Woodson's chief biographer, taking scholarship on Woodson to a more recognized level. Goggin's succinct 1993 biography is subdivided chronologically and thematically into six chapters and differs greatly from her dissertation. In narrating Woodson's life story, she scrutinized a great portion of those sources compiled by Scally nearly a decade earlier. In explaining his early life from 1875 until 1915, Goggin examined the records Woodson left at the M Street High School, the University of Chicago, Armstrong Manual Training School, Harvard University, and Howard University. Goggin echoed Meier and Rudwick's account by focusing on the Association's financial problems and the conflicts between Woodson, philanthropists, and some of his co-workers.[67] At the same time, she reviewed how Woodson labored selflessly for the benefit of the masses. A great part of Woodson's philosophy of black uplift, she argued, was couched in a genuine concern for the black rural and urban working class, racial solidarity, self-help, expressions of classical black nationalism, and, perhaps most important, complete autonomy. Indirectly overturning Meier and Rudwick's reading of Woodson's political schizophrenia, Goggin outlined his long career as a political activist in the Committee of 200, NAACP, National Urban League, Friends of Negro Freedom, New Negro Alliance, and Garvey's UNIA. She also surveyed his political ideology of the 1930s and 1940s as articulated in a handful of leading black weeklies wherein he had regular columns.[68]

Unlike Scally's scholarship, Goggin's biography has received great attention in nearly all of the widely read historical journals. From May 1993 until October 1996, Goggin's study was reviewed in more than a dozen magazines and journals; all of the reviewers welcomed her biography as a significant contribution, and some offered insightful critiques.[69]

The most recent development in the scholarship and historiography on Woodson is the publication of the Papers of Carter G. Woodson and the Association for the Study of Negro Life and History, 1915–1950. The processing of these papers on thirty-four microfilm reels was completed in late August 1998 and consists of "a large body of material that has never been available to scholars" including correspondence files, organizational and business records of the ASNLH, the Association's business ledgers and account books, many manuscripts submitted to Woodson, and the manuscript for *The Encyclopedia Africana.* David Levering Lewis has predicted that these papers are "bound to result in major revisions in much of what we think we have known about . . . how one of the most remarkable one-man operations in American scholarship survived and throve against enormous odds."[70] Arvarh Strickland offered equal praise for this collection. These documents are essential for historians seeking to research the ASNLH's formative years and in more general terms the challenges faced by autonomous black scholarly organizations during the era of Jim Crow segregation.

❖ ❖ ❖

It is impossible to measure exactly how the historical scholarship on Woodson has affected his public image or legacy. The mainstream media has sparingly covered Woodson. He did not grace the cover of major white newspapers or magazines. In July 1926, *Time* mentioned Woodson's receiving the Spingarn Medal, "the symbol of Negro distinction." On the last page of the "National Affairs" section, where a nice photo of Woodson appears, the editors reprinted selected passages from "the maze of unfamiliar facts" in *The Negro in Our History.* Had Woodson received this award in later years after he severed ties with influential philanthropists, it is highly improbable that one of the nation's leading news magazines would have acknowledged his accomplishments. In the years to follow, the ASNLH founder was among those few blacks mentioned in white-authored reference books. After he died, the April 4, 1950, edition of the *Washington Post* ran a small picture of Woodson with the a caption above it reading "Dr. Woodson Dies; Negro History Expert." The brief column appeared on page 2B along with the death notices of a handful of others. In the back of the *New York Times* for the same day, there was an even briefer obituary, without a photograph, entitled "Dr. C. G. Woodson, Retired Educator, Former Dean at W. Virginia State Dies—Authority on Negro History." Did these newspapers' white readers pay attention to these notices? Probably not. Not surprisingly, other major papers, such as the *Chicago Tribune, Detroit Free Press,* and *Boston Globe* ignored Woodson's death and contributions.

The black community's coverage of Woodson's passing was inconsistent. *The Crisis* failed to cover Woodson's death in any way. From April 1950 until December 1950, the NAACP's organ did not even mention Woodson's name. In March 1950 they paid brief tribute to Edwin R. Embree and Charles Hamilton Houston. One searches for Woodson's name in vain in the "Editorials" for May, June, July, or August, the months immediately following his death. How do we explain such an oversight? There are several possibilities. Perhaps the NAACP executive board did not have a cordial relationship with Woodson. He did, after all, criticize "highly miseducated Negroes," many of whom were associated with the NAACP. Other, more scholarly journals ignored Woodson's death as well. The *Quarterly Review of Higher Education among Negroes* did not mention Woodson's death in its "News Items" or "Editorials," even though Charles S. Wesley, then president of Wilberforce University, was on the editorial board. What makes this even more intriguing is that throughout the 1950s, the *Quarterly Review* paid tribute to several martyrs of the black struggle, such as Mary McLeod Bethune (1875–1955) and Charles S. Johnson (1889–1956).[71]

Ebony, one of black America's most popular middle-class magazines founded in the mid-1940s, paid homage to Woodson toward the end of the 1950s. He was "the third distinguished American" named by readers to "The Ebony Hall of Fame," Madame C. J. Walker being this award's first recipient. The editorial presented him in a manner echoing his disciples. The *Ebony* editors asserted:

> His achievements won him many admirers, but few of them became close friends. To Woodson, a stubborn, single-minded individualist, this was not of the slightest importance. He never consciously sought to be liked, never cultivated those habits and personality traits which could endear him to the public. He was, quite possibly, too busy. For decades it was his custom to devote virtually every waking hour in research, writing and editing. Nothing else mattered. He had no ties to anyone, depended on no one, came as close as any man can to being an island "intire of it selfe."[72]

"In his death, he [Woodson] does not leave many warm friends," Du Bois proclaimed in June 1950, "there were few tears shed at his grave."[73] The roughly five hundred people who attended Woodson's funeral, his close friends who openly mourned his death, and much of the black press disproved Du Bois's claims. Overall, black newspapers gave Woodson's passing wide coverage. In the 1930s, Woodson wrote regular and spontaneous columns for a range of leading African American newspapers, including the *Chicago Defender, Pittsburgh Courier, New York Age, Baltimore Afro-American, Boston Chronicle, Washington Bee,* and Garvey's *Negro World.* Woodson's death was mentioned in these papers, but in some instances it was overshadowed by the death of one of black America's greatest physicians and scientists, Dr. Charles Drew, who died as a result of an auto accident in North Carolina while on his way to a professional meeting. Drew's sudden death shocked black America, especially since after the accident he was rushed to a segregated hospital that did not have any blood plasma that may have saved his life. In the Saturday, April 8, 1950, edition of the *Pittsburgh Courier,* the front page headline read: "Dr. Charles Drew Killed: Crash Fatal to Blood Bank Expert." The tribute to Drew appeared throughout several pages of the paper. No mention was made of Woodson, who died on April 3, 1950. In this weekly's next national edition, the editors recognized Woodson with a brief account of his life, and they also included rare photographs of the late historian's sister, Bessie Yancey, his brother, Robert H. Woodson, and the pallbearers carrying Dr. Woodson's casket out of the funeral home.[74]

Other black newspaper weeklies' coverage of Woodson was more detailed. Both the *Chicago Defender* and the *Norfolk Journal and Guide* discussed Woodson's life and death in their April 8 and April 15, 1950, editions. Both featured photos of Woodson on the front page and celebrated his contributions alongside those of Charles Drew. The *Afro-American* furnished the most detailed account of Woodson's life, contributions, and death. On the first two pages of the April 8, 1950, edition of this Baltimore weekly, the editors sketched out in fairly good detail the circumstances of his death as well as his contributions as a scholar. Unlike the other papers, the *Afro-American* also quoted directly from Woodson. On April 15, 1950, Baltimore's leading black newspaper talked about Woodson's funeral rites. The thorough editors quoted directly from and paraphrased Charles H. Wesley's eulogy. They also reprinted what other friends of the deceased historian said, including John W. Davis, Ellis O. Knox, Emmett J. Scott, A. L. Jackson, L. J. Greene, Herbert Aptheker, R. B. Atwood, and L. P. Jackson. The tribute ended with Logan's words: "Dr. Woodson was essentially a creative mind. . . . His own works and the Association which he founded will be an invaluable reward for his unselfish efforts." It was not the time or place for Woodson's successor as *Journal* editor and Association director to critically assess his elder.[75]

In the subsequent decades, other black magazines and papers, including *Ebony*, recognized Woodson infrequently during what is today known as Black History Month. Nevertheless, Woodson's contributions are still sidestepped. Outside of academic circles, the general public has a very limited access to Woodson's legacy. Only a handful of his books have been reprinted at affordable prices, and no PBS special has been devoted to him.[76] Those interested could have visited his house at 1538 Ninth Street N.W., which was renovated in 1981 with funding from the U.S. Department of Interior and the D.C. Division of Preservation of Historic Sites. The executive director of the ASALH announced, "We think you will find joy in this restoration of what is to become one of Washington, D.C.'s most popular visitors' sites." How many Americans have visited this historical site and what they have gotten out of such an experience is difficult to ascertain. Woodson's Victorian-style row house has been "vacant for many years and is urgently in need of substantial repairs." Endorsed by the ASALH and the Organization of American Historians' executive board, there is a movement to restore this "national treasure."[77] Though the scholarship on Woodson has not afforded him celebrity status in American or African American culture, Woodson's name does live on in some capacities. Today, a great deal of information on Woodson can be found at thousands of Internet sites, and his name is used in the titles of awards, fellowships, libraries, organizations, institutes, schools, and even an apartment building. Still, much more serious work must be done in order to fully bring about an appreciation of Woodson's life, work, and contributions. Armed with a better understanding of Woodson, future generations of African American historians can better decipher their roles and possibilities. There are also many aspects of Woodson historiography that warrant further research.

2 A Pioneer in Black Studies and History

ALONG WITH COUNTLESS OTHER BLACK professionally and nonprofessionally trained scholars, Carter G. Woodson was an important member of the proto–Black studies movement. This African American "vindicationist tradition" included many black scholars who during the era of Jim Crow segregation laid the foundations for the modern Black studies movement.[1] W. E. B. Du Bois has probably been the most widely acknowledged member of this black scholarly tradition. While this group was by no means philosophically monolithic, they were bound together in meaningful ways. Most important, they were largely excluded from "whitestream" academe. For the most part, they did not have access to certain benefits and resources located in exclusive, white, scholarly outposts. In turn, they created viable, productive, autonomous academic institutions, scholarly approaches, and practical strategies for black mental and psychological liberation. This overarching philosophical outlook dictated that they create productive epistemologies that established, validated, and promoted the rigorous study of black life while simultaneously and directly challenging white ethnocentric scholarship and social thought. In the case of Woodson in particular, he foreshadowed modern Black studies scholars in stressing that the study of African descendants be scholarly, sound, creative, restorative, and directly relevant to the black community.

One of Woodson's most important contributions to the early black history movement and the proto–Black studies movement was his mission and ability to transform black history into a practical and popular medium for uplifting blacks and challenging racial prejudice. He revolutionized the

American historical profession and democratized the study of black history by extending the discipline to various groups of scholars who were not professionally trained. In adopting this approach, he did not de-emphasize the role of scientific scholarship in the "life-and-death struggle" for black liberation. On the other hand, he maintained that, in addition to being founded on meticulous research, the study and dissemination of black history needed to extend to the working-class and youth sectors of the black community. Woodson reasoned that the knowledge of African American history was, after all, an important and practical (though nonmaterial) way in which black people could become liberated and empowered.

Between 1915 and 1950 (increasingly more by the 1920s), Woodson strove to enlighten the black masses, popularizing black history in a variety of innovative ways. He extended himself as a resource to black communities throughout the country and opened the doors of the ASNLH meetings and activities to lay historians, ministers, secondary and elementary school teachers, businessmen, and the black community as a whole. He initiated Negro History Week and other extension services. And he published the *Negro History Bulletin,* an essential outlet for not only Woodson himself but for countless black thinkers representing a wide spectrum of the black community.

Several questions help us frame Woodson's contributions to the proto–Black studies movement. What influenced Woodson to adopt an essentially pragmatic approach to history? In what particular ways did he democratize the study and dissemination of black history? How did he successfully mesh his somewhat old-fashioned idea that history consisted of the collection and presentation of "facts" with his more progressive philosophy that history could uplift and empower blacks? How did Woodson use his popular scholarly medium to introduce his readers to contemporary social and political realities and concerns? How did Woodson's ideas about class differences within the black community shape his approach to history?

❖ ❖ ❖

In searching for the origins of Woodson's concern with popularizing black history and facilitating cross-class dialogues and interactions, a logical starting point is his upbringing and early years. Raised by former slaves and sharecroppers, Woodson came from starkly humble origins he never seemed to have forgotten. A seasoned manual laborer from his early childhood until his twenties, Woodson probably identified strongly with the children of black coal miners he taught from 1898 until 1900 in Winona, West Virginia.[2]

After receiving his doctorate from Harvard University in 1912, Woodson began publishing a genre of historical scholarship which was accessible to a wide range of readers. He wrote in such simple language that some of his modern critics have considered him unsophisticated. August Meier and Elliott Rudwick have claimed that "Woodson, unlike Du Bois, did not produce monographs that are read and admired to this day," that he "did not function as an influential historian through his own monographs."[3] Meier and Rudwick judged Woodson's scholarship based on its existence in the "white-stream" academy. They failed to place his scholarship within the context of his pragmatic philosophy of black history. As well, Woodson published several brands of scholarship: in the vindicationist tradition, rigorous scientific scholarship to combat racist scholarship; polemical commentaries in order to address black America's contemporary status in American society; and books aimed at attracting a wide readership from elementary school students to university students. This last collection of books included *The Negro in Our History* (1922), *Negro Makers of History* (1928), *African Myths Together with Proverbs* (1928), *The African Background Outlined* (1936), and *African Heroes and Heroines* (1939). The unfinished *Encyclopedia Africana* was also written in very simple language. Woodson valued his practical history texts. Several years before it was actually published, Woodson advertised *The Negro in Our History* as a study for use in black history clubs, elementary and high schools, and colleges and universities. "Just as soon as this book has come from the press," Woodson told the *Journal of Negro History* readership, "the Association will send to all Negro schools of secondary and college grade a field agent to interest them in the effort to inculcate in the mind of the youth of African blood an appreciation of what their race has thought and felt and done."[4]

It is difficult to discern how the black youth and laypeople were affected by Woodson's writings. The recently compiled Papers of Carter G. Woodson and the Association for the Study of Negro Life and History, 1915–1950, contain elaborate records of books sold by the ASNLH from the 1920s on. While there are countless receipts and orders, Associated Publishers struggled throughout its existence, and during Woodson's lifetime there was not a strong demand for black history books among the general black populace. According to Lorenzo Johnston Greene, boxes of the Association's books were literally collecting mildew in the Association headquarters' basement in 1930. Poet Sterling Brown declared in the early 1940s that the hardest task facing black authors was "developing a critical but interested reading public."[5] Working-class blacks, especially during the lean years of the Great Depression, did not place a high priority on purchasing hardcover scholarly literature. As Lorenzo Greene testified during his bookselling campaigns, it was black professionals who usually purchased the Association's literature. *The Negro in Our History* was Woodson's most popular book. By March 1941, Woodson noted that forty thousand copies of his text had been sold.[6] But his interaction with nonprofessional black communities went beyond simply using the written word.

Early on, the ASNLH developed connections to the heart of black communities. Every year during Woodson's lifetime, the Association's meetings were held in black churches, community centers, colleges and universities, and high school auditoriums throughout the country. Patricia Romero has noted that the first time an Association meeting was held in a major hotel was in 1964 in Detroit.[7] While the breakfasts, luncheons, and dinners attracted a certain highbrow crowd, and the executive council held its own private business meetings, the keynote speakers, panel discussions, and presentations and pageants were attended by a much broader spectrum of the black community. Unlike any other academic organization of its time, the ASNLH welcomed individuals without doctoral degrees into its ranks and even into its leadership positions. A perusal of the *Journal of Negro History* from 1916 through Woodson's death indicates that at annual meetings, schoolteachers and community activists, including many clubwomen, presented papers and in many cases even had their essays published in the pages of the *Journal* alongside the research of leading black and white scholars. In this way, Woodson democratized the black scholarly community.

Woodson's most famous and perhaps most effective effort at attracting a mass following and popularizing the study of black history was through Negro History Week celebrations. But before 1926, when he inaugurated this celebration, Woodson took black history to the people in other ways. During the era of Jim Crow segregation, Woodson and his colleagues were among the most sought-after lecturers in the black community nationwide. Woodson himself spoke at countless venues throughout his lifetime for minimal fees. L. D. Reddick recounted that during his childhood in Jacksonville, Florida, Woodson was easily "the most impressive speaker" he had heard. The manner in which Woodson presented himself before his audience, his electricity, and his dedication to "the cause" influenced the young Reddick to join the "Negro History Movement."[8] Woodson also corresponded with countless men and women interested in black history from all around the world. He answered their questions, commented on papers, and mailed them information pertaining to black history. In *Ten Years of Collecting and Publishing the Records of the Negro,* Woodson commented that since the inception of the ASNLH, the Association had functioned as a "free reference bureau."

Early on in the Association's history, Woodson sought to gain a mass following with outreach programs. By 1919, he employed J. E. Ormes, formerly in the business department of Wilberforce University, as a field agent. Ormes's role was to increase membership in the Association, appoint agents to sell books and subscriptions to the *Journal,* and organize black history clubs. In the early years, Woodson called upon any interested individuals to join his cause. According to a statement in the *Journal's* "Notes" in 1919, "any five persons desiring to prosecute studies" in black history could have organized a club. Each club was required to pay the Association two dollars, a small fee that entitled the member club to a year's subscription to the *Journal* and access to Woodson, by mail, for advice and instruction. He often sent bibliographies and outlines to clubs for study and required only that a club elect a president, a secretary, a treasurer, and an instructor, who should be the group's "most intelligent and the best informed member."[9]

Such early efforts from Woodson seemed to have been fairly effective. Several years before the first Negro History Week celebration, he commented that he had succeeded in convincing schools and colleges to "devote more time to the study of Negro life and history" and that "a larger number of persons" were becoming interested in the Association's work. By the mid-1920s, Woodson noted that black history clubs officially linked to the Association were found in practically all cites with considerable black populations.[10] Woodson also attempted to stir interest in black history among the youth with financial incentives. In 1924, in collaboration with the American Folklore Society, the Association offered a prize of two hundred dollars "for the best collection of tales, riddles, proverbs, sayings, and songs, which have been heard at home by Negro students of accredited schools."[11]

Months before the first Negro History Week celebration was to take place during the second week of February 1926 in commemoration of Frederick Douglass's and Abraham Lincoln's birthdays, Woodson explained the reason behind the celebration in a "widely distributed" pamphlet. Woodson told his readers that blacks knew "practically nothing" about their history, and that without this knowledge "the race" could become "a negligible factor in the thought of the world" and stood "in danger of being exterminated."[12] He added that race prejudice, from segregation to violence, resulted from the widely accepted notion that black people had not contributed anything of worth to world civilization. He argued that if the historical record was set straight and if the history of black people was studied in schools along with the achievements of others, not only would black youth develop a sense of pride and self-worth, but racism would also be abolished. Woodson ended his plea with this assertion: "Let truth destroy the dividing prejudice of nationality and teach universal love without distinction of race, merit or rank. With sublime enthusiasm and heavenly vision of the Great Teacher let us help men rise above the race hate of their age unto the altruism of a rejuvenated universe."[13]

Liberal and radical, black and white intellectuals and educators of the Intercultural Education Movement shared Woodson's contention that racial tension was the by-product of whites' historical and cultural ignorance and that education could help alleviate these problems of misunderstanding. Woodson's efforts to popularize black history both preceded and mirrored those of many intercultural education specialists of his time and were an important expression and ingredient of American educational reform during the interwar period. Interculturalists were by no means unified in their views. Like their Progressive Era predecessors, they did not constitute a monolithic group of reformers. They were motivated by the Europeanization of American culture as a result of immigration during the late nineteenth and early twentieth centuries. Many advocates of the Intercultural Education Movement shared the underlying belief that acknowledging the contributions of various subgroups in American society could effectively reduce "misconceptions about cultural differences" and ethnocentrism while promoting self-esteem in minority groups, cultural integration, and diversity in the United States.[14]

Negro History Week was the first major achievement in popularizing black history and was unique in that it focused on the black youth. Woodson realized that the miseducation of black people began in their homes, communities, and elementary schools, and he targeted these sites aggressively, focusing especially on the schools. Although some critics deemed Woodson's strategy of gradually introducing black history as a supplement to "whitestream" American history as too conservative, the approach was pragmatic and very radical when analyzed in the broader context of his agenda. Woodson knew that if he had demanded that black history be integrated into the American educational system all at once, his plan would have been too easily dismissed. A modest, week-long celebration during the winter season appeared much less threatening to the white public, to philanthropists, and to those "highly mis-educated Negroes" whom he sought to convert into devout black nationalists.[15]

Linking the past, present, and future, Woodson's vision of Negro History Week was optimistic and long term. This seemingly token celebration was to serve as a stepping-stone toward the gradual introduction of black history into the curricula of educational institutions, from the elementary school years through college, throughout American communities, black and white. He wanted Negro History Week to evolve into "Negro History Year," as he noted from time to time. Routinely, Woodson instructed those observing the week that they needed to diligently prepare for the celebration months in advance, and that after mid-February they needed to continue acknowledging the role of African descendants in world history. "Negro History Week should be a demonstration of what has been done in the study of the Negro during the year and at the same time as a demonstration of greater things to be accomplished," Woodson instructed schoolteachers. "A subject which receives attention one week out of the thirty-six will not mean much to anyone."[16]

According to Woodson, soon after he mailed out his first Negro History Week circulars to various educational institutions, presses, fraternal and social welfare organizations, literary societies, and radio stations, "there was a stir in the direction of active participation." He boasted, "There were few places in the country where this celebration did not make some impression."[17] Where there was interest in it, Woodson offered a concrete program along with research and promotional materials that highlighted black achievements from the ancient era in Africa to contemporary times. People who decided to take part in the celebration had autonomy over the week's activities, but Woodson did often offer a host of suggestions.

In pamphlets and articles in the *Negro History Bulletin,* he routinely instructed participants to organize committees for the celebration months before Negro History Week. He outlined the critical steps to success: involving the governing, power-wielding board of education; advertising the events extensively; recording oral testimonies from elders within the community; persuading libraries to order black history books; setting aside one day of every week as a "Book and Picture Fund Day" to raise money to purchase black history books for the community; sending to the ASNLH any relevant historical documents so that they could be properly maintained; organizing black history clubs; and creating a pageant highlighting the struggles of black Americans. Especially in February volumes of the *Bulletin,* he added special suggestions to schoolteachers about maximizing the involvement of the youth in practical ways.

During the celebrations there were banquets, breakfasts, speeches, parades, exhibits, and lectures that were usually held in churches, black colleges and universities, and community centers. Woodson insisted that a significant number of the events be free to the public. For this week, he stressed that speakers and organizers must donate their time to the cause. Schoolteachers, mainly black women, were vital Negro History Week organizers. They raised funds in their communities and had their students compose essays on famous blacks and events in black history; some encouraged their students to act in historical plays and pageants taken largely from an anthology written for elementary students entitled *Plays and Pageants for the Life of the Negro.*[18]

After its inception, Negro History Week continued to expand. In his "Annual Reports of the Director," Woodson noted that every year, Negro History Week drew a greater following. In many volumes of the *Journal of Negro History* after 1926, Woodson devoted brief articles to describing the success of the various programs. He was very pleased that the celebration had eventually made its way into the black churches, self-help organizations, public schools, even into rural areas. In 1932, he noted also that Negro History Week was gaining recognition in white schools, facilitating better "inter-racial relations." With each passing year, the black and occasionally the white press advertised local and national events. Early on, the outlets most active in publicizing Woodson's movement were the *Philadelphia Tribune, Baltimore Commonwealth, Chicago Defender, Palmetto Leader, Tampa Bulletin, Washington Eagle,* and *Norfolk Guide and Journal.* Later, other more widely distributed newspaper publishers joined in. Various radio stations were instrumental in publicizing and broadcasting Negro History Week events.[19]

By the 1940s, Negro History Week celebrations were increasingly popular. Woodson developed elaborate programming schedules. In November 1948, in order to help rural schools with little or no resources, Woodson introduced Negro History Week kits at two dollars apiece. At first, the kits included writings and speeches by famous blacks as well as a play depicting black history. Two years later, Woodson revised them to include many photos of famous blacks as well as a list of books for further research. The cost for this edition was $2.50.

But as Negro History Week become more popular, Woodson believed that there was a class of people who were exploiting the celebration for their own benefit. In the *Journal of Negro History* and the *Negro History Bulletin,* he routinely warned his readers about "the disastrous methods of pseudo-historians among Negroes exaggerating in spectacular fashion facts of minor importance" in order capitalize on a movement and transform it into a commercial venture. He was especially enraged with those "impostors" and "mis-informants," mainly entertainers, who, under the name of the ASNLH, reaped large profits during mid-February. At one point, he even demanded that they turn over their earnings to the Association, and he called upon Negro History Week organizers to boycott those "mischievous orators" and instead call upon one of the many historians whom Woodson trained.[20] In October 1941, he offered the following advice to schoolteachers: "Do not call in some silver-tongued orator to talk to your school about the history of the Negro. The orator does not generally have much in his head. His chief qualification is strong lungs—a good bellows. He knows very little about things in general and practically nothing about the Negro in particular except how to exploit the race. Let the children study the history of the race, and they will be the speakers who will put the spellbinder to shame."[21]

Woodson was also disturbed because as late as 1945 many schoolbooks on the black past "found their way to some shelf where they serve mainly to catch a portion of dust raised in that room." In one sense, he admitted the shortcomings of Negro History Week to penetrate into the psyche of American society. "It is evident then," he noted, "that our supplementary books on the Negro supplement nothing in most of our schools."[22]

Despite Woodson's frequent pessimism, which counterbalanced his unrelenting faith that his people could humanize American culture, Negro History Week was a monumental movement. Assessing the impact of Negro History Week celebrations on black working-class and youth consciousness from 1926 until 1950 is a difficult task. We can assume that many of the blacks who took part in these events felt great pride in their heritage and that some open-minded whites who witnessed and helped sponsor such events may have changed their views of black history and culture.

Indeed, throughout the late 1930s and 1940s, *Bulletin* readers, especially female schoolteachers, wrote to Woodson, often in great detail, about how they conducted their Negro History Week celebrations and how the processes had influenced them and others. Woodson often published these commentaries in the *Bulletin.* Many testified that Negro History Week had helped transform their cultural and political consciousness. Carrie E. Johnson, a schoolteacher from Troy, Alabama, told Woodson that his work "has been my greatest inspiration in making me want to devote all my time to the study of my race."[23]

Nevertheless, schoolchildren were probably the most highly transformed by these events. They learned by doing, researching the lives of famous blacks and acting in plays that depicted the African American past. Woodson extended himself to detail specific things children should do during Negro History Week. In the February 1938 issue of the *Bulletin,* he instructed children to "make a study" of their school's history; collect newspaper articles on "prominent" blacks in their county, city, or state; explore the history of blacks in the professions; and create a play or pageant that represented "every phase of life and every phase of struggle through which the race has come."[24]

Many of Woodson's colleagues believed that Negro History Week was his "most characteristic creation." Devoted Negro History Week promoter Luther Porter Jackson called Negro History Week "the feeder for every other activity of the Association." In paying tribute to Woodson, L. D. Reddick noted, "[H]is greatest influence upon the public mind came through Negro History Week." Reddick believed that the effect of Negro History Week on African Americans' self-confidence, poise, desire to achieve, and morale "defies measurement." This "mass education program" and "God-send for the Association" pleased Woodson to "no end" and upon several occasions he deemed it the Association's most valuable contribution. Woodson extended himself during this month. For example, in 1933, during the peak of the Great Depression, he spent not only Negro History Week lecturing at various venues, but he devoted himself for the next month "in the field," lecturing and helping people to organize throughout the country.[25] "By far," Woodson noted in the early 1930s, "the greatest stimulus given to the educational work of the Association in recent years has been the observance of Negro History Week."[26]

The impact of Negro History Week went beyond the black community during Woodson's lifetime. In 1949, Morris U. Schappes, a member of the American Jewish Historical Society, informed Woodson that at their annual meeting in February, the society decided to observe Jewish History Week from April 24 until April 30. He told Woodson that their decision was influenced by the success of Negro History Week. Woodson took pride in this wide-reaching impact of the Association's work, telling blacks that they could learn a lot from the cultural nationalism of their Jewish counterparts.[27]

The Negro History Weeks of Woodson's times were much different from most Black History Month celebrations of recent years. Since the end of the Black Power era, along with other facets of African American popular culture, Black History Month celebrations have been commodified, watered down, and tokenized by a capital-driven American popular culture. For Woodson, it was greatly important for the people themselves, especially children, to create personalized celebrations. While Woodson offered many suggestions, he challenged those interested in discovering the value of their past to do the uncovering themselves.

❖ ❖ ❖

In 1927, a year after the founding of Negro History Week, Woodson established the ASNLH's extension division in order to expose more people to black history through public lectures and correspondence study. The Home Study Department was necessary in Woodson's view because it could educate teachers who would in turn teach black youth about their history and because "various classes of citizens" needed to know their history. This process of education involves passing on information through a series of closely interactive stages and levels. In a tone reminiscent of Booker T. Washington when he advertised Tuskegee Institute's Movable School or Jesup Agricultural Wagon, Woodson asserted that the Home Study program took the school to the student. Woodson's program offered courses at introductory and advanced levels. Only those with a high school education and the desire to "profit by the work" were encouraged to apply for admission. While Woodson sought to make the study of black history and black life more accessible, he refused to delegitimize the scholarly endeavor by abandoning standards. One had to apply for admission and pay a five-dollar matriculation fee. Tuition for one course was twenty dollars, two for thirty-five, or three for fifty-two. Although students had one year to finish the requirements for each course and pass a final examination, Woodson encouraged students to complete the assigned work in two to three months.[28]

Each introductory course was accompanied by a series of lessons with specific readings and suggestions. After completing these lessons, the student would have (ideally) answered some questions and mailed the "recitation paper" back to the instructor, who would then review it and mail it back to the student with the appropriate comments. Advanced courses were offered to college graduates. More flexible in nature than their introductory counterparts, advanced classes were arranged with input from both the students and the professors. Woodson assured the public that the standards of the Home Study Department were equal to those of "accredited colleges and universities," that nothing is "hastily done," and that "every student is guaranteed personal attention." A brochure for the Home Study Department promoted classes in anthropology, art, English, history, literature, and sociology. The teaching staff boasted leading scholars in the African American community, including Woodson himself, Charles H. Wesley, Alain Locke, E. Franklin Frazier, Luther Porter Jackson, James Hugo Johnston, and Charles Johnson. At the end of the course, each student received a certificate that noted the amount of work he or she had accomplished, and full credit was granted only to those who passed the final examination.[29]

The Home Study Department did not appear to be successful in terms of enrollment. Further, it did not spread its roots into the black community as Negro History Week had. While Woodson noted that the second year of the Home Study Department went "remarkably well," a year later he admitted that the enrollment was very low, owing primarily to the fees and the standards of admission. Woodson nevertheless had a positive outlook, noting that those who did manage to finish were prepared to instruct others.[30] Such efforts demonstrate that central to Woodson's philosophy was the democratization of American academic culture.

The last major extension work Woodson undertook was the founding of the *Negro History Bulletin.* By the mid-1930s, Woodson wanted to increase his regular readership among black youth, the black working class, black elementary and secondary schoolteachers, and nonacademics in general. In addition, the *Journal of Negro History* was inaccessible to many because of its price. While white scholars such as Edward Channing told Woodson that the price of the *Journal* was too low, some black scholars told Woodson otherwise. W. H. Crogman, once president of Clark University in Atlanta, wrote to Woodson in April 1927 of his regret that "for some reason I did not come into touch with your 'Journal of Negro History' until about three years ago. I subscribed to it one year, and discontinued my subscription because of the terribly hard times and high prices."[31]

The *Bulletin,* on the other hand, had many functions. Written in a simple language to help black teachers who had little or no knowledge about black history, it supplemented "whitestream" American history textbooks of the time and was the vehicle by which schoolteachers and other concerned citizens helped Woodson take black history into the homes of the black masses. The magazine served as an advertising mechanism for the ASLNH's activities, especially for Negro History Week. It also served as a platform for blacks—from elementary schoolchildren to community activists to schoolteachers to professional scholars—to openly discuss and even publish their thoughts about black history. Woodson stressed to potential contributors that only serious articles dealing with black history would be considered: the *Bulletin* was not an entertainment magazine. Woodson also used the *Bulletin* as another one of his ideological platforms.

The first issue of the *Bulletin* was introduced in October 1937 and, like the rest of the volumes during Woodson's lifetime, appeared nine times throughout the year, coinciding with the months of the school year. Until the late 1940s, a year's subscription was one dollar (or twelve to fifteen cents a copy); for some time, clubs of five people or more could secure the magazine for only forty-five cents a year. Woodson also offered bulk rate discounts. By the time of his death in 1950, the subscription price had risen only to two dollars a year (twenty-five cents a copy). Woodson kept the price low and in fact sold the *Bulletin* at a loss in order to maintain a higher readership. Though Woodson was the managing editor, black women dominated the editorial and managing boards. They also wrote many of the articles, organized and ran the magazine, and encouraged children to begin their historical studies early. Individual issues of the *Bulletin* focused on certain topics and themes in black American history. Woodson adopted this approach so that regular subscribers would have "a brief illustrated history of the Negro" at the end of the year. He also sold back issues bound in one volume.[32]

Between 1937 and 1950, issues contained biographical sketches of famous and not-so-famous blacks and whites who were sentimental to the cause; simple book reviews; challenging lists of questions for the readers; plenty of photographs reminiscent of those found in *The Crisis;* discussions of periods and important events in black history; updates about current events mainly pertaining to black schools, Negro History Week, branches, and clubs; artwork by leading black artists; a "Book of the Month" section; poetry; information about Africa and the diaspora; suggestions for Negro History Week; simple plays written by schoolteachers and lay scholars; and primary sources. Of particular importance in terms of socializing black communities and cultivating within blacks' minds a black historical consciousnesses were Woodson's polemical columns, discussions initiated by teachers, and the "Children's Page," introduced in November 1940 at the suggestion of the *Bulletin*'s female staff and female readers, who thought that a section of the magazine officially designated for children would instill "the youth of African blood" with pride in their history and culture.

In November 1940, for instance, Lillian M. Rhoades, the associate editor of *Apex News,* told Woodson that she would like for the *Bulletin* "to solicit verse and articles by children." She reasoned, "This column devoted to their contributions will get them interested in their particular page, and familiar with the [*Bulletin*] as a whole. Then as they grow up," she continued, "they will grow up with the [*Bulletin*], and would not be without it."[33] Increasingly after its debut, the thoughts, prose, and ideas of children were featured in the *Bulletin* as a method of influencing other youngsters to study black history seriously. Each issue's "Children's Section" challenged readers to answer questions pertaining to the monthly theme and quizzed them about how they could best facilitate a Negro History Week celebration. Under the guidance of Howard University–trained artist Lois Mailou Jones, the young readers during the early 1940s were also provided a picture to color or paint, a mask to cut out and wear, or a sculpture to cut out of a bar of soap. While Jones gave her readers very clear instructions, the children were challenged to think creatively.[34]

The *Bulletin* also served as a discussion forum for teachers about how best to incorporate black history into their individual classrooms and their schools' curricula. They exchanged teaching methods, joined the contemporary political debates, and traded advice about how best to celebrate Negro History Week. In a sense, the pages of the *Bulletin* belonged to black schoolteachers, serving as their autonomous space for generating epistemologies of black history. Woodson encouraged this ownership and dialogue by assuring them that the magazine belonged to them and by publishing their ideas just as he published the scholarship of intellectuals in the *Journal.* Woodson also solicited their suggestions and published them from time to time. The *Bulletin* was unique in that it was one of the only journals open to black female teachers. He included photographs of them alongside photographs of other prominent figures in the struggle.

Woodson's image and voice resonated above his schoolteacher counterparts. In every issue of the *Bulletin,* Woodson wrote at least one column in which he addressed problems faced by black Americans, defined his philosophy of history, and offered his readers potential solutions. Throughout the pages of the *Bulletin,* Woodson articulated his vision of how history could serve mankind. He never really altered his fundamental belief that history entailed the objective laying-down of "the facts." While he certainly did emphasize black achievements and at times employed history as some form of "propaganda"—a tactic he himself despised—he insisted to *Bulletin* readers that "real history requires the elimination of self. . . . Facts properly set forth will tell their own story."[35] Woodson wanted history to be a major part of black people's everyday life. He used columns to call upon blacks to act and change the course of history themselves. For Woodson, the status of black people was a "life-and-death struggle." He shared with Marcus Garvey a fear that black people faced the possibility of extermination. In an essay appearing in the February 1940 issue of the *Bulletin,* Woodson challenged his readers to do great things based on the deeds of their ancestors. History was, for Woodson, a tool of inspiration. "To you, then, comes the challenge as to what you will do in building upon the foundation which they have laid. These people whose civilization was marked by the kerosene lamp, the wash tub, the hoe, and the ox-cart disappointed the prophets who said they would be exterminated; and on the contrary they enrolled themselves among the great." Woodson pleaded, "What will you do in the day of the moving picture, the radio, and the aeroplane? If we do not take hold where they left off and advance further in the service of truth and justice, we are unworthy to claim descent from such a noble people."[36]

Woodson wanted blacks to study history seriously and to incorporate it genuinely into their worldviews. He constantly reminded his readers that the purpose of Negro History Week was not simply to acknowledge and celebrate blacks' accomplishments for one week. Woodson argued that black history should be taught everyday in the classrooms; that knowledge that blacks *do have a history* could significantly decrease race prejudice; and that if blacks knew their history, they would be inspired to act. Woodson's straightforward philosophy of history as explained in the *Bulletin* was very non-elitist. He believed that anyone willing to invest significant work could act "like" a historian. In 1943, Woodson told teachers that a historian was a rigorous collector and organizer of facts, that children could be historians by recording their families' pasts, and that even those not formally educated could be historians of some sort by writing down, in whatever language, the histories of their communities. Woodson firmly held that the history of black Americans, despite their oral traditions, needed to be recorded by black people. He did not deem anyone who recorded historical "facts" a historian, yet he was committed to demystifying one function of the black scholar and stimulating interest in black history and the historical profession in a widely accessible manner.

Woodson used the *Bulletin* to indict white America for mistreating blacks, to celebrate blacks' abilities to persevere, and to critique his fellow black Americans. In a 1939 essay in a volume devoted to the black church, Woodson asserted that black churches were too emotional, plagued by disunity, and lacked concrete philosophies of social uplift. He was especially critical of the exploitative preacher: "He will come to the church at times during the week to fire the hearts of the 'seeker,'" Woodson charged, "but after he receives his collection he is ready to retire to some other part of the city because he does not care to dwell in their district." Woodson concluded that such behavior existed because "most trained ministers were miseducated."[37] Perhaps he critiqued the black church because he realized the potential it had in regenerating black America.

Woodson also continued his attack on black intellectuals and the black middle-class in the *Bulletin*. More than five years after *The Mis-Education of the Negro* was first published, Woodson described the typical black graduate from Yale, Harvard, Columbia, and Princeton as being useless. A graduate of Harvard himself, Woodson used such generalizations in order, he hoped, to spark debates and critical conversations. The black college graduate, in Woodson's estimation, was one "equipped to begin the life of an Americanized or Europeanized white man," one without the proper training to help the masses of his people. These "intellectuals," Woodson added, despised Africa and its descendants. Woodson claimed that their aping of white people would not help them or American culture. He instructed blacks to "learn to do what whites cannot do" and then make the world "much better off" with these gifts. Woodson advocated a "revolution" in the American educational system, calling for institutions that would be molded to the conditions of black Americans.[38]

In a later issue of the *Bulletin,* perhaps in reference to black participation in Gunnar Myrdal's *An American Dilemma* (1944) or Du Bois's and Rayford W. Logan's participation in the Phelps-Stokes Fund's encyclopedia on Africa, Woodson attacked black scholars for working hand in hand with white scholars in what he called "mis-representing" black people. Woodson argued that too many black scholars were blindly selling their research to white research investigators who altered their works to support theories of black inferiority.[39] Woodson charged that these black intellectuals lacked character and would sell out their people for any amount of money and recognition within white scholarly circles.

Woodson extended his criticisms to black political leaders. Several times in the 1930s, he championed the opinion that no black political leadership had existed since Reconstruction. He proclaimed that there were too many "inconsistent and compromising" self-ordained leaders who were "working against the interests of the race." Black leaders, in his view, all too often accepted segregation. At times he seems to have given up on black leadership entirely. In the early 1940s, Woodson argued that blacks would gain democracy in America only with the leadership of "the laboring classes" since they were "not obligated to the oppressors of their people" as were their spokesmen or "hand-picked agents."[40] Woodson's iconoclastic rhetorical strategy was aimed at raising debate within black intellectual circles.

Woodson also indicted the black middle class in the *Bulletin* for their lack of business sense and failure to operationalize economic nationalism and self-sufficiency. Foreshadowing Malcolm X, Woodson deplored the fact that blacks allowed foreigners to open businesses in their communities. He argued that black people lacked an economic program in the most basic of forms. The Great Depression was "a blessing in disguise," Woodson commented in challenging blacks to turn within, to rely on themselves, and to be creative. Concluding that "the Negro's point of view . . . must be changed," he offered *Bulletin* readers several potential solutions. He called upon blacks to open small businesses, demanded that his people, especially professionals, stop wasting their money on toys and leisure activities, and called upon "the man who has few thousand dollars" to make sacrifices for the benefit of those in need. Woodson was especially critical of the black middle and professional classes. He was convinced that they had the power to help the masses in monumental ways. He arrived at this conclusion not only by studying the ideologies and actions of countless of his predecessors, but also by recognizing the ways in which one person and one organization of committed individuals could serve a "needy cause."[41]

Woodson's open criticism of the black middle and professional classes (of which he was a member) revealed not only his impatience with his counterparts' failure to establish more meaningful coalitions with the black laboring classes, but, equally important, his faith in their abilities to bring about their own advancement and liberation as well as that of black Americans in general. In holding such beliefs, Woodson's ideas resembled those of other black intellectuals of his time. For instance, while Charles H. Wesley revised the history of black workers and in the process recognized their potential to generate significant social change, Harry Haywood "not only defended the black working class against the racist attacks of white workers, but he also emphasized its revolutionary potential in the long-term struggle to abolish American capitalism and imperialism." For Wesley, Haywood, Woodson, and others like them, the black working class would itself, without the guidance of an elite black leadership, play an essential role in helping improve the status of black America.[42]

❖ ❖ ❖

During the era of World War II, Woodson's commentaries took on a much more political flavor. He attacked the U.S. government for mistreating devoted black soldiers during and after the war. He declared in one column that U.S. policies "resembled more the policies of Hitler" than those of a so-called democratic nation. To Woodson, this behavior paralleled the abuse endured by black American soldiers since the colonial era. Woodson interpreted the role of blacks in World War II, and in previous wars, as "peculiar." Like many other black leaders throughout history and his time, he publicized and supported blacks' historical and contemporary activities in the armed forces in hopes that blacks would receive citizenship in exchange for their services. Embracing the "Double V Campaign," he believed that the black soldier's loyalty during World War II would "strengthen his case" for equality and first-class citizenship. He urged blacks to engrave their unwavering patriotism deeply into the historical record so that whites could not deny their basic human rights without denying "the truth." In one sense, Woodson had faith that enough liberal whites would eventually acknowledge "the truth" and undergo significant ideological transformations.[43]

Throughout the remainder of the 1940s, Woodson continued to publish social commentaries in the *Bulletin.* He attacked segregation in American social and institutional life, condemned America's imperialist and expansionist ethos in the immediate aftermath of World War II, scrutinized problems plaguing the black community from within, reiterated and clarified the function of Negro History Week, and commented on the changes affecting black people in a global context.

During Woodson's lifetime, the *Bulletin* underwent various changes and developments. The first major change, in October 1939, was the increase in size from eight to sixteen pages. Woodson resolved that black schoolteachers were in need of more information to adequately incorporate black history into their curricula. In order to maintain his audience, Woodson did not raise the price, and by the magazine's third volume, the articles were becoming more in-depth, thematically organized, and more scholarly in tone. During the 1940s, more than a few of Woodson's protégés contributed scientific historical scholarship to the *Bulletin.* By October 1940, the style of the magazine changed. While the first three volumes resembled a small newspaper, the volumes after 1940 looked more like a journal or magazine, resembling issues of *The Crisis.* From October 1937 until April 1950, Woodson's columns in the *Bulletin* became increasingly more political. The gradual radicalization and increased scholarly flavor of the magazine is best explained by Woodson's strong conviction that the magazine was not a vehicle of popular matters or propaganda. He stressed that it was a space where students with varying interests of history could enlighten and engage each other. He tended to couch his polemical diatribes in historical articles and perhaps guard them with some sense of anonymity.

According to Woodson, the *Bulletin* was a successful venture. In 1943, he declared that "nothing attempted" by the ASNLH since Negro History Week "has met with more public approval" than the *Bulletin.* He felt justified in publishing it at a loss because he believed that it was finding its way into the minds of black people, making black schoolteachers more well rounded, inspiring black youth, and even helping to deconstruct race prejudice and foster better relations between blacks and whites. Woodson used the *Bulletin* as he had the *Journal*'s "Notes," as a comfortable place to articulate his dynamic, iconoclastic worldview in simple language. At the same time, the *Bulletin* was one of Woodson's gifts to black people. John Hope Franklin certainly thought so. "The BULLETIN," Franklin noted, "represented perhaps the most vigorous extension of the work of Dr. Woodson into the lives of persons who were soon to share the responsibility of making their communities better places in which to live."[44]

During the four decades after the founding of the Association of the Study of Negro Life and History in 1915, Carter G. Woodson helped lay the ideological foundations for the modern Black studies movement. Since the Black Power era, many scholars have acknowledged Woodson's key role in the proto–Black studies movement. Most important, he successfully converted a scientific academic discipline into a practical tool of self-empowerment and liberation. Many decades before the golden years of Black studies, the scope and seriousness of Woodson's scholarship and social activism served as useful object lessons for practitioners of the modern Black studies movement. Dimensions of Woodson's approach can be beneficially adapted to Black studies paradigms of the twenty-first century.

3 The Progenitor of a Twentieth-Century African American Iconoclastic Tradition

IN OCTOBER 2001, Harvard University's new president, Lawrence H. Summers, and Harvard African American studies gatekeeper Cornel West had a private meeting. Neither man was aware of the ramifications that this somewhat historic meeting would have. According to reports from West, who discussed his side of the story in *Vanity Fair,* Summers accused him of frequently missing classes; not producing serious enough scholarship; spending too much time engaged in various political campaigns; inflating students' grades in his African American studies courses; and getting too involved in popular culture by recording a CD with a distinct R & B and hip-hop flavor. West recounted that Summers said he wanted to personally review West's scholarly projects every few months to ensure that they met Harvard's standards. Humiliated and dishonored, West publicized Summers's allegations, and by January 2002, many major newspapers and newsmagazines reported that West was seriously considering leaving Harvard for Princeton. The conflict between Summers and West has generated significant media attention, with Black studies being discussed in a manner reminiscent of the 1960s and 1970s. West's final decision to leave Harvard in April 2002 was covered on the front page of the *New York Times.*[1]

There were several different camps involved in this debate, including West sympathizers, West critics, and a small group who presented the case in a more neutral manner. According to sympathizers, including Robin D. G. Kelley, Glenn Loury, and Danny Goldberg, West's departure from Harvard's African American studies "dream team" hurt the overall intellectual flavor of the university. West's critics, such as Shelby Steele, John McWhorter, and

Thulani Davis, agreed with many of Summers's indictments of West. Some of these critics have stooped to nasty name-calling. West has been deemed an "academic lightweight," a "clownish minstrel," and even "a self-promoting lightweight with a militant head of hair."[2]

Gerald Early provided a more balanced assessment of the situation and defended West. Early noted that West, unlike most intellectuals, has been able to take his message beyond the academy. In October 1995, West participated in the controversial Million Man March initiated by Nation of Islam leader Louis Farrakhan. About five years later, he publicly defended hip-hop celebrity P. Diddy during the celebrity's widely publicized trial. West participated in one of the early hip-hop summits. Consistently and throughout the country, West speaks out at a variety of venues. He endorsed Al Sharpton's announcement to run for president. He has done commercials promoting the television network BET. In 2001, Artemis Records released West's first CD project, "Sketches of My Culture"; West called this debut, spoken-word CD, "danceable education." He has also collaborated with KRS-One. In the mid-1990s, West, along with other black public intellectuals, was accused of embracing his comfortable position at Harvard. Years later, his activities definitely challenged the Ivy League standards of high-profile professors. Early summarizes the current and past plight facing many black scholars: "Scholars as a group are kind of alienated to some degree from non-academic folks. What academics do is kind of refined, and you are away from ordinary folks. I think that really becomes an issue for the black scholar trying to speak for the black people."[3]

The Summers-West incident raises a host of important questions. How do black scholars balance their lives as intellectuals and community activists? What types of limitations exist for black scholars operating in Ivy League institutions? How are Black studies programs being treated throughout the nation's colleges and universities? What is the state of affirmative-action policies in American higher education? How much autonomy do university professors have? And, perhaps most important, what is the role and responsibility of black scholars and intellectuals to the masses of their people? Historically, this last inquiry has generated a great deal of discussion within the black community. Between 1933 and the early 1990s, an African American iconoclastic tradition of scholars has struggled with the issues reinjected into black intellectual dialogues by Cornel West's highly publicized experiences: the function and responsibility of the black scholar, the black intellectual, and the black middle class.

In their introduction to Harold Cruse's famous *The Crisis of the Negro Intellectual* in the mid-1980s, Bazel E. Allen and Ernest J. Wilson III, two

University of Michigan scholars, argued that there has existed "a long and honorable succession of intellectual landmarks in Afro-American thought" that has demonstrated an "independent spirit of analysis, its iconoclastic disregard for the popular pieties of the time, and its debunking of the self-legitimations of the dominant personalities, institutions, and practices of a period." Allen and Wilson placed an interesting mix of scholars within this loosely defined tradition, including W. E. B. Du Bois, the contributors to *The New Negro* anthology, Carter G. Woodson, Richard Wright, Ralph Ellison, James Baldwin, Leroi Jones (Amiri Baraka), Harold Cruse, E. Franklin Frazier, William Julius Wilson, and Thomas Sowell.[4] Though intriguing, Allen and Wilson's use of "iconoclastic tradition" is a problematic description for these scholars. While all these intellectuals may have sought to overturn traditional ideologies and institutions, they attacked very different ones and for different reasons. Grouping "radical" and "conservative" black thinkers together without making any distinctions between them, Allen and Wilson did not justify the linkages among these thinkers.

I would use the term iconoclast in terms more specific than those proposed by Allen and Wilson. Using Carter G. Woodson as a centerpiece and the progenitor of a black iconoclastic tradition, I focus critically on three twentieth-century African American scholars who not only disregarded their black bourgeoisie colleagues but who, in their outspoken and controversial monographs, also actively challenged them. In addition to Woodson, the group includes E. Franklin Frazier, author of *Black Bourgeoisie* (1957), and Harold Cruse, author of *The Crisis of the Negro Intellectual* (1967). Each of these thinkers used terminology and analyzed case studies specific to his particular time and concerns, but each critically deconstructed the same type of intellectual spokesperson. They indicted those African Americans who separated themselves from black culture and the struggles of the masses, who instead sought recognition, honor, and financial gain only for themselves, striving, through imitation, toward the ideal of integration into the white American mainstream.

In addition to noting a common problem, these thinkers wrote their polemics for similar reasons. They published their commentaries as public confessions and affirmations of their own psychological transformations, metamorphoses of consciousness that reflected a dedication to social and political activism. They shared the ultimate goal of persuading other blacks of their class to abandon the behavioral characteristics of the pathological personalities they described. They therefore often exaggerated and repeated their arguments. Woodson, Frazier, and Cruse believed that the problems facing black intellectuals had reached such a peak that it was necessary to advance both concern and debate within their communities. The writings of all of them were received negatively by many leading intellectuals of their times. Finally, as Allen and Wilson noted about Cruse's classic, the writings of these iconoclasts are indeed in many regards relevant to the cultural politics of contemporary black America. These writings still speak to the issues and audiences of today "with the same acuity" that they showed for "earlier readers."[5]

While the iconoclasts of this study all shared a common vision, it is Woodson's ideas that form the centerpiece of the "iconoclastic tradition" for several reasons. He was one of the first black intellectuals to critique publicly the historically black colleges and universities as well as the caste of educated leaders whom Du Bois so adamantly praised in the early 1900s.[6] During the first half of the twentieth century, most black intellectual leaders did not openly challenge Du Bois's theory that "exceptional men," "distinguished Negroes," and "college-bred Negroes" were the best equipped group to save the race, to "guide the Mass away from contamination and death of the Worst," bringing them "in contact with modern civilization" and "broad culture."[7] In outlining (in 1903) the need for a "Talented Tenth"—theoretically the most able 10 percent of black Americans who, through higher education and cultural status, would become leaders—Du Bois did not extensively critique the black intelligentsia of his day or earlier. He indicted only those who were "half-trained demagogues," "vociferous busy bodies," "money makers," and, of course, Booker T. Washington. He praised his antebellum predecessors for challenging the institution of slavery and he complemented his educated post-Reconstruction counterparts for their unselfish work as teachers, preachers, and professionals supposedly instructing the masses as to "what life means."

Nearly three decades later, Du Bois continued to praise the "Negro bourgeoisie" at a time when Woodson condemned many of them. "For two generations the social leaders of the American Negro, with very few exceptions, . . . have worked unselfishly for the uplift of the masses of Negro folk," Du Bois wrote in *The Crisis* in 1931. "There is no group of leaders on earth who have so largely made common cause with their race as educated American Negroes, and it is their foresight and sacrifice and theirs alone that have saved the American freedman from annihilation and degradation."[8] In fact, Du Bois did not level an overt indictment against the Talented Tenth until about a half a century after he initially articulated this strategy. In 1948, Du Bois reformulated his turn-of-the-century ideology in an address before Wilberforce University's prestigious Sigma Pi Phi Fraternity. He stressed that his archaic program needed to be revised to suit the problems of post–World War II America.[9]

Long before Du Bois publicly reexamined his own theory, Booker T. Washington, not possessing the formal training and academic credentials of his colleagues, had challenged Du Bois's thinking along the same line that more recent members of the "iconoclastic tradition" have criticized their respective intellectual foes. Beginning in the late nineteenth century, Washington portrayed black intellectuals who opposed him as being "unfortunate and misguided young men" trained only in "mere book knowledge." "My experience," Washington asserted in *My Larger Education,* "is that people who call themselves 'The Intellectuals' understand theories, but they do not understand things." Such "abstract principles of protest," Washington continued, "did not solve the country's race problem." Washington preceded Adolph Reed Jr. in arguing that black intellectuals made money off the sufferings of the black masses. Many black intellectuals, Washington said, "make a business of keeping the troubles, the wrongs, and the hardships of the Negro race before the public. Having learned that they are able to make a living out of their troubles, they have grown into the settled habit of advertising their wrongs. . . . Some of these people do not want the Negro to lose his grievance, because they do not want to lose their jobs."[10]

Though they were molded by different social climates and fashioned ideologies and programs that served their distinct approaches, Woodson reinvoked certain aspects of Washington's program—namely, a frank and almost cynical dismissal of certain black intellectuals, a quest for autonomy, a strategic way to deal with whites in positions of power, and a devotion to the black masses through practical outreach work. In this sense, Woodson was unique since nearly all prominent black intellectuals after Washington's death have sided with Du Bois. Besides Cruse, who defended Washington in only a very limited manner, Woodson is the only iconoclast who openly defended Washington. In *The Negro in Our History,* first published in 1922, Woodson appears to have sympathized with Washington rather than with Du Bois's camp. According to Woodson, Washington stepped forth with "a new idea . . . as to move millions." Woodson asserted that Washington's educational philosophy laid "a foundation for the future." He agreed that Washington should be criticized for falling prey to "certain entanglements in which he of necessity had to make some blunders." But Woodson concurred with his role model that "mere agitation for political rights" could not solve black America's economic plight. In Woodson's estimation, Washington was "the greatest of all Americans, the only man in the Western Hemisphere who has succeeded in effecting a revolution in education." He especially applauded Washington's ability to make education practical "for the masses of the people who had to toil."[11]

Throughout the rest of his career, Woodson continued to defend Washington. In the March 1947 volume of the *Negro History Bulletin,* Woodson, rejecting the popular dichotomy of black leadership, celebrated Washington's contributions to the black struggle: "It is doubtful that he ever convinced the majority of his race that he was on the right track," Woodson noted. "No man had been so generally misunderstood by his own people."[12] Woodson's support of Washington, however, must be placed within its proper historical context. During Woodson's lifetime, W. E. B. Du Bois, Ida B. Wells, Horace Mann Bond, and E. Franklin Frazier criticized Washington's leadership strategies and legacy. It was not until after Woodson's death, between the early 1950s and the 1980s, that scholars such as August Meier, Emma Lou Thornbrough, Elliott Rudwick, James D. Anderson, and Washington's chief biographer Louis R. Harlan began to uncover Washington's "secret life" and the use and misuse of power with the "Tuskegee Machine." If the historiography on Washington had been more developed before Woodson's death, Woodson arguably may have not been so laudatory of the Tuskegeean. Most basically, Woodson certainly admired Washington for his institution-building ethos and emphasis on black entrepreneurship and business development.

In *The Mis-Education of the Negro,* when Woodson challenges black intellectuals to be practical and to help the less fortunate, he sounds very much like Washington in *My Larger Education.* In his now-famous 1933 polemic, Woodson was not turning over a new leaf; he was continuing his evolution as a scholar-activist and adopting a new approach. Woodson "doffs the garb of historian and assumes the role of commentator on education and educators, social uplift, religion, the professions and business in general as affecting the colored people of the United States," a writer for the *Memphis Commercial Appeal* accurately observed.[13] One can trace the evolution of this line of thought by reflecting on Woodson's life before the 1930s. According to Jacqueline Goggin, Woodson inherited a "sense of rebelliousness" from his father and grandfather. Several decades after he died, Lorenzo Johnston Greene said that Woodson was so critical that he often "cruelly" hurt his employees seemingly on purpose. Woodson, to be sure, was an outspoken critical thinker. The best indicator of Woodson's early iconoclastic approach is revealed in his book reviews and "Annual Reports" in the *Journal of Negro History.* Between 1916 and 1950, Woodson signed his name to more than

250 book reviews in the *Journal.* Almost certainly he wrote unsigned book reviews as well. In these articles, Woodson consistently challenged white and black authors, boldly attacking all those with whom he did not agree.[14]

The ideas Woodson articulated in *The Mis-Education of the Negro* had been brewing in his mind for more than a decade before. In 1931, in a *Journal* review of the fifth year of Negro History Week, Woodson challenged "successful Negroes" educated at the "best colleges" to help uplift the masses. "Statistics show that the large majority of the Negroes who have put on the finishing touches of our best colleges are all but worthless in the uplift of their people." Woodson continued, "If after leaving school they have the opportunity to give out to Negroes what traducers of the race would like to have it learn, such persons may earn a living, but they never become a contributing force in the elevation of those far down." Woodson denounced an educational system that misled "advanced Negro students" to despise "their own people" and to study things that "have no bearing on the tasks which they confront in life." As a solution, Woodson called for a revolutionary change in the educational training of black intellectuals. He asked black scholars to study their African heritage and to apply their learning to uplifting people of African blood. He called upon teachers of "ripe scholarship" to teach the children. In the "Annual Report of the Director" in 1931, Woodson prepared his readership for his forthcoming book on the plight of the black intellectual and professional.[15]

In 1933, in the midst of the Great Depression, Woodson published *The Mis-Education of the Negro.* At the outset, he told his readers that he had decided to present this volume to the public because many people "were deeply interested" in his ideas. Despite the confrontational tone of Woodson's essays, he claimed that he did not intend for his book to be a "broadside" against specific people, but rather a new set of solutions for how best to create an educated body of black reformers in an age that supported intellectual narcissism. His main focus was first showing how "highly educated Negroes" had misled, exploited, and hampered the livelihood of the black masses, and then how these destructive approaches could be reversed.[16]

Woodson's polemic, laced with traces of history, is delivered in simple and straightforward language. The prevailing argument running throughout the twenty-eight chapters of overlapping subjects is that blacks educated at leading white and black colleges and universities during the early twentieth century failed miserably in helping to improve the status of black America. Woodson posits many reasons and offers various remedies to address the diverse political, social, cultural, economic, and religious needs in the lives of black Americans.

According to Woodson, the "educated Negro" acted irresponsibly because he was not trained to serve black people in practical ways and in fact had been taught to hate Africans and the black masses. The "American educational system" made black people "Americanized" and "Europeanized white-men." Woodson argued that blacks did not get enough adequate training in fields like art, drama, and other more creative fields of thought. He claimed that educated blacks strove to gain acceptance by imitating white America and by downplaying their own cultural individuality. Woodson rooted this mentality in the post-emancipation education of black people. During the antebellum era, he argued, there had been many sincere Northerners and Southerners who believed in helping blacks to help themselves, but after emancipation, these "unselfish" workers were replaced by exploiters of "the race."[17]

In Woodson's view, the educational system established by white philanthropists during Reconstruction did little to help blacks deal with their unique situation. Their scholarship lacked the "spirit of their predecessors." Woodson found fault in both industrial education and classical education. All too often, the former turned out unprepared workers for the industrial market and the latter proved impractical. "We do not have in the life of the Negro today a large number of persons who have benefited by either of the systems about which we have quarreled so long," Woodson concluded. Such systems continued to blossom, in Woodson's estimation, because black teachers had not stepped forth to instigate or demand change. On the contrary, they had been trained "to do what they are told" and were too afraid to challenge the system. Woodson declared that only a "few mis-educated Negroes" posed challenges. In his view, most educated blacks bought into the "diploma-mill produce" system. Blacks went to college, he argued, to get a "darkter's 'gree" in order to get a job, make money, and buy happiness.[18]

Woodson argued that receiving a doctorate only contributed to blacks' laziness and lack of scholarly activism. He asserted that black PhDs "not only lose touch with the common people, but they do not do as much creative work as those of less formal education." He accused black scholars of resting "their oars" once they received their passes into the ivory towers of academe. Black doctorates were too often produced as "Doctors of Philosophy made to order." Woodson accused the Columbia, Yale, Harvard, and Chicago graduates of dismissing black businesses and embracing brands of socialism and communism that did not originate from within the black experience. He indicted them for failing to do the groundwork for blacks in business. He also attacked the educated business owners themselves for being too individualistic and materialistic.[19]

According to Woodson, one of the most detrimental consequences of being miseducated at black and white colleges and universities was turning one's back on the black masses. Woodson believed strongly that the gap between the masses and the Talented Tenth was widening greatly. He noticed that this problem was especially apparent in the religious life of blacks. He indicted black leaders for adopting the religion of "the enslaver and segregationist." In comparing black leaders of the late nineteenth century with those of the 1930s, he concluded that while nineteenth-century black reformers "went off to school to prepare themselves for the uplift of a downtrodden people," his contemporaries went to school "to memorize certain facts to pass examinations." A lot of black professionals, in Woodson's estimation, viewed their jobs solely as a way to make money. "Too many Negroes go into medicine and dentistry merely for selfish purposes, hoping thereby to increase their income and spend it on joyous living." Woodson's most blatant attack was thrust on those blacks who considered themselves leaders of their people. He asserted that leadership had all too often been conferred on a few, without popular consent.[20]

Woodson offered a host of solutions to the problems he saw facing all blacks, the masses as well as the middle-class professionals. He called upon his people to be independent pioneers. In simplest terms, he wanted all black people to abandon "slavish imitation" and learn how to think on their own, thus making themselves indispensable in enterprises in which others could not adequately perform. In order to achieve this goal, Woodson called for the development of "common sense schools" with dedicated teachers, not those "roll-top desk theorists who have never touched the life of the Negro." Woodson believed that the educated black could solve the problems of black people if he "would forget most the untried theories taught him in school, if he could see through the propaganda which has been instilled into his mind under the pretext of education," and "if he would fall in love with his own people and begin to sacrifice for their uplift." Woodson claimed that he even preferred grassroots leaders and reformers as teachers to professors from Columbia, Harvard, or the University of Chicago. Woodson called upon highly educated leaders and teachers to be servants of the people guided by unselfishness:

> The servant of the people, unlike the leader, is not on a high horse elevated above the people and trying to carry them to some designated point to which he would like to go for his own advantage. The servant of the people is down among them, living as they live, doing what they do and enjoying

> what they enjoy. He may be a little better informed than some other members of the group; it may be that he has had some experience that they have not had, but in spite of this advantage he should have more humility than those whom he serves, for we are told that "Whosoever is greatest among you, let him be your servant."[21]

Woodson also challenged black leaders and educators to transform the educational system in which they were trained and to take steps to incorporate the African and black experience.

Woodson instructed blacks to become more radical in their politics. He wanted blacks to use politics only to better secure their goals when practical and to create a brand of politics from within. Woodson believed that the political tradition in America, which had oppressed his people for so long, was not designed to empower black people. He advocated a straightforward, bourgeoisie, economic nationalist platform. He believed that blacks should patronize black businesses and warned his readers that such an alternative would work only if the black businesses had the community's well-being at heart. He advised blacks not to become enslaved by the vices of materialism.. He counseled blacks not to waste money on unnecessary items. While he valued hard, manual labor, he discouraged blacks from leading a life in traditional industrial education. By the 1930s, such an approach was becoming impractical in his mind.[22]

The Mis-Education of the Negro has been praised by scholars and leaders in both the Black Power era and the succeeding Afrocentric movement. However, these generations did not adequately criticize the shortcomings in Woodson's vision. For example, while Woodson elaborated upon the failure of the "highly educated Negro" to deal with the masses on a one-on-one level, he himself exhibited some of this same class prejudice. He believed that the masses needed to be rescued from their state of "backwardness." "Sometimes you find as many as two or three store-front churches in a single block where Negroes indulge in heathen-like practices which could hardly be equaled in the jungle," Woodson commented in his description of blacks in Washington, D.C. "The Negroes in Africa have not descended to such depths." What Woodson labeled "heathen-like" comprised characteristics that made black American religion and culture distinct.[23] Like his Talented Tenth predecessors, Woodson believed (at one level at least) that the black masses were "underdeveloped" and needed civilization as offered by a reformed, educated black constituency.

Woodson also drew shallow and even erroneous conclusions from history. In one case, he even argued that blacks refused to work under each other and to take orders from each other because "slaveholders taught their bondsmen that they were as good or better than any others and, therefore, should not be subjected to any member of their race."[24] Woodson assumed, without proof, that enslaved blacks internalized what their owners placed before them. Throughout the book Woodson oversimplified the historical record in order to hammer home his conviction that the black middle class was failing in maintaining "the race" during the Great Depression. He also did not consider that there were many black scholars who did not fit his convenient prototype. As is the case with most radical polemics, *The Mis-Education of the Negro* contains broad generalizations that are not grounded in rigorous, documented study, but instead are the products of the day-to-day observations and experiences of its author.

How did Woodson's contemporaries respond to *The Mis-Education of the Negro?* In more than a dozen newspapers in the winter and spring of 1933, the majority of reviewers welcomed Woodson's book as a needed criticism of the American educational system. Black scholars of the 1930s certainly could not simply ignore the relevance of his assessment. Most did not take him on in a public forum. Even those whom Woodson indicted seemed to have welcomed his argument. In *The Survey,* Alain Leroy Locke applauded Woodson's "articulate and reasoned" statement to a "very great dilemma."[25] *The Mis-Education of the Negro* represents one of the first major publicized assaults leveled against the black bourgeoisie and the black intellectual by a professionally trained black scholar. After Woodson's *Mis-Education,* only a handful of other black intellectuals reinvoked his message in monograph-length polemics. Among them are E. Franklin Frazier and Harold Cruse.

❖ ❖ ❖

More than two decades after Woodson's major tome first appeared, E. Franklin Frazier (1894–1962) published the second significant twentieth-century attack on the black middle class. Though *Black Bourgeoisie* is much more complex and scholarly in tone than *The Mis-Education of the Negro,* and though Frazier himself disagreed with Woodson on many specific issues, he was in many ways similar to Woodson, inasmuch as Frazier inherited his sense of rebelliousness from his family, came from a working-class household, and worked very hard for his education. Like Woodson, Frazier developed into a maverick scholar decades before publishing his iconoclastic study. Several years after graduating from Howard University in 1916, he was one of the first black Americans to speak out publicly against World War I. From then on, as his chief biographer Anthony M. Platt has noted, he seemed to take great satisfaction in challenging authority and the status quo. Throughout the 1920s, Frazier published several controversial scholarly articles.[26]

Frazier and Woodson both existed in times when it was extremely difficult for black intellectuals to make a living. They frequently commented on this problem and worked especially hard to gain recognition for the scholarly quality of their research and to gain respect for the black intellectual community as a whole. At the same time, they did not hesitate to publicly challenge members of their own community by name. Both were particularly critical book reviewers as well. Frazier and Woodson were similar in that each strove to dichotomize their writings into scholarly studies and polemics. It was the meshing of these two styles that made their writings so unique and powerful for their times. These similarities help explain the commonalties in their studies separated by more than twenty years.

Frazier first published *Black Bourgeoisie* in France in 1955 as *La Bourgeoisie Noire.* He published it in the United States in 1957. In this study, the renowned sociologist used a historical perspective to critique the modern black middle class. He addressed its evolution, complex character and interests, views of black folk culture, and relationship with the black masses and white society. In simplest terms, Frazier's study was an analysis of "the behavior, the attitudes and values of the 'black bourgeoisie.'" *Black Bourgeoisie* is divided into two parts: (1) a historical analysis of the economic and social conditions of the black middle class, their "real status," and (2) an analysis of their past and contemporary behavior and values.[27] Unlike Woodson's study, Frazier's work is multidisciplinary, drawing from sociology, history, psychology, and polemics. His analysis of black middle-class behavior is also more intricate and profound than Woodson's. In contrast to *The Mis-Education of the Negro,* Frazier's study is well organized, adequately footnoted, and written in a scholarly tone heavily influenced by economic and social theory.

Frazier's thesis is straightforward. He argued that the modern black middle class of businessmen, intellectuals, lawyers, dentists, preachers, teachers, nurses, clerical and social workers, and others sought to divorce themselves completely from the culture and traditions of the black masses, seeking instead to wholeheartedly adopt white values, especially those emphasizing the accumulation of wealth and property. According to Frazier, the black bourgeoisie created and maintained an elaborate yet illogical "world of make-believe" that buffered them and their children from reality. Central to the maintenance of this escapist orientation is the myth that salvation can be achieved through economic enterprise and the accumulation of material items, the black press, a devotion to conspicuous consumption, a total rejection of black folk culture and the nineteenth-century philosophy of uplift, and the creation of "Negro society." For Frazier, these behaviors resulted from the black middle class's "deep-seated inferiority complex."[28]

The tragedy for Frazier's black bourgeoisie is that white society neither accepts them as equals nor joins arms with them against their oppressors. They in turn become frustrated because they "cannot escape identification with the Negro" and are "subject to the contempt of whites." Frazier concluded that the black middle class repressed hostilities and hated themselves. Unlike the masses, Frazier insisted, the black bourgeoisie suffered spiritually because they had adopted whites' values and patterns of behavior and could not "retreat within their own world." Pointedly, Frazier commented that they "seem to be in the process of becoming NOBODY."[29]

What really makes Frazier's study "iconoclastic" and reminiscent of Woodson's think piece is that his indictments of members of the black bourgeoisie are bold, uncompromising, and penetrating. Like Woodson's, his analyses stem from the truthfulness found in self-confessions. The arguments of both authors caused at least some of the ranks of the black middle class to rethink the meaning of their daily actions. Frazier's study received much more attention from black scholars than Woodson's because it was less polemical. Those who were offended by Frazier's study may have felt more comfortable in responding to him because the thoroughness of his research and the complexity of his theory warranted some feedback. In addition, when Frazier wrote *Black Bourgeoisie,* he was a more controversial figure than Woodson was when he wrote *The Mis-Education.* By the late 1950s, Frazier was most widely known for his debates with Melville Herskovits and his work on the black family.[30]

The intricate manner in which Frazier organized his study and launched his biting attack on the black middle class reveals how much he wanted others to buy his argument. He relied heavily upon history to frame his case, and his study is more historical than Woodson's. Frazier traced the roots of the black bourgeoisie to the evolution of black banks in the post-emancipation era. He argued that banks were "the main symbols of the bourgeoisie spirit among Negroes."[31] According to Frazier, since the development of modern industry, black "white-collar workers" have striven to attain money and status while turning their backs on the suffering masses. Frazier celebrated the "old" black elite vanguard, the black "genteel tradition" existing during and before the late nineteenth century because, he reasoned, despite their characteristic missionary zeal, they sincerely sought to help the black masses. Frazier believed that the new black bourgeoisie had broken its ties to the "old guard" by replacing the spirit of unselfish reform with a dedication to conspicuous consumption.

A substantial part of Frazier's theory is economic, and his economic analysis is deeper than Woodson's. Frazier argued that in the late 1800s, black leaders created the myth that black people's salvation could come through the development of black businesses. He chastised Booker T. Washington, members of the 1898 Atlanta Conference, the National Negro Business league, the Colored Merchants Association, and others for convincing the black middle class that the development of black businesses constituted the best solution. Frazier believed that black businesses had failed historically and that many black businessmen were in fact only middlemen selling products to the black masses for the white capitalists they served. Born two decades before Frazier, Woodson had advocated what his younger cohort deemed the "faith in the myth of Negro Business." Woodson did not believe that business was the main solution, but he did often comment that black people needed to imitate other ethnic groups who migrated to America and initiated and supported their own business ventures. Like Frazier, Woodson critiqued black business entrepreneurs for turning their backs on the black masses.[32]

Frazier held the black press responsible for dictating the behavior, thought patterns, and cultural tastes of the black bourgeoisie. In his estimation, black newspapers and news magazines, especially *Ebony,* did not present a realistic portrait of black America, but instead highlighted and exaggerated blacks' success. Frazier also accused the black popular press of promoting conspicuous consumption.[33] Though Woodson had not attacked the black press as Frazier did, he did not believe that the purpose of the press was to construct a "world of make believe." Instead, he urged black writers, including journalists, to publicize black history and to critically and realistically address black America's dilemmas.

In terms of identifying the intricate characteristics and behavior patterns of the black bourgeoisie, Frazier's study is more sophisticated than Woodson's. Frazier claimed that a self-hating black middle class sought integration into white America through the accumulation of wealth and the denial of their blackness. While Woodson and Frazier agreed on this point, Frazier added that the black middle class created a distinct, elite "Negro society" in order to mask their rejection by whites and their alienation from the black masses. This separate black middle-class society, which exists in a social and cultural vacuum, is a world in which prestige rules and status is accorded those who possess the most material wealth and property and who can afford to attend debutante balls, pass out from drinking too much, ditch religion, shelter their children from reality, and play poker all day.[34]

Nowhere in *Black Bourgeoisie* does Frazier present any solutions to the problems he described. His readership is left to assume that perhaps he would have called upon the black bourgeoisie to break free from their "world of make-believe," reestablish their relationship with the black masses, seek integration with whites as social equals instead of assimilating, celebrate black culture, and abandon their collection of social myths and their devotion to conspicuous consumption. A few years before he died, Frazier offered some solutions in an article featured in the *Negro Digest.* He called upon his colleagues to recognize the impact of slavery and second-class citizenship; to "dig down into the experience of the Negro and bring out a transvaluation of that experience so that the Negro could have a new self-image or new conception of himself;" and "to provide a positive identification through history, literature, art, music and the drama." Frazier echoed much of what Woodson called for several decades earlier. Both men ultimately believed that black Americans, especially the black middle class, needed to abandon their inferiority complex by rediscovering the culture of the black masses.[35]

In many ways, the most influential book written by a member of this iconoclastic group was Harold Wright Cruse's *The Crisis of the Negro Intellectual.* Born in Petersburg, Virginia, in 1916, Cruse belonged to a generation of black scholars who were greatly influenced by World War II. As a youth, he attended public schools in Petersburg and Norfolk, Virginia, and in New York City. His post–high school education was gained in the Armed Forces Institute of the United States Military in the field of journalism in the early 1940s. In March 1941, he, like many black men of his time, entered the U.S. Army and served in Europe and North Africa until May 1945. From 1945 to 1946, he worked in the Civil Service's Veteran's Administration. A year later, he became a research specialist for the New York City Labor Press. His focus was black labor history and political affairs, but he also reviewed films and drama. In the 1950s and the 1960s, Cruse developed into a freelance journalist, a television film editor, and a theatrical stage manager and producer.[36]

Before *The Crisis of the Negro Intellectual* was first published in 1967, Cruse had not officially entered academe. A year later, the University of Michigan invited him to teach as a visiting honors professor; he was instrumental in establishing the university's Afro-American Studies Program, becoming its first director in 1969–1970. Throughout the 1960s, he contributed to leading black American magazines and journals. He was also active in community and public affairs. He wore many hats as political worker and social organizer for the Adam Clayton Powell Harlem Teams Inc.; as teacher of black history at the Harlem Community Free Schools for Adult Education; and as guest lecturer at the New School for Social Research on black labor, politics, and cultural issues. The ideas presented in *The Crisis* reflect his work and thought from the mid-1940s through the dawning of the Black Power era.[37]

In the broadest sense, Cruse's monumental study is similar to the works of Woodson and Frazier in that it highlighted the drastic shortcomings of black intellectuals—a group synonymous with the prototypes of Woodson and Frazier. Like his colleagues, he called black intellectuals all types of names, from "snobbish" to "weak-kneed" to "anti-theoretical." Toward the end of his study, he echoed Frazier's blanket accusation that the black middle class was essentially "NOBODY." Black creative intellectuals, in Cruse's mind, were "a rootless class of displaced persons who are refugees from the social poverty of the black world."[38]

Cruse argued that black intellectuals had not advanced in their thought since the 1920s, the era of the Harlem Renaissance. Since then, and especially during the civil rights struggle, Cruse maintained, black intellectuals—mainly writers, playwrights, and social critics—had consciously separated themselves from the culture, struggle, and identity of the black masses; adopted the American "materialist ethos"; embraced integration while abandoning nationalist tendencies; been co-opted by white liberals, Marxists, Communists, and so-called radicals; failed to establish a clear-cut cultural ideology and philosophy manifested in political, economic, social, and especially cultural institutions and concrete programs; failed to created a sophisticated yet pragmatic body of thought that both critiqued their own emerging ideas and attacked monumental problems inherent in (white) American culture; and failed to challenge their predecessors since the days of the Harlem Renaissance. Cruse adamantly believed that since the 1930s, black intellectuals had ceased thinking on their own and had instead sought to gain acceptance in white American society even if this meant escaping from one's African American cultural roots. Black intellectuals, he argued, needed to establish an autonomous cultural identity "from the Negro point of view."[39]

Cruse included a historical framework in his study and argued that the study of history had the potential to save black America and its intellectual representatives. In a very Woodsonian fashion, Cruse asserted:

> The farther the Negro gets from his historical antecedents in time, the more tenuous become his conceptual ties, the emptier his social conceptions, the

> more superficial his visions. His one great and present hope is to know and understand his Afro-American history in the United States more profoundly. Failing that, and failing to create a new synthesis and a social theory of action, he will suffer the historical fate described by the philosopher who warned, "Those who cannot remember the past are condemned to repeat it."[40]

Though Cruse sounded very much like Woodson, he interpreted the function of history differently. Indeed, Woodson believed that if black people knew their history, they would not make the same mistakes as their forebears and that the study of black history would instill within black people a sense of pride and self-esteem. Roughly three decades later, Cruse argued that black intellectuals needed to study the thoughts, actions, programs, successes, and failures of their early twentieth-century counterparts in order to construct new lines of thinking, meshing them with the old to fit the present needs. He wanted his contemporaries and the younger Black Power architects to refashion certain aspects of Washington's, Garvey's, and Du Bois's thinking to the more modern conditions in which they existed. Cruse wanted modern black intellectuals to learn from the shortcomings of Harlem Renaissance creative artists. Cruse's study of more than five hundred pages is substantially historical in orientation, like that of E. Franklin Frazier's.

Cruse's book is also Harlem-centric. He argued that Harlem was the "pivot of the black man's quest for identity and salvation," the "Mecca for the intelligentsia." Cruse reexamined the romantic implications of James Weldon Johnson's *Black Manhattan* and envisioned the history of black Harlem as one of the realizations of economic and cultural nationalism. Ironically, Cruse celebrated white American intellectuals more than he did their black counterparts. According to Cruse, the Mabel Dodge group critiqued the American materialistic ethos, capitalism, and racism during the so-called Roaring Twenties, while black intellectuals did not. Because the black bourgeoisie failed to support them, black creative intellectuals relied upon "white cultural paternalism." In Cruse's estimation, leading Harlem Renaissance writers, including James Weldon Johnson, Langston Hughes, and Claude McKay, did not make any significant analyses of the period in which they rose to fame, and they failed to make any institutional changes in terms of cultural production and creativity. Cruse suggested that black intellectuals of the Harlem Renaissance, "overwhelmed at being discovered," were too easily co-opted by white patronage. He chastised them for letting others, especially Jewish leaders, become "experts on the Negro Problem." The only black intellectual to escape Cruse's harshest judgments during this era was

Du Bois, whom Cruse applauded for linking black art and culture to politics and economics in "The Criteria of Negro Art."[41]

Harlem Renaissance intellectuals did not, in Cruse's mind, lay the foundations for independent, black, philosophical ways of thinking. "The Negro is, today," Cruse asserted, "the victim of the incompetence of radical social thought and the forty-year default of the Negro intelligentsia."[42] Cruse posited that black spokespersons of the 1960s inherited more than forty years of uncritical thought patterns, starting with their predecessors of the 1920s.

After laying out the historical groundwork for his thesis, Cruse launched his attack on various black and white intellectuals and organizations of the Harlem Renaissance period as well as of the civil rights movement and the early Black Power era. His most biting critiques were waged against the "Harlem Communist Left," Marcus Garvey, Herbert Aptheker, Richard Wright, the Arts for Freedom, the *Freedomways* writing staff, Lorraine Hansberry, Paul Robeson, Richard B. Moore, John Henrik Clarke, the Negro Writers' Conferences, and the architects of the "Black Power" slogan. In offering such a comprehensive indictment, Cruse distinguished himself from his iconoclastic colleagues. Only a few black intellectuals escaped Cruse's scathing criticisms. Those who did receive his applause are the other members of this study's "iconoclastic tradition." Cruse recounted:

> Taken as a whole, the black bourgeoisie in the United States is the most politically backward of all the colored bourgeois classes in the non-Western world. It is a class that accepts the philosophy of whites whether racial, liberal, progressive or conservative, without alteration or dissent and calls it leadership. It is a class that absorbs very little from the few thinkers it has produced—Martin R. Delany, W. E. B. Du Bois, Booker T. Washington, E. Franklin Frazier and Carter G. Woodson—men who left something behind them.[43]

Cruse's reluctance to spare many black intellectuals from his critical sting is one attribute that casts him beyond his times. He is at the forefront of a small, revisionist body of black historians who believe that we need to avoid romanticizing black history. For Cruse to assume such a stance during the Black Power era was quite unconventional. While some black historians like Benjamin Quarles and John Hope Franklin took pride in writing objective, nonemotional history, very few provided in-depth critiques of black leadership, probing beyond the surface-level chastising of Booker T. Washington.[44]

Cruse transcended his fellow iconoclasts in terms of solutions. Woodson and Frazier spent a great deal of time and energy describing and critiquing their case studies—and little time, sometimes none at all, offering detailed, practical solutions. Cruse provided his readers with a list of changes he believed would help clarify and redefine the black intellectual's role and function. He spent such a great deal of time critiquing black intellectuals because he believed they could become the main agents of the cultural democratization of America, that they held the key to significantly transforming American culture and instigating historical change. Cruse relied on the same class that he had so roundly criticized for the salvation of black people, a fact that earned him some scorn from some Black Power–era scholars. Cruse provided many potential solutions that hinged on the actions of black intellectuals.[45]

He called upon black intellectuals to abandon integration and to embrace black nationalism. By nationalism, he did not mean a surface-level affirmation of one's African heritage or the patronage of black capitalists. He meant adopting "the Negro point of view" and embracing black folk culture. He challenged black intellectuals to stop borrowing from white Americans and their European counterparts and to create original ideas instead. Cruse would have liked the "Lost Black Generation" to establish themselves firmly on the cultural front and to apply their new ideology to economics and politics. Cruse offered his readership a ten-point plan for some basic "organizational objectives" that would transform black life in Harlem and could be applied elsewhere. These plans were practical and reminiscent of previous solutions offered by black nationalists.[46]

Central to Cruse's solutions was the imperative that black intellectuals critically examine their historical evolution as a class. He maintained that the new generation of black intellectuals needed to distinguish themselves from the "old guard" of the 1920s. Like Booker T. Washington, he urged black intellectuals to deal with the masses more closely, to educate the black masses in more practical matters, becoming more "committed to basic political, economic, and cultural issues in the ghettoes."[47] Cruse's study received a lot of attention from black scholars. Many black intellectuals were offended and disturbed by his scathing broadside attack. According to Robert L. Allen, Cruse's study had a great impact on an entire generation of black thinkers, doing "much to shape nationalist thinking."[48]

At certain junctures in history, each of the iconoclasts in this chapter believed that it was necessary for them to publicly challenge some of their colleagues. They called for a reevaluation of the black intellectual's function in American culture and society. All of their ideas were unique for their times and received attention from the African American intellectual community and in some cases from the leftist white academic establishment. In terms of their perceptions and willingness to articulate their thoughts despite contemporary trends, these thinkers are among some of the most insightful and independent minded. They were especially important because their broadsides ignited critical thought within the black intellectual, middle-class, and professional communities concerning their potential to seriously affect the status of the black masses. Yes, some had their feelings hurt by these iconoclasts' direct and confrontational tones. The result, however, was an important step toward helping black intellectuals and professionals realize their importance in the black struggle for liberation. Even today, black intellectuals who read their studies are challenged to reevaluate their purpose and being. Frazier was perhaps the most sophisticated of the group. Cruse was the most meticulous in his scrutiny of black thinkers of old. And Woodson was the most practical. The ASNLH founder was the only member of this iconoclastic cadre who attempted to solve the problems he described with concrete, practical programs. Those scholars who joined forces with him in democratizing and popularizing the study of black history were redefining the conventional role of the black intellectual not only through their rhetoric but, more important, through their actions.

4 Black Women, Woodson, and the ASNLH, 1915–50

"WOODSON HIMSELF LACKED BACKGROUND for broad historical writing; he was almost contemptuous of emotion; he had limited human contacts and sympathies." Several months after Carter G. Woodson's death, W. E. B. Du Bois concluded this harsh criticism of the founder of the Association for the Study of Negro Life and History (ASNLH) by adding: "He had no conception of the place of woman in creation."[1] What Du Bois may have meant by this last point is unclear and begs further elaboration. Was Du Bois critiquing Woodson for supposedly ignoring black women's role in history? In 1991, almost four decades after Woodson's death, historian Patricia Morton elaborated on Du Bois's provocative comment. She argued that starting in the nineteenth century and continuing well into the second half of the twentieth, many black male historians have contributed to white society's most detrimental views, myths, and stereotypes of black womanhood. For Morton, however, Woodson's views about black women are harder to pinpoint. Though she notes that Woodson at times defended black womanhood, she emphasizes that the "Father of Negro History" largely omitted slave women and black female activists from his scholarship. At the same time, she praises Woodson for challenging "conventional orthodoxies," specifically for deconstructing some of the myths pertaining to black women. "Woodson dared to argue that in her continuing Mammy roles as a domestic worker for whites, the Afro-American woman had been done a disservice by her exclusion from the black-authored story of history." Morton continues, "Even more unusual was his keen recognition that black-authored scholarship could be restricted by the racist myths of the past." Morton also applauded Woodson for highlighting the essential role played by black washerwomen. "Woodson's reconstruction showed that what racist discourse had made of the Mammy need not determine what Afro-American scholarship could discover about Afro-American women."[2]

How did Carter G. Woodson portray black women in his scholarship? How were black women discussed in the pages of the *Journal of Negro History* from 1916 until 1950? What contributions did black women make to the *Journal* and the *Negro History Bulletin?* Did Woodson conform to the gender conventions as other black male historians and scholars of his time? Did his writings and programs perpetuate and/or challenge derogatory myths and stereotypes about black women? And what were the various roles black women played in the ASNLH during Woodson's reign as the Association's director? The place of women in Woodson's mind, scholarship, and program is much more complex and interesting than either Du Bois or Morton indicates.

Woodson's views of black women may appear to have been at times ambiguous, but overall they were quite progressive when compared to the views of other black male scholars and historians of his time.[3] While he did not publish monographs devoted to black women or fight actively and openly for women's rights, he did publish several important articles in the 1930s that sought to reconstruct the prevailing negative images of black womanhood. He welcomed black women with open arms into a movement very dear to him. He also supported and celebrated their efforts at legitimizing and popularizing the study of black life and history. Black female teachers, clubwomen, librarians, amateur historians, and social activists played vital roles in the activities of the ASNLH, especially by the late 1930s, when the *Bulletin* was inaugurated. The contents of the *Bulletin* show a Woodson who valued the contributions of black women. The place of women in Woodson's mind, scholarship, and program can be interpreted as one of his most important yet largely overlooked contributions to African American history and the historical profession. In order to appreciate the place of women in Woodson's thought and movement, one must carefully examine his scholarship, beyond the surface, and revisit the foundations and day-to-day activities of the ASNLH, especially after the 1930s. In many regards, Woodson was far ahead of his time in acknowledging aspects of black women's history, leadership skills, and essential contributions to the ongoing African American struggle for equal rights and justice. His advanced vision and program made him a unique black male leader and scholar during the first half of the twentieth century. Though molded by the gender norms of his age, Woodson in many ways challenged the masculinist ideologies of his time.

A casual reading of Woodson's scholarly work may seem to support Du Bois's assertion. Between 1915 and 1950, Woodson produced more than twenty books. Not one of these studies was devoted to or highlighted black women's contributions to American civilization. He did not, however, completely ignore black women. Take, for instance, Woodson's most famous text, *The Negro in Our History,* first published in 1922. This study's first reference to black women mentions how two women in South Carolina in 1754 "were burned alive" for resisting slavery. In exploring "miscegenation," Woodson discussed how black women were at times victims of sexual exploitation. All other references to black women are in the form of brief biographical sketches. He included many key black female historical figures such as Phillis Wheatley, Harriett Tubman, Marie Louise Bitard, Frances Ellen Watkins Harper, Marie Metoyer, Ellen Craft, Sojourner Truth, Madame C. J. Walker, Meta Vaux Warrick Fuller, Mary Howard Jackson, Jessie R. Fauset, Angelina W. Grimké, and Georgia Douglas Johnson. Wheatley, Tubman, Craft, and Truth are pictured in this classic text, indicating that Woodson saw the value in presenting his readers with female heroine role models.[4]

In *The Negro in Our History* and other popular books that followed, Woodson also challenged the widely accepted myth that slavery corrupted the black family and black womanhood. Woodson proclaimed that black women were not "loose women," that, to the contrary, "the moral sense of the imported African rebelled against such promiscuity." Woodson's defense of black womanhood in *The Negro in Our History, Negro Makers of History,* and *The Story of the Negro Retold* served as both a defense of the black race as well as a challenge to the dehumanized images of black women.[5]

Woodson explored the contributions of black women more extensively in his analyses of contemporary African American life. Like other black male scholars of this time, Woodson did not incorporate sophisticated gender analyses into his scholarship. Such approaches would not enter into mainstream academic discourse until after the Black Power era. In his 1934 study on black professionals, *The Negro Professional Man and the Community,* Woodson introduces his work as constituting a survey of "the Negro professional men as they function in the community."[6] Women were not altogether ignored, though. In exploring the history of African American professional service, Woodson noted black women's presence. His data from 1930 census reports highlighted the distribution of some black female professionals by state, especially in the areas of acting, music, teaching, library service, nursing, and in religious, social, and welfare work. In his study, which particularly focused on physicians and lawyers, he indicated that there were only seven black female lawyers, judges, and/or justices, and fewer than fifty black female physicians.

In elevating the status of these professions, Woodson seemed to suggest that work dominated by men was the most important; he did, however, acknowledge the contributions of nurses.

In 1930, Woodson noted that there were only four trained male nurses out of more than four thousand. Though he did not explain this phenomenon, he focused on their background and training; their role in social uplift; the settings in which they worked; their employers' views of them; and the problems they faced. Woodson demonstrated potential for making important gender analyses by making two salient observations: he noted that single women made up the nursing profession because married life was not conducive to such a demanding lifestyle, and he believed that public-health nurses were more active in social uplift than male physicians. Like other black male leaders of the Progressive Era, Woodson argued that nurses were "natural" leaders in social uplift. Holding onto the ideals of Victorian American society, he believed that women were born sympathetic nurturers and best suited for nursing: "An examination of the records of nurses shows that they are leaders in their particular field, but do not enter upon many other efforts which invite the attention of physicians, dentists, and pharmacists. This may not indicate any defect in the training or practice of the nurses but rather the inclination of women in this sphere as in most others to stand aside and permit men to assume the leadership in such matters."[7] Woodson encouraged black women in their supporting role, as he perceived it. "Much credit is due also to the Negro nurse," Woodson noted in his conclusion, "who, encouraged by the Negro physician, has risen on the mind of intelligent people."[8]

From 1915 until his death, Woodson authored one major work focusing on black women. "The Negro Washerwoman, a Vanishing Figure," a scholarly article published in 1930, directly challenged Du Bois's critique and presents a Woodson who openly celebrated the contributions of black women as leaders. Woodson credited the race's survival from slavery to freedom to black women who washed clothes. "In the history of no people has her example been paralleled," Woodson proclaimed. "In no other figure in the Negro group can be found a type measuring up to the level of this philanthropic spirit in unselfish service." According to Woodson, during the antebellum era, free washerwomen in the South worked in and outside their homes in order to supplement and often replace their companions' meager earning power. He found that washerwomen often purchased slaves and freed them "for a minimal charge." Some women even became the heads of their families. In the North, where black men were often systematically excluded from skilled trades, Woodson viewed the role of the washerwoman as being especially pivotal. "Without the Negro washerwoman many Antebellum Negroes would have either starved in that section or they would have been forced by indigent circumstances to return to slavery in the South," he noted.[9] As the "breadwinner" and "important factor in the house," these hardworking, successful washerwomen paid for the maintenance of their family's homes and were also active within the community and in social uplift through their participation in the abolition movement, emigration, church reform, small-scale philanthropy, and business.

Woodson argued that in spite of the development of "modern laundry" after the Civil War and emancipation, the black washerwoman continued to assume a vital role in family and community life. She was "a godsend" to impoverished male sharecroppers. Many "teachers, ministers, business men, and professional workers" were financially supported by the washtub, Woodson's research on black professionals indicated. Without the hard work and sacrifice of "noble women of this type," many men would not have had the means to enter such pursuits. "She gave her life as a sacrifice for others."[10] Woodson also claimed that the washerwoman dealt with crises better than her male counterpart. Foreshadowing *The Mis-Education of the Negro,* he concluded his succinct article by chastising mis-educated black men and by praising working-class black women for their enterprise and belief in themselves:

> At the same time the Negro teachers and professional classes, who in being taught solely the superiority of the other races had developed an inferiority complex, could not have confidence in the initiative and expertise of the uneducated Negroes who launched these enterprises. The Negro working women who had not been misguided by such theories had no such misgivings. The only thing they wanted to know was whether it was something to give employment, prestige, and opportunity for leadership. They believed in the possibilities of their own group and willingly cooperated with any one who had a high sounding program. They were not the ignorant and the gullible, but the true and tried co-workers in the rehabilitation of the race along economic lines.[11]

Woodson's article was in many ways ahead of its time for reconstructing the image of the "Mammy" as imagined by racist scholarship. His approach was also unique within the black community because he acknowledged the value of domestic female labor very early in African American historiography.

That Woodson wrote "The Negro Washerwoman" raises many questions. Clearly, he understood the role of black working-class women in the survival of the black community. Why, then, did he not publicize the role of the washerwoman in his other more widely circulated books after 1930? Certain conclusions in "The Negro Washerwoman" were drawn from data in questionnaires filled out for the ASNLH, so why did Woodson not use the abundant information on working-class black women to perhaps initiate a comprehensive study? Most likely, he had other major projects in the making. Whatever the case may have been, several years after "The Negro Washerwoman" appeared, Woodson revisited women's roles as leaders in the black community.

By the early 1930s, Woodson began writing articles and editorials for a range of newspapers including the *Baltimore Afro-American, Boston Chronicle, Washington Bee, New York Amsterdam News, Louisiana Weekly, Negro World, Chicago Defender, New York Age,* and *Pittsburgh Courier.* In the popular press, he laid scholarly orthodoxies to the side and honed his polemical style. He addressed a host of issues such as education, segregation, the problems of African American leadership, basic trends in African and African American history, the black church, World War II, the popularization of black history, the role of black businesses, and, of course, the Association's work. In one of these polemical articles, Woodson focused on African American women; in a 1932 editorial, he called for black females to replace black male spokespersons.

In mid-December 1932, Woodson was invited to a "mass meeting" in Philadelphia where a group of black women were protesting whites' use of the term "Negress." Woodson, who was unable to attend, offered advice in the pages of the *Pittsburgh Courier.* He agreed that the term was "offensive," but he did not think that getting the word barred from the dictionary was enough. "These women seem to be desirous of treating the symptoms of the disease rather than the disease itself." Woodson instructed *Courier* readers, "The important thing to do in this case is to get at the causes of such an undesirable usage of words which once may have had different meaning." He argued that this insult to black womanhood was rooted in black America's failure to properly elevate its women. He proclaimed that black people were their own worst enemies in this case because black men were supplying whites the ammunition to degrade black women. According to Woodson, black women "have been carried along as a class capable of exploitation or treated as necessary evils in the struggle of man with grave problems."[12]

In his characteristically iconoclastic tone, Woodson argued that black men who opposed the term "Negress" were hypocrites "since many of us treat our women as if they were not better than dogs." He collectively accused his male counterparts of sexual harassment. "You would be surprised to know the large numbers of our distinguished men for whom respectable women cannot work. Often before a women has been in one's office a week he wants to fondle and caress her." Woodson continued, "The next step is to take her out to dinner, and finally it becomes a fait accompli. His business establishment then changes into a trysting place, and soon employees and employers have the opportunity to live on unpleasant memories."[13] Woodson's candid discussion of sexual harassment is quite radical, considering that at the time this issue was not addressed in public discourse. Many among Woodson's black female readership probably welcomed his antisexist rhetoric.

In terms of solutions, Woodson believed that black men should be at the forefront. However, he called upon the men of the race to abandon their sexist behavior and to "protect," "dignify," and elevate "our women." The tone of his language suggested that he was still limited by the gender conventions of his era. Like nearly all other black male leaders of that period, he believed that women depended upon male leadership, benevolence, and guidance. Woodson called upon Philadelphia women to organize cross-class, community "consumer's leagues" to make "the Negro just as much a producer as a consumer." While critiquing black women, he also indicted the black middle-class male leadership for "selling out" and ignoring the black masses. Women *acted* differently, Woodson reasoned: "Sometimes I am inclined to believe that if the women had more voice in our affairs we would be much better off. Our women are so much better than our men. It may be that they are not inherently so, but men have doubtless been touched by so many foul things of life that they have lost their sincerity and honesty. Certainly the women are more faithful to our people and they do more for the elevation of the unfortunate element than our men."[14]

In both Woodson's scholarly and popular texts, black women were discussed in detail on rare occasions. This does not mean that Woodson considered black women's contributions insignificant. When he did address black women, he noted and at times highlighted their monumental contributions to history and contemporary leadership.

Black women were not featured extensively in the *Journal of Negro History* as subjects or authors. But they were not absent either. In fact, several outspoken black female leaders contributed to the *Journal*. Between 1916 and 1950, no more than ten *Journal* articles, most authored by men, explored dimensions of black women in history. The lack of women writers at the time is not too surprising since there were not many professionally trained female historians and scholars in the first half of the twentieth century. Nearly all black women who did write *Journal* articles gravitated toward gender-neutral, noncontroversial topics. In the first several volumes of the *Journal,* two leading African American female intellectuals contributed pieces. Neither Mary Church Terrell, one of the leading twentieth-century black female activists, nor feminist poet Alice Dunbar-Nelson focused on black women's lives or history.[15] Nonetheless, their early presence suggests that Woodson was more progressive in his selection of intellectual talent than his American Negro Academy counterparts.

In its opening volume in 1916, the *Journal* touched upon black women's experiences. W. B. Hartgrove invited scholars to delve into the lives of "noted colored women of Virginia." He chronicled the lives of Marie Louise Moore and Fannie M. Richards. The former was noted for her ability to raise fourteen children and for single-handedly migrating to Detroit from Fredericksburg, Virginia, following her husband's death in 1851. Richards, whose family followed Moore's lead, was one of the first blacks to teach in Detroit's private schools. Hartgrove interviewed her roughly five years before her death. "With eighty-eight terms of teaching to her credit," Hartgrove concluded, "the number of pupils who owe part of their education to 'this gentle and cultured woman' accounts well up into tens of thousands, enough to populate a fair-sized city."[16] The *Journal's* second volume contained one article that skimmed over a handful of famous black women. Historian Benjamin Brawley deemed Frances E. W. Harper one of black America's leading poets "in the long period between Phillis Wheatley and Paul Dunbar." Yet in an essay of less than one page, Brawley dismissed her for not being original and for "lacking in technique." He claimed, "Mrs. Harper was best when simple." A superior male attitude may have been at the root of his oversight, for he also indicted his male subjects for not producing creative, "intense" work.[17]

During the 1920s, only one article dealing with black women was published in the *Journal*: Elizabeth Ross Haynes's "Negroes in Domestic Service in the U.S." Haynes (1883–1953) was one of the leading black female intellectual reformers of her time. After attending State Normal School of Alabama, Fisk University, and the University of Chicago, she attended Columbia University, where in 1923 she received a master's degree in sociology. As a graduate student, she researched the black working class, focusing on black women. Her interest in black women in the work force dated back to 1919, when she, Mary Church Terrell, Nannie Helen Burroughs, Elizabeth C. Carter, and some other black female leaders petitioned the first International Congress of Working Women in Washington, D.C. From 1920 until 1922, while working with the U.S. Employment Service as a domestic service secretary, she began researching the lives of black working women more seriously.[18]

Haynes's master's thesis, published in the *Journal* in 1923, concerned all "those persons performing household duties for money." Woodson often published younger scholars' master's theses and dissertations in his journal. Haynes's study, though slightly more than fifty pages, drew from 1,771 cases. She did not explore gender variations, merely noting that from 1910 until 1920 there were more women domestics than men. But she did investigate the personal profiles of many of these domestics, highlighting their turnover rates, their ages and marital status, and their literacy rates. Like her male counterparts, she strove to be as objective as possible and avoided meshing activist rhetoric and scholarship. For example, she failed to mention racism as a fundamental cause for high turnover rates for black female domestics. Neither did she consider sexual exploitation as a reality or scrutinize the white female employers whom she surveyed. She did sympathize with the domestics' plights of isolation and loneliness, lack of free time, and harsh working conditions with substandard equipment. She also criticized the employment agencies for economically exploiting their workers. According to Haynes, black domestics survived by unionizing and, more commonly, by joining churches and secret orders.[19]

Black women received greater attention in the *Journal* in the 1930s. In the dawning of the decade, sociologist E. Franklin Frazier began articulating his soon-to-be-famous black matriarchy myth in Woodson's *Journal.* For Frazier, the slave mother was "the dominant person in the family" and "the more secure symbol of parental authority and affection." He argued that sexual relations between masters and slave women tended to give the mother in the slave family an even more dominant role than was ordinarily the case where the "paternity of the father and his place in the family received recognition." He based such ideas on information in various biographies, autobiographies, and plantation records. Though Frazier may have developed his antifemale posture in articles like "The Negro Slave Family," Woodson seemed to have balanced how black women were portrayed in various brief biographical sketches he authored throughout the 1930s.[20]

The lives of some black women who made great contributions to the "life-and-death struggle" were briefly noted, usually after they had died. In the "Notes" section of the *Journal,* Woodson and his associates mentioned black women's contributions. A few times, as was the case with Emma Frances Grayson Merritt (1860–1933), Woodson praised the black woman's contributions in depth. He lauded this longtime Washington, D. C., educator for her leadership, social activism, modern methodology, dedication to "the cause," and unselfishness. She touched "the large masses of Negroes in the backward parts of the country" and encouraged her disciples "to toil unselfishly for their handicapped group." Woodson credited Merritt with innovating the education of blacks nationwide.[21]

Beyond such tributes, there were a few *Journal* sketches on black female history-makers during Woodson's lifetime. Sarah Remond and Phillis Wheatley were the subjects of brief biographical sketches in the mid- to late 1930s. In 1935, Dorothy B. Porter, the longtime curator of the Moorland-Spingarn Research Center, published a brief account of Remond's life and work. Porter noted that this abolitionist and physician fought to overcome racism and discrimination; joined the abolitionist speaking circuit; published in papers like the *Anti-Slavery Advocate;* ventured to England in 1859–1860; and even earned a medical degree from a leading medical school in Florence, Italy, in 1871. "The name Sarah Remond, then, should have a prominent place in the history of the Negro," Porter championed in a tone not unlike Woodson's.[22] Several years later, Edward D. Seeber reminded *Journal* readers to acknowledge Wheatley's contributions to American poetry.[23]

❖ ❖ ❖

Central to Woodson's cause was the dismantling of stereotypes about black America perpetuated by racist white scholarship. However, in doing so, vindicationist black male scholars like Woodson often failed to radically reconstruct black women's historical identities. According to Patricia Morton, the vast majority either directly or indirectly supported the "myths of black womanhood" well into the second half of the twentieth century.[24] From time to time, even black female scholars may have unwittingly contributed to these myths. One example in the *Journal* stands out.

In a 1938 article, Jessie W. Parkhurst of Tuskegee Institute had the opportunity to help dispel the myths about the black "Mammy" of the antebellum South. Parkhurst's approach was multilayered and courageous for any historian of her time. However, she relied upon the often-racist testimonies of mistresses, their children, and Southern white scholars like U. B. Phillips and Thomas Nelson Page in drawing the "actual role" that the "Mammy" played "in the plantation households of the Old South." Parkhurst argued that while whites romanticized their "Mammy's'" role, the "Mammy" image was maintained because she was, for whites, a symbol of success, a key to entering aristocratic Southern culture. Whites, therefore, needed to claim ownership over her. Most blacks, on the other hand, chose to forget that awful part of their past. In the process of acknowledging the centrality of black women in plantation culture, Parkhurst reinforced many stereotypes of black women. Rather than dispelling the stereotypes surrounding the "Mammy" figure, she argued that the "Mammy" was a real figure in Southern antebellum history and played a vital role in the culture of many white slaveholders. Parkhurst probably had the goals that Woodson had had when he celebrated, dignified, and recast the role of the black washerwoman, but she may have done more to promote a detrimental stereotype than to eradicate it.[25]

Parkhurst painted the picture of every "Mammy" as the loyal, responsible, patient, devoted house servant who performed "drudgery work" and reared the master's children as her own. "She rested neither day nor night in her care and attention" to her mistress's children. Reinforcing Frazier's myth of the "black matriarch," Parkhurst placed "Mammy" directly "next to the mistress in authority," bossing "everyone and everything in the household." Parkhurst argued that the "Mammy" was respected as a member of her owner's family and in total control over white aristocratic children. She even went as far as to argue that there existed between this household slave and her mistress some type of "freedom of intercourse" and codependence. Parkhurst raised many important issues about relationships between black female house servants and their mistresses that would be explored in the 1980s by scholars like Elizabeth Fox Genovese. But she argued that there existed a group of elder female domestic servants who were completely devoted to their white employers, identifying with them completely. At the time of its publication, Parkhurst's article had positive and negative results. She credited black women with playing a central role in white antebellum culture, at the expense of not scrutinizing her primary sources rigorously enough. All too often, she took the testimonies of mistresses and their children as accurate portrayals of black women.

❖ ❖ ❖

Parkhurst's article, published in 1938, was the last major article on black women to appear in the *Journal* before Woodson's death in 1950. Woodson's 1930 article on black washerwomen and his 1932 commentary in the *Pittsburgh Courier* calling for black female leadership therefore stand out. Why did Woodson not publish more articles like these two? And what motivated him, during the Great Depression, to address openly the roles of black women in historical and contemporary times?

Woodson's views of women go far beyond his scholarly and popular writings. During Woodson's lifetime, women assumed important roles in the activities of the Association for the Study of Negro Life and History. Black women were very visible in the Association's infrastructure from the outset, being hired to perform duties as secretaries, bookkeepers, and stenographers at the Association headquarters in Washington, D.C. Knowing how hard Woodson himself labored and what he demanded of his assistants, these jobs must have been quite arduous. Lorenzo Johnston Greene commented that he felt sorry for the young women who worked in the office because of their heavy workloads and their need to endure Woodson's character.[26] On occasion, Woodson acknowledged the women's service: after Miss A. H. Smith retired from serving as the Association's office manager and assistant to the secretary-treasurer, Woodson praised for her "faithful service" from 1915 until 1923. He publicly thanked her for remaining with the Association even after she was offered a higher salary elsewhere.[27]

After Woodson founded Negro History Week in 1926, black female teachers, clubwomen, librarians, and social activists played essential roles in popularizing the study of black history. Without the practical work of women, Woodson's efforts at popularizing black history would not have been nearly as successful. Black women set up activities in schools, such as book displays and pageants; they worked hard to advertise Negro History Week celebrations; and they established branches, clubs, and study groups throughout the country. During the 1930s and 1940s, for instance, Sylvia Tucker was a key leader of the Association's Detroit branch (founded in 1924), which thrived under her leadership. Woodson praised her for her fundraising abilities: as early as 1938, she had raised close to six hundred dollars for "the cause." In the 1940s, under her guidance, the branch reached its peak of fifteen hundred members. She also introduced Association chapters in other Michigan cities—Flint, Lansing, Ann Arbor, and Grand Rapids. Tucker has been remembered as being a "spark plug," a "dynamic leader,"—indeed "Miss Negro History."[28]

Along with well-known spokeswomen, black women at the grassroots level were key organizers and participants in the ASNLH's annual meetings throughout the country. Women's clubs often helped sponsor events, hosted dinners, and organized the entertainment for the visiting members. Black women were always present at the Association's meetings and contributed to the lively discussions. Later, they joined the intellectual ranks of panelists and presenters.

The first reference to a black woman contributing to the intellectual atmosphere of an Association conference occurred nearly a decade after the ASNLH was founded. In April 1923, at the spring conference in Baltimore, Maryland, N. F. Mossell of Philadelphia discussed the significance of teaching black history to children. Six months later, Mary McLeod Bethune became the first black female to present a major paper at an ASNLH annual meeting. At the spring conference in 1924, black women like Sadie Mossell

Alexander (lawyer, civil rights activist, and the first black woman to earn a doctorate in economics [1921]), enjoyed even greater visibility. Nannie Helen Burroughs, founder of the National Training School for Women and Girls in Washington, D.C., presented a paper celebrating black America's African ancestry. In the tone of a militant cultural nationalist, she argued that black people survived in the New World because they hailed from a "superior" civilization.[29] Woodson admired Burroughs's commitment to the black struggle, and Burroughs admired Woodson. During the first two decades of the twentieth century, she required her students not only to study black history using Woodson's texts but also to pass a written and oral black history examination in order to graduate.[30]

The increase in female participation in 1923 and 1924 was followed by a period of nearly five years when women seem to disappear from the ranks of presenters. It is interesting to note that not one black woman presented a major paper at the ASNLH's tenth anniversary annual meeting held in Washington, D.C., September 9–10, 1925. By the late 1920s, black women did make some significant intellectual inroads as vital participants at the very successful annual meeting held in St. Louis, Missouri, in late October 1928, where the subject of the well-attended opening session was the "Women's Negro History Mass Meeting." Arsania Williams, head of the Women's Clubs of St. Louis, presided over the meeting, which drew large participation from clubwomen. Sallie W. Stewart, president of the National Federation of Colored Women, discussed African cultural survival in America, and Myrtle Foster Cook, Chairman of the History Department of the National Association of Colored Women, discussed women's roles in popularizing black history. At a later session, Zora Neale Hurston, at the time a short story writer, practicing anthropologist, and folklorist, presented a paper on the role of three key organizations—the American Folklore Society, the Department of Anthropology at Columbia University, and the ASNLH—in studying black culture.[31]

At the annual meeting in 1929, black women were active presenters again. The first public session featured three highly visible, outspoken, active black clubwomen: Jane Edna Hunter (1882–1971), founder of the Phillis Wheatley Association in Cleveland, Ohio; Mrs. H. R. Butler (1872?-1964), president of the National Congress of Colored Parents and Teachers; and Charlotte Hawkins Brown (1883–1961), founder of the Alice Freeman Palmer Institute. Hunter delivered "an inspiring introductory address." After the get-acquainted dinner on the second day, the students of Burrough's National Training School for Women and Girls enacted a play entitled "When Truth Gets a Hearing."[32]

During the 1930s and early 1940s, black women appear not to have served as major presenters at annual meetings, but in 1947 in Oklahoma City, Cernoria Johnson and Jessie Parkhurst Guzman presented at an annual meeting the first major scholarly papers focusing on black women. Johnson presented the paper "Recent Achievements of Negro Women in the South West"; Guzman delivered a study on the contribution of black women to America. Some sixteen hundred people jammed the Douglass High School Auditorium to hear Guzman's research.[33]

By the mid-1930s, black women in the ASNLH made significant advancements. In 1935, Lucy Harth Smith and Mary McLeod Bethune became the first black women elected to the Association's executive council. At the annual meeting just one year later, Bethune was elected president of the ASNLH "to fill the vacancy" opened by John Hope's death in February 1936. Bethune, founder of the Daytona Educational and Industrial Institute, served as the president of the ASNLH until 1952. Though her presidency has been called "largely ceremonial," Bethune definitely left her mark as Association president. The author of the Associated Publishers' *Women Builders* went as far as to assert that "no connection of Mrs. Bethune's was more important than her election to the presidency, succeeding John Hope, of the Association of the Study of Negro Life and History." One of her biographers added that she brought "prestige and money" to the Association.[34]

When Bethune was elected president of the ASNLH, she was one of the most well-known and respected black public figures, having been president of the National Association of Colored Women, director of the National Youth Administration's Division of Negro Affairs, and president of the National Council of Negro Women, an overarching organization that encompassed all black women's organizations. Bethune was also linked to many organizations in the black community, such as the NAACP and the National Urban League. She had a particularly close relationship with Eleanor Roosevelt (it has been said that Bethune had a "carte blanche" to the office of the first lady, who influenced her husband's potential decisions). While Bethune's various responsibilities may have limited the amount of time she could devote to the ASNLH, she certainly contributed significantly to the intellectual climate of the annual meetings; served as a well-known representative, fundraiser, and publicist for the Association; and supported Woodson in his quest to democratize and popularize African American history. From 1936 until 1945 she was, in one scholar's estimation, "the pre-eminent race leader at large."[35]

As ASNLH president, Bethune regularly attended the annual gatherings, presiding over executive council meetings. From 1935 to 1951, she delivered many addresses, five of which were published in the *Journal.* Historian Bettye Collier-Thomas is correct in crediting Bethune with "disseminating the study of black history through her speeches and writings." In her speeches, Bethune articulated her vision of the function of history and the role of the black intellectual, reiterating Woodson's goals for the Association to search for "truth" and stressing that black scholars concentrate their efforts on popularizing black history. Bethune's philosophy of black history was essentially pragmatic. The "social usefulness of scholarship and its findings depends on its translation into the common tongue," Bethune asserted. Like Woodson, she believed that black historians needed to arm black children with the knowledge of their "glorious" past of "marvelous achievement." Young schoolchildren's perceptions of African American history were very important to her. She believed that black children could be encouraged to overcome great obstacles, to "make new history," if they were exposed to what their forebears accomplished. It was for this reason that under Bethune's reign as president, the *Negro History Bulletin* prospered; as well, she was one of its most important fundraisers. Like Woodson, she also optimistically maintained that "world peace and brotherhood" would result from greater appreciation of African and African American contributions to American and world history.[36]

As Association president, Bethune also celebrated the historical and contemporary contributions of black women. At the thirty-second annual meeting of the ASNLH in Oklahoma City in 1947, she delivered an address entitled "Recent Achievements of Negro Women." Bethune stressed with exuding pride that black women contributed greatly to African American advancement on many levels in manners equal to their male counterparts. Bethune proclaimed:

> They have toiled in the fields, these women, to build an economy for others, and to maintain homes for their families. They have washed over tubs and ironed at night, that we, their children, might be educated. They have supported the churches and preached from the pulpits and sung in the choirs. They have started schools and taught in them. As doctors and nurses they have ministered to the sick. Their voices have pleaded the cause of the oppressed in the courts of the law. . . . They have been homemakers and businesswomen . . . social workers and scientists, civic leaders and government officials. . . . What do we not owe to them? Our women! I am glad that I am a woman! . . . The women of my race have stood shoulder to shoulder with our men—thinking together, counseling and working, in every field of endeavor, acknowledging no barriers or race or sex. Our achievements have

> only begun. They will continue as long as we press forward, with knowledge and understanding—and without fear![37]

Bethune's faith in the significance of black history continued beyond her tenure as Association president. During her retirement at age seventy-eight, she published "My Last Will and Testament" in *Ebony.* In the tradition of ASNLH workers, she sought to pass on to future generations of African Americans her legacy "in hope that an old woman's philosophy may give them inspiration." She reminded her younger readership that "our ancestors endured the degradation of slavery" with dignity so that the future generations could benefit. She believed that this past should never be forgotten or taken for granted. In the tradition of Woodson and the Association, she proclaimed, "Our greatest Negro figures have been imbued with faith. Our forefathers struggled for liberty in conditions far more onerous than those we now face but never lost the faith. Their perseverance paid rich dividends. We must never forget their sufferings and their sacrifices, for they were the foundations of the progress of our people." She also called upon the younger generation of black leaders to emulate the selfless works of famous historical figures. "We have had other great men and women in the past: Frederick Douglass, Booker T. Washington, Harriet Tubman, Sojourner Truth. We must produce more qualified people like them who will work not for themselves, but for others."[38] Bethune's pragmatic vision of history, like Woodson's, sought to inspire younger generations of African Americans to persevere and promote racial pride.

Woodson valued Bethune's dedication to black civil rights and her contributions as president of the Association. In May 1950, Bethune recalled: "This year I felt that my own shoulders were over-tired and I told Carter Woodson that I wanted to lay down the duties of the Association's presidency, but he would not let me. He pleaded with me to stay through this year."[39] Woodson and Bethune appeared to have had a solid relationship and a sense of mutual respect. In the draft for his *Encyclopedia Africana,* Woodson wrote an extensive, eight-page account of Bethune's life and work. He called her "one of the most distinguished personages of her time." Such compliments should not be taken lightly, since Woodson was very conservative with any kind of praise. Bethune equally admired Woodson. After he died, she praised him. "I loved Carter Woodson," Bethune testified. "He helped me to maintain faith in myself. He gave me renewed confidence in the capacity of my race."[40]

Many other less high-profile black women supported Bethune's quest to popularize and democratize black history. Throughout his annual director's reports, Woodson noted the "unselfish" hard work of women in raising money for the ASNLH; promoting Negro History Week; maintaining clubs and branches; and, in general, sacrificing their personal needs for others. Among those to receive Woodson's highest praises were Susie R. Quander, who headed the dollar donation drive with Charles S. Wesley in the mid-1930s; Jane Dabney Shackelford, a teacher at Booker Washington School, Terre Haute, Indiana; Dorothy Porter, curator for the Moorland Foundation Library of Negro Life and History; Sylvia M. Tucker, the state representative for the Association in Michigan; and Hilda V. Grayson who, during the 1940s, worked closely with schoolteachers in rural areas as a "field representative."

❖ ❖ ❖

From the inception of the *Negro History Bulletin* in October of 1937 until Woodson's death, and corresponding with Bethune's presidency, black women were a dominant force on the magazine's editorial staff. In many respects, the periodical served as an arena in which black women, mainly schoolteachers and social activists, could articulate their concerns about educating black youth, reforming American society, and uplifting the masses of their people. In a 1943 article introducing the *Bulletin*'s most active supporters, Woodson highlighted the contributions of many of his female co-workers. "In and out of Washington are found teachers and other workers with this vision of reaching the youth and the masses, and they have been of inestimable value in the performance of this tale." To *Bulletin* readers, Woodson humbly compared his role with that of his mostly female staff: "The Managing Editor is often commended for the style and the contents of the magazine, but the credit is due in a larger measure to his co-workers."[41]

Several years later in the *Bulletin,* Woodson published an article chronicling the work of "modern" black historians. While he highlighted the scholarly contributions of his male disciples, including Lorenzo Johnston Greene, Luther Porter Jackson, John Hope Franklin, A. A. Taylor, Rayford W. Logan, and William Sherman Savage, Woodson acknowledged the efforts of many nondoctoral female promoters of black history. "Maud Cuney Hare, disclaiming any pretension to the title of historian, deserves nonetheless a place among the most distinguished of her race in this sphere," the Association founder noted. He praised her for amassing data on black musicians and for publishing her groundbreaking *Negro Musicians and their Music* (1936). Among others receiving Woodson's highest praises were Jane Dabney Shackelford, Elsie Derricotte, Jessie H. Roy, Geneva Turner, Sadie St. Clair, Beatrice J. Fleming, and Marion Pride. By associating these nonformally trained female writers with "modern historians," Woodson somewhat democratized the profession along class and gender lines.[42]

For example, though nearly all of Woodson's protégés and field workers were black men, he did occasionally send women into the field. Wilhelmina M. Crosson of the *Bulletin's* editorial board was one of these researchers. Beginning in the summer of 1945, she received a leave of absence from teaching in the Boston public schools to study "the intercultural approach in the Mexican public schools" under the auspices of the ASNLH. Woodson charged her with researching the African presence in Mexico to uncover significant insights for the reform of black Americans' education. When she returned, Crosson published a lengthy article in the *Bulletin* on her experiences and presented a paper on her research at the Association's annual meeting in Philadelphia, October 1946. A year later, she was elected to the ASNLH executive council.[43]

Woodson also noted the contributions of other "enterprising women" who "have rendered the public a great service" in publishing black history for children. He often encouraged nondoctoral women writers to write and publish literature for children. For Woodson, well-written children's books were as valuable as scholarly studies,[44] and he was himself among the few black male scholars to have written juvenile literature.

The *Bulletin's* "Children's Page" was managed completely by black women who, from time to time, highlighted the contributions of their heroines. In December 1948, the "Children's Page" offered teachers a lesson plan for third- through sixth-graders that highlighted the contributions of Mary McLeod Bethune, Charlotte Hawkins Brown, and Nannie Helen Burroughs so that "the children may wish to emulate them in some way." Students were instructed to become amateur historians of black women by "making up a play using one or all three women together," locating "clippings in magazines and newspapers about these three women," and finding stories of "other women who have done similar things."[45]

❖ ❖ ❖

Black women wrote about other black women, a tendency Woodson did not discourage. In the March 1944 issue of the *Bulletin,* Mary L. Williams explored the twenty-six poems in Margaret Walker's first published book of poetry, *For My People.* According to Williams, Walker's poetry addresses the black struggle for freedom, black Southern culture, religion, and folklore. Overall, Williams noted that Walker's poetry helped inspire within people the desire to make democracy a universal reality in America.[46] Several months after

Williams's article, Dorothy B. Porter published a piece highlighting the role of black women in American wars from the mid-eighteenth century through World War II. Porter combed through primary and secondary sources to reveal the "courage in Negro women" as war historians, soldiers, nurses, spies, caretakers, Red Cross members, YMCA volunteers, industrial laborers, and servicewomen working alongside white women.[47] She concluded by assuring America that black women would continue their patriotism during World War II. Like Woodson, she too was a proponent of the "Double V" campaign—victory against fascism at home and abroad.

In 1948, Jessie Parkhurst Guzman published the longest article on black women to appear in the *Bulletin* during Woodson's lifetime. Originally a 1947 speech presented at the Association's annual meeting in Oklahoma City, her article focused on black women's contributions to American and African American culture from 1940 to 1947. Guzman highlighted black women in education, the arts, theater, music, literature, politics, social reform, and war service. Her article was well documented, drawing largely from various editions of the *Negro Year Book,* and it includes more than twenty photographs of various black female activists as well as extensive vital information. For example, noting the strides black women had made in education, Guzman explained that while only twenty-six black women received doctoral degrees between 1876 and 1940, thirty-eight became doctorates in the seven years thereafter.[48]

Other black women in Woodson's Association focused their education and talent on lifting up black children. Lois Mailou Jones's role in the *Bulletin,* for example, extended beyond that of an occasional contributor. For many years, Woodson employed Jones as the magazine's artist and "Children's Page" coordinator; her watercolors, prints, and sketches added a sophisticated and artistic dimension to the magazine, complementing the text. By 1937, when Jones began regularly working with Woodson, she was already an internationally accomplished painter teaching in Howard University's art department. Woodson was pleased with her ability to illustrate black life and history and to offer creative activities to young readers. In the early 1940s, the *Bulletin* promoted her Saturday-morning art class, which she had established in Washington, D.C., in 1933. Like Woodson, Jones believed that teaching children was a vital part of the black struggle for a new cultural identity, that the best way to learn was by doing, and that children had to demonstrate "originality of thought."[49]

Jane Dabney Shackelford received Woodson's highest praises repeatedly from the late 1930s through the 1940s for her work in education. After receiving her bachelor's degree in her home state of Indiana, she taught there in a "one-room city school with five grades," then pursued her master's degree at Columbia. She subsequently began teaching at Booker Washington School, where she noticed, while teaching third grade, that there was a great paucity of children's books dealing with black history. She therefore decided to fill this void.[50]

In 1938, when Shackelford's *The Child's Story of the Negro* was released, schools all over the country (Newark, Saginaw, Los Angeles, Goldsboro, Tulsa, and Montgomery) ordered the $1.40 book for the special rate of $1.00.[51] Shackelford, the *Bulletin* announced, was now "nationally famous." Woodson emphasized that her book made it to its second edition faster than any other black history book up until that point. "The book is written by an experienced teacher, a woman who understands children and speaks their language," Woodson noted.[52] In the mid-1940s, the *Bulletin* announced that Shackelford was an "excellent interpreter of the past of the Negro to children."[53] Several pages of the February 1945 *Bulletin* featured positive reviews of her second children's book, *My Happy Days*, about black children and family life. She was heralded for her objectivity, clarity, and for creating a book that had the potential to affect both black and white children. One teacher, writing to the *Bulletin*, explained how *My Happy Days* served a very practical function, "I have a large boy in my 6B class who reads on a second grade level but who I fear would be embarrassed to read from a first or second grade book and maybe would stay out of school to avoid doing so. So to save the day I am using *My Happy Days* as his basic reader. He enjoys it very much and, without realizing it, is improving slowly by reading material on his grade level. In addition to that I have him writing a textbook himself based on his experiences at work, home, etc., patterned after *My Happy Days*."[54] Shackelford's publications made her "immortal" in Woodson's eyes; he promoted her books by including reviews and her photo in many issues of the *Bulletin*. Shackelford was active in running the *Bulletin* as well.

Shackelford was also a very active promoter of black history as the head of an ASNLH branch, "The Indiana Negro Historical Society," in Terre Haute, Indiana. The Society popularized black history by creating a ten-page bulletin. "What it has done is a striking example which other such organizations might emulate," Woodson stated. As a teacher, Shackelford devised practical programs for her students. They were recognized by the *Bulletin* for their first-rate "Negro history booklets."[55]

Woodson also served as an active mentor to other black women, including scholars Jessie H. Roy and Geneva C. Turner. Roy, a longtime member of the *Bulletin*'s editorial board and a student of Woodson's at M Street High School in the fall of 1910, and her colleague Turner formed the nucleus of "a very enthusiastic Negro History Club" in Washington, D.C., in the late 1930s. They considered themselves self-taught children's book writers; one day, they decided to share some of their work with Woodson. After reviewing it, he was quite impressed. Roy and Turner began working closely with Woodson on a book of biographies. Woodson generously shared his time with them, as he did with many of his younger male disciples. "Often when the discussion of an historic figure was too interesting, Mrs. Turner and I would go with Dr. Woodson to lunch or dinner at the YMCA (Dutch treat) or continue our study as we ate," Roy recalled. "If necessary we would return to the office and continue our study of a character even if it meant staying until late in the night."[56]

Woodson himself authored several praise songs to women in the *Bulletin*. He often honored (with biographical sketches in the pages of the *Bulletin*) the sacrifices and work of many ordinary black female teachers who supported the black history movement. He recognized women as being successful community role models and leaders: "Miss Wilhelmina Crosson of Boston keeps the people of both races there thinking about the good rather than the evil to the credit of the Negro. She holds up before the young people of the city the high ideals of the best in the race." Woodson also featured photographs of nearly a dozen of these female "friends of the truth" in the *Bulletin*.[57] During World War II, he wrote a short article in which he chastised the Daughters of the American Revolution for not including black women in their organization.[58]

Clearly, Woodson welcomed many black women into the Association as equals in popularizing the past of black people. He supported and praised many black women's "unselfish work" and publicly celebrated the devotion of many black female teachers and social activists who were committed to promoting African American history. He encouraged and promoted their writings. In fact, at one level Woodson himself was more like the black female amateur historians he praised than his highly specialized fellow male disciples. Like Jane D. Shackelford, Helen A. Whiting, Jessie Roy, Geneva Turner, and countless others, Woodson produced texts for a broad readership. He shared with his female educator counterparts a primary concern for the youth. This interest was something unique among male scholars of his time, many of whom avoided producing scholarship suitable for the masses and focused instead on combating racism in the academy.

Educated black women during the Jim Crow era did not enjoy the option of widespread membership in the academy. For more than fifty years after emancipation, black professional women were carefully socialized within a broader racist and sexist society to possess a "sense of mutual obligation among the women, their family, and the larger black community."[59] The black women who worked hand in hand with Woodson belonged to what historian Stephanie Shaw referred to as the African American professional class. Most male professionals avoided "feminized" careers in social work, teaching, library science, and nursing. During Woodson's lifetime, most male professionals maintained this sexual division of professional labor. Some were more extreme than others. According to Gloria T. Hull, there was unprecedented "blatant antifemale prejudice" during the Harlem Renaissance era. Many black women writers were systematically excluded from the male-dominated circles of influence. Alain Leroy Locke, one of the most influential caretakers of the Harlem Renaissance, "behaved misogynistically and actively favored men," Hull said.[60] Woodson, on the other hand, promoted the scholarship and public activism of many black professional and nonprofessional female scholars he believed were as devoted to "the cause" as he was. He probably thought that black women were better suited for secretarial and behind-the-scenes type of work for the Association, yet he did not consider women unfit for scholarship and/or public activism. Though the roll call of black female presenters at Association meetings is short, many important black women, including a few outspoken feminists, no doubt added new dimensions to these Association gatherings.

W. E. B. Du Bois accused the ASNLH founder of having "no conception of the place of women in creation," and during the 1970s and 1980s many female scholars, including Bettina Aptheker, Jean Fagan Yellin, and Nellie Y. McKay, celebrated how Du Bois championed female rights and positively portrayed black women in historical and creative writings. More recently, however, at least one historian has revised this interpretation. Patricia Morton contends that though Du Bois was a "pioneer in the transformation of even the most dehumanizing images of black womanhood into empowering symbols of worth," he, like his predecessors, cast black women as specific "types" and described black female public activists in nonthreatening terms.[61] Even the most progressive black men coming of age in the first half of the twentieth century had great trouble emancipating themselves from the gender conventions of their times. Woodson's views of black women were progressive when one considers the historical context of his life.

❖ ❖ ❖

During an era when nearly all American women were encouraged to remain in the domestic sphere and black women's history was largely in the hands of black female scholars and clubwomen, Woodson published several important articles that reconsidered the prevailing negative images of black womanhood. He welcomed black women with open arms into his movement; and he supported and celebrated their efforts at legitimizing and popularizing the study of black life and history. Mary McLeod Bethune served as the ASNLH's president during a critical era in its maturation. Black female teachers, clubwomen, librarians, writers, and social activists also played vital roles in the success of Negro History Week celebrations, Association clubs and branches, annual Association meetings, and, most important, the *Negro History Bulletin.* Woodson's interpretations and appreciation of black women's multifaceted roles in African American advancement can, therefore, be understood as one of his most progressive contributions to black history, the early black history movement, and the historical profession in the United States.

PART TWO

Lorenzo Johnston Greene's Life, Work, and Contributions, 1899–1950

5 The Origins of a Creative Scholar and Historian, 1899–1928

THOUGH THEIR LIVES AS SCHOLAR ACTIVISTS overlapped by about twenty-five years, and they were equally dedicated to the early black history movement, Carter G. Woodson and Lorenzo Johnston Greene were the by-products of some distinctly different historical circumstances. Most important, they hailed from different generations and different parts of the country. They both spent their early years during the "nadir," Woodson experiencing the immediate aftermath of Reconstruction and last several decades of the nineteenth century as a young man. Greene, on the other hand, knew only the twentieth century firsthand. Based on these variations, it would be logical to expect that their perspectives would diverge instead of intermingle. They certainly had their generation-based disagreements, yet their early lives overlapped in ways that perhaps help explain commonalities in their worldviews as proto–civil rights movement black scholars. Both were reared by struggling, working-class families who nurtured their growth and ability to persevere. As children and young adults, both men were forced to develop work ethics of Herculean intensity, a sense of compassion for and faith in the black laboring classes, and a service ethos that would become a central component of their adult characters.

Born in 1899, Greene spent his early years through his young adulthood in a country undergoing monumental transformations in industrial growth, urbanization, technological advancements, mechanization, settlement westward, widespread interest in party politics, consumerism, labor unrest, corporate consolidation, foreign expansion and empire building, social Darwinism, nativism, racial conflict, and reform. This environment, especially in terms of race relations, molded Greene's outlook. His formative years belonged to what historians have collectively labeled the Progressive Era. In conventional periodizations of U.S. history, this period (roughly 1890 until 1920) was an unstable, bittersweet era in the history of African American intellectuals. African American reformers, scholars, and spokespersons developed innovative uplift programs and made unprecedented sacrifices for the advancement of their people. Yet these expressions of activism, impulses for reform, and strategies of creative resistance were by-products of the widespread antiblack culture of the Progressive Era. Using the term "progressive" to describe the realities of African Americans during the late nineteenth and early twentieth centuries can be misleading and problematic.[1]

For the vast majority of African Americans, the Progressive Era was synonymous with a period of widespread Jim Crow segregation, unprecedented racial intolerance and violence, political disenfranchisement, labor restrictions, and economic exploitation. It coincided with what historian Rayford W. Logan called the "nadir," or "lowest point." In his groundbreaking *The Negro in American Life and Thought: The Nadir, 1877–1901* (1954), Logan suggested that the crucial period from 1877 until 1901 marked the nadir of African Americans' collective status in U.S. society. Roughly a decade following the book's first edition, Logan published a revised edition, positing that "the lowest point" in African Americans' struggle for universal freedom lasted from the end of Reconstruction until as late as 1923.[2] Logan supported his argument by analyzing how U.S. presidents from Hayes to McKinley consolidated white supremacy; how major Supreme Court decisions undermined blacks' fundamental civil and human rights; how blacks suffered from systematic legal and extralegal forms of economic, political, and social oppression; how popular newspapers, magazines, and books throughout the nation dehumanized and stereotyped African Americans; and how Booker T. Washington's 1895 "Atlanta Compromise" negatively affected blacks' status.

Greene lived the first several decades of his life in an era during which "every institution in the United States—the academy, the churches, the courts, the sciences, even foreign policy—gave vent to the most violent forms of racism, including torture and lynching."[3] Ida B. Wells noted that in 1892 alone, no fewer than 235 blacks were lynched. In the 1890s, Wells also posited that ten thousand blacks had been killed by whites since 1865. During the 1890s, "lynchings claimed an average of 139 lives each year, 75 percent of them black." Between 1888 and 1922, the NAACP noted that more than 3,000 blacks had been lynched. These lynchings, it should be stressed, represented only those mob murders that were documented; no one knows how many undocumented lynchings took place in the United States. "Efforts to establish precise numbers are extremely useful but become, at a certain point, meaningless," Philip Dray has recently argued. "Whether people were being killed for an alleged criminal act, a transgression of social norms, or for holding minority political views, whether their number was 500, 5,000, or 25,000, by the time the anti-lynching movement got under way just before the turn of the century, it was evident that the threshold for mob murder in America had long since passed."[4] In the year of Greene's birth, Sam Hose, an African American farm laborer accused of murdering his employer, Alfred Cranford, and raping Cranford's wife in a dispute over low wages and a request to visit Hose's ill mother, was lynched in Georgia. The April 24, 1899, edition of the *New York Tribune* printed the following:

> In the presence of nearly 2,000 people, who sent aloft yells of defiance and shouts of joy, Sam Hose (a Negro who committed two of the basest acts known to crime) was burned at the stake in a public road, one and a half miles from here. Before the torch was applied to the pyre, the Negro was deprived of his ears, fingers and other portions of his body with surprising fortitude. Before his body was cool, it was cut to pieces, the bones were crushed into small bits and even the tree upon which the wretch met his fate was torn up and disposed of as souvenirs. The Negro's heart was cut into several pieces, as was also his liver. Those unable to obtain the ghastly relics directly, paid more fortunate possessors extravagant sums for them. Small pieces of bone went for 25 cents and a bit of liver, crisply cooked, for 10 cents.[5]

More horrifying than this account is the fact that the brutal lynching of Sam Hose was not unique. "Thousands of black men and women met the same fate. Varying only in degrees of torture and brutality, these execution rituals were acted out in every part of the South" and also significantly affected the lives of blacks throughout the rest of the nation.[6] Certainly, blacks in the South faced much greater physical threats and psychological trauma than their Northern counterparts during the era of segregation. However, more than a few mass lynchings of blacks occurred outside the South, and African American communities throughout the nation were exposed to the realities of lynchings through newspaper coverage, photographs, postcards, and, perhaps most important, through direct communication and contact with family and friends from the South. Lynchings and the failure of American presidents to institute anti-lynching legislation demonstrated the United States' overall lack of respect for black life during Greene's early years. Overt violence against blacks assumed other forms as well. Between the late

1890s and 1919, large race riots occurred in major U.S. cities such as Atlanta, Chicago, New Orleans, St. Louis, Washington, D.C., and smaller cities such as Wilmington, North Carolina; Phoenix, South Carolina; and Springfield, Illinois. White rioters, often hand in hand with police forces, attacked and murdered innocent blacks and terrorized their communities. During the "Red Summer" of 1919, there were more than twenty race riots, and at least eighty-three blacks were lynched. In legal and constitutional terms, blacks were disempowered when the Civil Rights Act of 1875 was declared unconstitutional in 1883. The *Plessy v. Ferguson* decision of 1896 began an era of legalized segregation under "Jim Crow" laws, which would remain largely intact for more than fifty years in the South.

Racist thought justified many whites' mistreatment of African Americans. Ideological racism, rooted deeply within the psyche of American culture, was rejuvenated in the late nineteenth century. A wave of literature explaining and defending the new racial policies and advocating black inferiority flooded academic circles. Leading scholars across disciplines at mainstream, prestigious universities initiated and bolstered claims of black inferiority. Various white historians took the lead in dehumanizing blacks. In assessing the U.S. Progressive Era historical enterprise, August Meier and Elliot Rudwick have argued, "There was always a degree of pluralism within the profession . . . there were a few white historians—ambiguous though their own racial attitudes sometimes were—who perceived the significance of the blacks' role and of race as a moral issue in American history and who were supportive of study in this area."[7] Still, between 1890 and 1920, many leading U.S. historians (very much products of their times) were racists, promoted the notion of African American inferiority, and/or ignored African Americans' contributions altogether.[8]

Harvard historian Albert Bushnell Hart, one of the few white historians who at times openly supported African American history and historians, was ambiguous in his attitudes toward blacks. While he occasionally praised certain exceptional African Americans and challenged overt white supremacist scholarship, he nevertheless held that African Americans were inferior. "Race measured by race," he concluded in one section of *The Southern South* (1910), "the Negro is inferior, and his part in history in Africa and in America leads to the belief that he will remain inferior in race stamina and race achievement."[9] Earl Lewis has detailed the "pivotal role" of the *American Historical Review* in promoting African American history during its first century.[10] Nonetheless, it is clear that "outwardly racist" essays were published even in this journal during the early twentieth century.[11] According to Peter Novick, historians such as John F. Rhodes, J. W. Burgess, William A. Dunning, and Ellis Paxson Oberholtzer were "systematically racist," and a "consensual" and "near unanimous" racism united white historians from the North and the South during the "nadir."[12] Despite their claim to being nontraditional, innovative, and pluralistic in scope, James Harvey Robinson's "New History" disciples and proponents ignored the race problem, implying that it was not a "primary force" and assuming that "race problems would be solved automatically in the course of progressive developments."[13]

African American historians before Greene's times accepted the responsibility of writing blacks into American history and correcting racist scholarship. A classic example of African American historians embracing what Manning Marable has deemed the "corrective" principle of the black intellectual tradition was Du Bois's and Woodson's responses to U. B. Phillips's famous *American Negro Slavery* (1918). The first two African American PhDs in history critiqued Phillips's portrayal of African Americans as being "ignorant," "unenterprising," "barbaric," and "childlike and credulous" in the "ways of civilization."[14]

White scholars in other fields supported their racist colleagues in the historical profession. In psychology, G. Stanley Hall, who earned the first PhD in psychology in the United States and was founder of the *American Journal of Psychology*, claimed that blacks were psychologically different from whites and possessed certain "emotional traits" causing them to act in uncontrollable ways. In science, Robert Bennett Bean of the University of Virginia Medical School claimed that blacks' brains were underdeveloped. Early on in his career, sociologist Howard Odum asserted, "The Negro has little home conscience or love of him . . . no pride of ancestry . . . few ideals and perhaps no lasting adherence to an aspiration toward real worth." Odum continued (in a 1910 volume appearing in the same series in which Greene's dissertation would later appear): "He has little conception of the meaning of virtue, truth, honor, manhood, integrity. He is shiftless, untidy, and indolent."[15] With very few exceptions, such ideas were largely unchallenged by white scholars until the classic civil rights movement.

Despite this multilevel, oppressive environment, African American intellectuals made monumental advancements during the post-emancipation era, especially during the "nadir." As scholar William M. Banks has noted, "Between 1865 and 1915 a social framework for the development of a genuine black intellectual group slowly took shape."[16] Armed with notions of self-help, African American nationalism, self-defense, and race pride, a variety of African American spokespersons uplifted their race and challenged the widespread academic racism. Resembling members of V. P. Franklin's African American autobiographical intellectual tradition, African American historians, professionally trained and self-taught, "demonstrated on overarching commitment to 'race vindication'" by challenging racist "historical discourse" that upheld "the mental and cultural inferiority of African peoples." They "lived lives that were personal vindications of racist notions about black people" and told "the truth about the history and culture of peoples of African descent in the United States" and at times throughout the diaspora.[17]

The path for Lorenzo Johnston Greene to become a leading authority in African American history was laid by a host of important Progressive Era black historians, including George Washington Williams, W. E. B. Du Bois, Nathan Monroe Work, Carter Woodson, and others. Black intellectuals, spokespersons, and scholars from various walks of life, disciplines, and orientations took the lead in vindicating the race. Black spokespersons such as Ida B. Wells, Anna Julia Cooper, countless clubwomen, representatives of the American Negro Academy, and many others sought to defend and uplift their race. As intellectuals, they were "committed to promoting thought and culture, group self-help through education and self-empowerment, and, at times political protest on behalf of black Americans."[18] The first decade and a half of Greene's life coincided with what John Hope Franklin called "The Age of Booker T. Washington," a period from 1895 until 1915 when "Washington's influence was so great."[19] Washington's authority was a direct by-product of his publicly articulated, accommodating stance toward white Americans who accepted segregation and did not openly agitate for social, political, and human rights.

During the so-called Progressive Era in which Greene matured to young adulthood, racist thought was supported by popular culture. Black intellectuals such as Greene and his predecessors were able to make some inroads in defending "the race," yet popular racism could not be attacked with scholarship alone. By the late nineteenth century, various manufacturers and advertising marketers produced images that highlighted blacks' racial differences. According to Kenneth Goings, during the years that molded Greene's early life, thousands of items, collectively known as black collectibles, were produced in order to "prove" that blacks were "indeed different and sub-human," to help "reinforce the new racist ideology that emerged after reconstruction," to justify the overall oppression of blacks and "keep African-Americans frozen in time."[20] These stereotypes entered nearly every sector of American life, including schools, churches, theaters, homes, and department stores, and few whites perceived them as being inaccurate or dehumanizing to African Americans.

This mode of racist thinking was not limited to European descendants in the United States. It had international sanctioning. Greene was reared in a period when Africans were exploited and mistreated in very similar ways their African American counterparts experienced. The years from about 1880 until 1910 represent the modern colonial conquest of Africa. Modern colonialism in Africa was fundamentally an economic system of exploitation justified by white supremacist thought and maintained by coercion, violence, and legal apparatus. The colonial conquest and experience was equally as violent as the black experience during "the nadir." According to Adam Hochschild, "[During King Leopold's reign in the Belgian Congo] and its immediate aftermath, the population of the territory dropped by approximately ten million people," from a population of roughly twenty million in 1880 to ten million in 1920. European imperial powers published unprecedented amounts of racist literature proclaiming the inferiority of Africans. Museums, "freak shows," and world's fairs allowed all classes of Europeans and Americans to become firsthand witnesses of Africans' so-called savagery. Books from travelers, missionaries, and colonial officials demonstrate the manner in which continental Africans were declared inferior to Europeans.[21]

Clearly, Greene had "entered a world on the brink of war and a country characterized by deepening racial antagonisms, increasing violence against Afro-Americans, and the rise of militant movements for civil rights and self-defense." At the same time, Greene was born into a time with "a cadre of activists who after World War I would come together from vastly different regions of the country to form the cutting edge of a social, political, and cultural movement."[22] A strongly influential generation of black intellectuals, scholars, and leaders were born in the late nineteenth century and the first decades of the 1900s. Among others, there were Jesse Fauset, Charles Johnson, Jean Toomer, E. Franklin Frazier, Rudolph Fisher, Oliver Cox, Ralph Bunche, A. Philip Randolph, Charles Hamilton Houston, Elijah Muhammad, Marcus Garvey, Langston Hughes, Zora Neale Hurston, and Woodson's "Boys." Taken together, these leaders and intellectuals founded the largest mass movement in African American history and instigated a cultural movement that stands second only to the cultural revitalization of the Black Power era. Like their predecessors and those who would later build upon their efforts, the ideas and approaches adopted by Greene and his colleagues were molded by the times in which they existed; their unique life experiences; their relationships with others; their abilities to make profitable decisions, choices, and predictions; and, of course, chance.

❖ ❖ ❖

Greene, the sixth of nine children, was born in Ansonia, Connecticut on November 16, 1899.[23] He recalled much less about his father's ancestry than his mother's. His father, Greene once said, "divulged little information to his children concerning his background." According to oral traditions, Willis Hamilton Greene's family roots sprung out of New Jersey and Pennsylvania. He was born in Williamsport, Pennsylvania, in the mid-nineteenth century. Before he married Greene's mother, Willis Greene had been married once and had at least one daughter whom Lorenzo later knew of. Greene's mother, Harriet Elizabeth Coleman, was born in Arlington, Virginia. Her parents, George and Louisa Coleman, were former slaves, and by 1880 they had five children. After emancipation, Greene's maternal grandfather became a farmer.

In 1888, while Willis Greene operated a canal boat on Maryland's Potomac River and worked for a Washington, D.C., wholesale grocer, he and Harriet Coleman were married. "Immediately following their marriage," Greene recalled, "the couple, lured by higher wages in the factories of the North, migrated to Ansonia, Connecticut."[24] Greene's mother's family also migrated to Connecticut, affording him the privilege of a nearby extended family as he grew up. The blacks and whites who lived in Ansonia were chiefly working class. Many children in this brass, copper, and steel manufacturing settlement located in the Naugatuck Valley quit school to work in the factories at age ten or eleven. Factory work was a way of life. In Ansonia, Greene's father secured a job as a teamster with a brass-manufacturing firm, Wallace and Sons, later named the Ansonia Brass Company. Willis Greene worked there for longer than his son would work full time at Lincoln University. Greene described his father as "hard working," but his "meager wages of twelve dollars weekly" was not enough to support their growing family, which had at least eight mouths to feed before the dawning of the twentieth century.[25] Greene recorded that his mother, "like women of most poor families, did a day's work, took washing and ironing into the home, cooked and sewed in order to augment her husband's wages." Greene's mother was a domestic servant whose overall lifestyle may have differed significantly from her Southern counterpart, but it was also probably very similar in some respects. It appears that she did not suffer the dangers that many domestics encountered in the South. By bringing her work "into the home," she determined her working hours, her pace, and she could watch over her children while working. The children, especially the females, were probably socialized to see the dignity and importance of hard work and the significance of controlling the terms under which one labored. Greene's mother had the autonomy that working-class women relied upon in order to maintain their sanity and dignity.

Because times were hard for poor black families anywhere during "the nadir," Greene's older brothers and sisters dropped out of school in order to further supplement the family economy. Unlike many black doctoral scholars featured in Horace Mann Bond's 1972 study, Greene did not come from a privileged background. His family and the community as a whole supported young Rennie's quest for an education during the hardest times.[26] Greene's early years were ones of hardship. "It was difficult to get enough to eat, to maintain a serviceable pair of shoes," Greene recounted in the third person: "His clothing often consisted of 'hand-me-downs' from elder members of the family or those given to him by families for whom his mother worked." He recounted the embarrassment of sometimes, for lack of choice, having to wear his sisters' or mother's old shoes and a deceased female cousin's winter clothes to school. "When Lorenzo appeared at school in this female finery, his classmates poked fun at him calling him 'sissy.'" The young Greene continued to go to school and endured the ridicule of his classmates, most of whom were also poor. He must have been fairly self-assured and confident to deal with the frequent jokes about his appearance. Greene said that one of his sisters "who had musical talent" could not cope with not being able to "dress like the white girls," so she dropped out of high school midway through her first year. Such an action was not uncommon for daughters of poor, working-class families. In their classic 1929 study, the Lynds noted that daughters of the working class frequently left school if they could not keep up with the fashion trends of their upper- and middle-class counterparts.[27]

Though he did not talk about racism in accounts of his early life, and even asserted that "racial antagonisms" were virtually unknown at Ansonia High School, he probably encountered some prejudice as a child. Ansonia was home to few blacks. In 1910, for example, of the town's 15,152 total population, only 413 were black.[28] Bordering towns had even fewer African Americans. Greene was often the sole black in his classes. Perhaps the absence of overt "racial antagonisms" can be accounted to class dimensions. Since the Greene family was of the same socioeconomic class of the vast majority of whites in the town, it is possible that they were absorbed into Ansonia working-class culture. Even though he did not quit school like his older siblings and many of Ansonia's children, Lorenzo did contribute to the economic maintenance of the homestead. During his elementary school years, he earned some money by performing odd jobs "such as carrying dinners to factory workers, sawing wood, cleaning yards, and cutting grass." These early experiences influenced Greene's ability to keep up with Woodson's demanding regimen and to make sacrifices on others' behalf later on in his life.

Greene found solace in schoolwork as early as his grammar school days. He very much enjoyed reading fairy tales and history in his spare time and took advantage of the "ubiquitous libraries of New England." In his late forties, Greene commented that his early grammar school interest in history, which earned him several prizes as a youngster, "largely influenced his decision to make history his life's work."[29] His high school years constituted "the happiest period" of his life. He was very popular and active in both academic culture and extracurricular activities. He was the president of the German Club, captain of the male debating society, a speaker in high demand at pep rallies, and was dubbed the "class poet"—all of this at a high school where blacks were nearly invisible (at one point, there were only three blacks out of a student population of six hundred). He continued to work during these years, shining shoes, running errands, and stocking shelves in a local drugstore. With the money he earned, he purchased his clothes, bought his own school supplies, and contributed to his family's survival, as his elder siblings before him had done. When he graduated from Ansonia High School in 1917, he was the only black in his class and was also the first black graduate in the school's history. Greene graduated in the top three percent of his class and received the school's most prestigious award, the Pine History Prize. Greene's family and Ansonia's small black community were very proud of the confident young man. He was the first of the family to graduate from high school.[30]

Looking at Greene's life through his teenage years, one notices that he shared a good deal in common with W. E. B. Du Bois, born three decades before him in bordering Massachusetts. Both came from poor, struggling families. Both were reared in the eastern United States in small towns where blacks were greatly outnumbered. Both were popular students, active in school, and demonstrated intellectual superiority over their white classmates. Both worked several jobs to help maintain the material success of their families. And both were the first blacks to graduate from their respective high schools. But the two were also different. Greene came from a large family with a strong father figure, whereas Du Bois's father abandoned his mother and child about one year after Du Bois's birth. Even though both enjoyed debating, Du Bois became intrigued with a local brand of politics much earlier than Greene. Du Bois seemed to have had a clearer sense of what he wanted to do after graduating from high school as well. This may be accounted to the fact that he, unlike Greene, did not need to worry about helping support a large household.[31]

After Greene graduated with an "exceptional" class, his high school principal encouraged him to study law at Syracuse University. His family and other friends of the family encouraged him to study medicine. At the time, medical work was among the most popular vocations of "college-bred Negroes," along with teaching, preaching, secretarial work, and law. African American college graduates chose these professions during the era of Jim Crow segregation because they could and, equally important, because they felt a sense of duty and responsibility to their community and people. As Woodson noted in *The Negro Professional Man and the Community,* by becoming a physician, preacher, lawyer, or teacher, the black professional could give back to his/her community in concrete ways. Despite his love of history and debating, Greene did not follow his principal's advice or his earliest calling: he decided to become a physician, and his decision was not unique. At the time there were slightly more than three thousand black physicians. It was a very practical vocational choice for a race-conscious, college-bound scholar after the Civil War. Often the victims of poor sanitation and poverty, blacks were very susceptible to a range of diseases. Black patients were denied proper treatment from white establishments, and black doctors found it difficult to find a significant clientele of white patients. So black doctors and patients needed each other. The African American physician in the era of segregation was "the most affluent member of communities with sizable Negro populations," Rayford Logan surmised. In an article written around the time Greene made his decision, Kelly Miller added, "The Negro physician comes into immediate contact with the masses of his race: he is the missionary of good health."[32]

Greene could not enroll in college right away because his family was still struggling to survive, so he worked for several years to help maintain the large household and save money for college. These several years after graduating must have been very trying ones for Greene: intellectually, he was prepared to enter a culture of higher education; instead, he joined the ranks of his former classmates who concluded their studies years before high school. One can only speculate that the recent high school graduate did not give up on his academic dreams. Surely, he still visited the "ubiquitous libraries of New England" and followed current events. But unlike many of his contemporaries, he did not have the benefit of sharpening his intellectual blade against other promising young scholars of his generation or the opportunity to study under professionally trained scholars. During these years he was, instead, a self-trained scholar. In March 1986, Greene told Arvarh Strickland that while he did not save a lot of money, "he renewed his determination to get away from Ansonia before he became a 'slave to the factory whistle.'"[33]

Two years after he graduated from high school, Greene left his New England homestead for Washington, D.C., in hopes of studying medicine at Howard University. Howard's medical school was a very good choice. After May 31, 1905, when it was placed under the management of the trustees, the medical school at Howard blossomed. It changed from a night school into a day school, and the university paid more of its significant bills. It boasted a separate library before 1920. The medical school was first-rate for the early 1900s, when, out of about seven black medical schools in the country, five were "'in no position to make any contributions of value' to the training of Negro physicians who had the responsibility of caring for Negro patients." Several others did not have adequate financial support. Howard's medical school was the only one that required high school courses or an equivalent for entrance in the early 1900s. By 1923, the school of medicine was the only department in the university to receive a Class A rating by the "Rating Association of America." By the time Greene would graduate, practically every student at Howard passed the board exams. It is said that by October 25, 1925, only one of forty failed the exam.[34]

Greene did not join the ranks of Howard's prestigious medical corps upon arriving in Washington, D.C. His time off from school had taken its toll. Unprepared in mathematics, he failed the entrance exam. Kelly Miller, Howard's dean of the College of Arts and Sciences from 1907 until 1919, directed Greene to Dunbar High School, where Greene took math courses. Dunbar, founded in 1870 as the Preparatory High School for Colored Youth, was recognized as being one of the most prestigious public schools for blacks. While Greene hailed from a humble, northeastern, working-class family, most of Dunbar's students came from the ranks of Washington's black middle-class and bourgeoisie elite. This must have been an eye-opening experience for Greene, moving away from the drudgery of factory work and into a highbrow black academic culture.[35]

By 1920, Greene entered Howard University still planning to study medicine. By the end of his second year, he had fulfilled the school's premedical requirements. And he did not abandon his childhood interest in history. He continued to take classes in the social sciences and decided to delay entering the medical school until the end of his junior year. During his last year, he enrolled in history courses, the only classes that fit into his busy work schedule. Greene missed Woodson, who resigned after attempting to introduce black history permanently into Howard's curriculum in 1919. Walter Dyson, Leo Hansberry, and Charles H. Wesley molded his early perceptions of history and in different ways reinvoked Greene's love of history and challenged him to reassess what it meant to be a black historian. He also took classes from Lorenzo D. Turner and Alain Leroy Locke.

Greene greatly admired Wesley, spoke highly of Turner, and was quite critical of Hansberry and Locke. He wrote in his diary that Hansberry did not possess the proper "qualifications for serious study, possessing only a B.S. degree, and that a War Diploma." Greene continued his critical assessment of the university's African History instructor in 1928: "Without biology, which is fundamental, lacking familiarity with French, German, Portuguese, and Arabic, in which languages everything worthwhile on Africa has been written, he is like a man who goes fishing with a bare hook." The "real genius" of Hansberry, in Greene's eyes, was his "extraordinary ability to attract students to his course for the sake of an easy passing grade." Greene added in a late 1929 journal entry that he himself was "better prepared for serious historiography" than his former teacher. Locke did not impress Greene, either. "For all his superior education—and I doubt whether any Negro in America has had the benefit of better training—he has produced nothing original." Apparently, Greene did not consider any of Locke's philosophical studies or essays on the New Negro as being authentic and did not care for this man of "superfine culture" because "he lacked the practicality of Woodson."[36]

Greene wrote his harsh criticisms of Hansberry and Locke in his diary and probably never intended for his personal thoughts to enter the public domain. His observations were certainly based on his (probably tenuous) interactions with these two influential black scholars, but Greene's assessments were counterbalanced by others' testimonies. At Howard, Hansberry's "popularity, teaching effectiveness and eminence made a lasting impact on students and faculty." Charles H. Wesley, Greene's mentor, was among those who had great respect for Hansberry's pioneering work in African studies. Greene's views of Locke are refuted by numerous scholars who appreciated Locke's contributions: Charles S. Johnson, William Stanley Braithwaite, W. E. B. Du Bois, and Ralph Bunche, who believed that Locke "was a strong and unique beacon lighting an exciting new course for aspiring young Negroes."[37]

❖ ❖ ❖

The shift to studying history was for Greene "the turning point in his career." Howard University specifically, and Washington, D.C., in general, were together the Mecca of the black intelligentsia (in his memoirs, however, Greene did not talk too much about his experiences in Washington, D.C., in the early 1920s). In many respects, Greene and others were fortunate to attend black colleges in the era of segregation. Before integration, leading black scholars were concentrated at black universities such as Howard, Lincoln University in Missouri, Southern University in Louisiana, Atlanta University, and others. At Howard, as late as 1940, Charles Drew, Sterling Brown, E. Franklin

Frazier, Rayford Logan, and Alain Locke were among the faculty. He briefly commented on his various professors and his social life in his diary from 1928 to 1930. Greene, who went to Howard as "a young idealist," made many friends there, but he was unimpressed with the disposition of some of the students. He did not enjoy the social life offered by fraternities because of their "snobbish" attitudes and low interest in intellectual endeavors. They were, in his estimation, "sterile, barren, bereft of any uplift movement." Greene also did not have the leisure time for such activities. While taking a full course load, he ran elevators, cleaned windows, and even sold cold cream. He lived with his mother's sister, laundered his own clothes, and prepared the bulk of his meals. During the summers, he returned to Ansonia and labored as a truck driver for the brass factories he dreaded so much; he also worked as a "machinist's helper."[38]

Greene's years at Howard (1920–1924) coincided with the controversial reign of J. Stanley Durkee, the university's last white president, from July 1, 1918, until June 30, 1926. In his history of Howard, Rayford Logan argued that Durkee was one of Howard's most progressive presidents who inaugurated a host of positive changes for faculty, students, and the surrounding community. Raymond Wolters has offered a much more critical assessment of Durkee's reign, however. According to Wolters, Howard's eleventh white president stressed an archaic "moral welfare" and missionary zeal, employed a compromising "responsive (or cooptive) strategy," altered the university's finances and academic programs to the detriment of students and faculty, and essentially instituted a self-serving "program of centralization."[39]

While students and black faculty at Howard had historically engaged in various forms of protest against white control of the university, Durkee's presidency—running parallel to the mounting post–World War I black radicalism, the New Negro movement, and the Harlem Renaissance—was characterized by student and faculty unrest. According to Wolters, during the mid-1920s Howard's president and board of trustees exhibited an "official indifference to the black renaissance" by rejecting students' and faculty's requests for Black studies courses, faculty salary increases, and black cultural autonomy. Greene was at Howard when his fellow students began increasingly challenging the university's missionary ethos, offering instead ideologies of racial uplift, solidarity, and self-determination. Student unrest and activism at Howard peaked after Greene's departure with student, faculty, and alumni opposition in 1925 to compulsory ROTC and other military requirements. Black opposition among faculty to Durkee's conservatism was nearly unanimous. Prominent, leading Howard scholars such as E. Franklin

Frazier, David Houston, Woodson, Kelly Miller, Alain Locke, Montgomery Gregory, Ernest E. Just, George Williams Cook, and others voiced their displeasure with Durkee, who, in turn, aggressively targeted more than a few of his critics—namely Locke, Miller, Woodson, and other lesser-known professors.[40] Durkee's resignation in the spring of 1926 was eventually brought about by the mounting pressures of black professors and students who were determined to put an end to white leadership. In 1926, after Greene graduated from Howard, Mordecai W. Johnson became the university's first African American president; he would serve in this capacity for thirty-four years.

While Greene was at Howard, his scholarly achievements transcended the standards of cut-and-dried academics of the classroom and drifted into the creative realm. At Ansonia High School, Greene was known as the "class poet." He further honed his skills in writing poetry and prose at Howard. The earliest available examples of Greene's poetry date from February 1921 until the summer of 1924, a period during which Greene wrote about a dozen poems (he compiled them decades later with roughly ninety others). He continued to write poetry into the late 1930s, although he did not consider himself a poet. In the late 1940s, while editing the *Midwest Journal,* he humbly told Melvin B. Tolson that he was "a layman, unschooled in the niceties of poetic art."[41]

He shared his poetry only with a select audience. While in Washington during the late 1920s, he read some of his works to his close friends; among them were Georgia Douglas Johnson, whom Greene first met in August 1928, Gertrude McBrown, and artist Lois Mailou Jones, who in March 1931 agreed to illustrate his poem "Out of the Mist." The poems Greene wrote during his Howard years concerned several themes. He wrote about his intimate feelings toward several young women, commented on the tragic aftermath of war, stressed the need for forgiveness in relationships between those in power and their subordinates, put into poetry the sorrow he felt after his sister's death, shared his ideas about life in general, and summarized what his experiences at Howard meant to him.

It is difficult to classify Greene's early poetry, since it touched upon many different themes and because, unpublished, his work did not gain the attention of literary critics or other poets of the time. His style ranges from classical rhyming patterns, such as iambic pentameter, to nonrhyming verse. Most of his earliest poetry was very lofty in tone, and he seemed to borrow from famous poets such as Shakespeare. No doubt, he had read Shakespeare and other classical writers of the Western tradition in high school. At Howard, he further developed a taste for Shakespearean verse. In a notebook dated

1924, he had detailed notes on many of Shakespeare's plays and on the writing techniques of England's bard.[42]

Greene's early poetry served as a medium of expressing his love for different women; indeed, at least ninety percent of all the poetry Greene wrote could be classified as love poetry (and a great amount of this poetry was written for Thomasina Talley, whom he met in the early 1930s and married in 1941). On several occasions, Greene took pride in the power of his poetic imagination in courting women. "Read poetry to Miss [Myrtle] Glenn," Greene jotted down in his diary on February 13, 1931: "Got so excited after my rendition of 'A June Night' that she started stroking my hair." In February 1931, he admitted that women were his "eternal weakness." In his late twenties, he commented that he was by no means ready to take only "one object of affection and swear to cherish and love her" for the rest of his days (he remained a bachelor until his early forties). In his early thirties, he explained: "'Tis better to love often before marriage than afterwards. One can pick and choose then and have some basis of comparison for the choice."[43]

With the exception of his "Class Poem to Howard," his early poetry did not focus on black American subject matters. While such leading literary critics of the 1920s as Alain Locke or William Stanley Braithwaite may have recognized the "beauty" and universality of Greene's poetry, some would have challenged Greene to employ his creative artistic skills also as "propaganda for gaining the right of black folk to love and enjoy." Du Bois's views on art during the 1920s were very straightforward. "All Art is propaganda and ever must be, despite the wailing of the purists," Du Bois argued. "I do not care a damn for any art that is not used for propaganda."[44]

Like other Americans born in the last decade of the nineteenth century, Greene was a "war baby." During the 1890s, the United States began demonstrating its military might in Latin America and other parts of the so-called "Third World." After the United States defeated Spain in 1898, "the Pax Americana was imposed in Cuba, Puerto Rico, Hawaii, Guam, and the Philippines," and the U.S. entered a new phase of foreign policy and empire building.[45] When the United States declared war on Germany, Greene was in his final year of high school. When World War I ended, he was still in Ansonia working to support his family. Greene's contemporary stance on white America's growing expansionism, imperialism, and militarism—or on blacks in World War I—remains open to speculation. Immediately after World War I, Greene did write a poem in which he commented on the tragic aftermath of war. In "To the Unknown Soldier," written on November 11, 1921, he argued against war based upon the innocent lives lost. For Greene, all of the flowers, medals, and fame bestowed upon a soldier who gave "ambition, loved ones, even life" in order to save "his native land" did not mean anything. Death neutralized and nullified such recognition, according to Greene. He asked his readers what all these manmade medals and expressions of recognition meant to dead soldiers. For Greene, we needed to stop war and restore peace once and for all. He wrote:

> In him a greatful nation shrines
>   Her nameless heroes;
> Reveres her sons who with their life
>   Paid war's supremest cost.
> This tribute breathes a nation's prayer,
>   That war fore'er may cease;
> That o'er this bleeding earth may dawn
>   A day of lasting peace.[46]

Through midcentury, Greene changed his views about war several times. During World War II, he supported America's war efforts, believing that victory could be a means of attaining black equality. Then, shortly after the war, he called for peace as he did in "To the Unknown Soldier."

One of Greene's longest early poems, "The King's Jester," employs a Shakespearean style and tells a tale about how a jester offended a king one day and "straitway fell from his much-envied place." After some time, this jester bravely returned to the "royal room," offered "ten thousand redresses," and begged the king for forgiveness. The king took the "courtly knave" back into his "kingly grace," granting him "full forgiveness." This poem is a brief commentary on human nature and relationships between different castes, the empowered and the disempowered. Greene's jester was human in that he made a mistake. He was not too proud or too scared to ask humbly for the king's forgiveness. The king was all-powerful and was by no means pressed to forgive the jester, yet he pardoned the actions of the jester. Greene portrayed the king's actions as being even more noble than the jester's. "To err is human," Greene concluded, "but Forgiveness, Love, is like to nectar, dropped from heaven above."[47]

Greene also used his poetry as an emotional outlet for reflecting upon day-to-day life, the state of the world, and significant events in his life. In a poem entitled "To the Clouds," for instance, he wrote about surviving in a society and world in which there were monumental problems, from "jealousies" to famine, "industrial hatred" to "church feuds," "greed" to "foul segregation." Greene's solution for coping with this "toilsome life" was to draw inspiration from God and then to live by making his own choices and by determining his own destiny. His religious beliefs at this time appear to have been very practical and "this worldly." Greene philosophized on how it was like to get by on a daily basis:

Yet, struggling, must I on and seek for aid
Within myself, wherein there sits enshrined
The "I That Am"—My Soul—a part of Him,
Breathed into me from His Essence Divine.
Not as ye, then, the playthings of the wind,
For Will is mine, in life my course to choose;
And choosing, therefore, I am Guide and Light,
And, or myself, life's path may keep or loose.[48]

In another poem composed the same year, Greene reflected on his state of mind when one of his sisters died (apparently) in early January 1924. He mourned her death in the poem "To My Sister." On January 2, Greene called upon "all nature" to pause from their regular activities "since my sweet sister lifeless lies today." He called upon "ye people" to openly wail and cry with him. The death of his sister overwhelmed him with grief. A saddened Greene proclaimed:

Yet rise! Here let me weep for her again!
Cease wailing, birds! bells! stay your tollings dread
Ye winds and waters, your laments restrain!
For grief o'ercome me for my sister is dead.[49]

Roughly a month later, Greene published a poem in which he likened the beauty of a woman named Cynthia to the moon, the most powerful light of "heaven's celestial blue!" Whoever Cynthia was, Greene thought very highly and fondly of her and longed to join her in her elevated, "happy state."[50]

The last poem Greene wrote while he was at Howard was "Class Poem to Howard," completed on May 10, 1924. Though brief, it is the most extensive account of Greene's impressions of his Howard years. It also constitutes one of his first articulations of race consciousness and responsibility. According to this poem, Greene enjoyed his four years at Howard, saying that the university "nurtured" its students, "equipped us with intelligence" in order to "serve our country wisely, and our God." For Greene, his alma mater represented the "hope, the pride, the glory of our race," which by the 1920s had made its "mark" in a range of professions. Howard, Greene maintained, deserved its progeny's "gratitude" and "priceless blessings" because it taught them "to observe, . . . to love, to seek the truth," and to achieve their "cherished goals" and "longed-for ends." Greene interpreted the role of Howard University in a manner similar to Woodson's view of the role of the Association for the Study of Negro Life and History (ASNLH) in promoting black history. Years before Greene first met him, Woodson proclaimed that if whites had knowledge of black America's glorious past and humanity, racial prejudice would naturally disappear. Echoing Woodson, Greene asserted:

> May you so foster racial harmony,
> By lifting high your sons in scholarship,
> That petty animosities shall fade,
> Dispelled like mist before the morning sun;
> Then, Howard, majestic on your sacred hills,
> A thousand praises ringing in your ears,
> May you stand forth, a great world institute,
> Striving for God, and all humanity.[51]

Greene also reiterated the philosophy of uplift advocated by his counterparts of the late nineteenth and early twentieth century, and he seemed to have believed that the masses looked upon black college graduates such as himself as being their leaders, a credo which would become less popular during the rise of the New Negro and the Harlem Renaissance. "O help us, Howard, to lift our struggling race that looks with eager eyes to us for aid," Greene asserted, "O may we all such service render that our deeds shall be a hymn of praise to you."[52]

Greene's early poems, written during his Howard years, touch upon a host of themes. While his poetry was not centered on black America (and it was not of the caliber of his professional poet counterparts), his writing was undoubtedly an important part of his personality, serving perhaps as an emotional, spiritual, and creative outlet as he was preoccupied with science-oriented classes for the majority of his undergraduate years. Considered a social science, history did not serve as a medium of creative expression for Greene: history majors were taught to write in a detached, nonemotional, objective manner. Greene did not seem to mind this. For him, Wesley was a "historian of the first rank" in part because he was "a clear, dispassionate thinker." At Howard and during his later years of writing poetry, Greene would not have thought of meshing his art with historical scholarship, drawing a sharp line between the two. Du Bois, on the other hand, was one of the only scholars of this time to marry the two genres in a masterful manner.

❖ ❖ ❖

Greene received his bachelor's degree from Howard, cum laude, in 1924. His qualifications were very strong. Since at one point he planned to study medicine at the University of Heidelberg in Germany, he had taken many courses in German, Latin, French, and Portuguese. As he commented in a diary entry in November 1929, such knowledge would have made him a prime candidate for studying African history. After graduating, he had abandoned medicine and chose history as his profession. Greene recounted that his parents and community in Ansonia were greatly dismayed when he informed them of his decision. They probably did not see the practicality in becoming a historian. A physician had a concrete, clear-cut, historically rooted function in the community and was a well-respected breadwinner. The historical profession was basically unknown to the black masses at that time. When Greene graduated from Howard, Du Bois and Woodson were the only African Americans holding doctoral degrees in history. A year later, in 1925, Charles H. Wesley became the third black to do so. Even though Woodson founded the ASNLH in 1915 and published the first volume of *The Negro in Our History* in 1922, he did not begin seriously to popularize black history among the masses until 1926, when he inaugurated Negro History Week.

Greene felt the pressure of his parents and community, who could not comprehend why their exemplary Ansonia High School graduate turned to history. In August 1924, he reluctantly submitted to their pressures and enrolled in the medical school of New York University. However, when he was returning to Ansonia from registration, he visited Dr. Peyton Anderson, a famous New York City tuberculosis specialist. A Connecticut native and friend of the family, Anderson convinced Greene to pursue a degree in the social sciences because he saw that "we needed more scholars in that field." So "upon reaching home, he [Greene] quietly, but firmly, informed his family of his decision. Although obviously disappointed, they resigned themselves to his wishes."[53] Greene's decision to become a historian stemmed from his early love of the discipline and from a sense of commitment to black people in general. He viewed his decision as being one that would eventually affect blacks as a whole. He perceived himself as being a representative for "the race" in the ivory towers of academe.

In the late 1940s, Greene commented that he had always possessed a desire to earn a degree from Connecticut's most elite and prestigious institution of higher learning, Yale University in New Haven. He did not have enough credits to satisfy Yale's graduate school requirements, but the dean advised him to enroll in Columbia University's extension program and to take thirty hours of history. After that, he was told, Yale would be "happy" to accept

Greene into their program. Greene decided to enroll in the graduate school of history at Columbia University.

Even though Yale was the first American university to award a PhD to an African American (1876), by the era of World War II, Columbia had produced many black master's and doctoral graduates. By December 1943, Harry Washington Greene calculated that "at least 381 persons of Negro descent have been admitted to the degree of Doctor of Philosophy or its corresponding academic equivalent." Columbia, trailing the University of Chicago by only five, produced at least thirty-five of these scholars, but Columbia almost doubled the University of Chicago in master's degrees awarded to blacks. By 1943, forty-two blacks had received master's degrees from Columbia.[54]

In 1926, two years after he entered Columbia, Greene was awarded a master's degree. He remained at Columbia (which was originally only a steppingstone toward enrollment at Yale) because of the "great historical scholars" he encountered there. Greene believed that he had the "rare privilege" of studying under "world-famous" historians such as Evarts B. Greene, David Saville Muzzy, Carlton J. Hayes, Robert Livingston Schuyler, Allan Nevins, Dixon Ryan Fox, Harry A. Carman, and Austin Evans. Apparently, Greene was academically well supported at Columbia. He credited professors Evarts B. Greene (1870–1947), historian of colonial America, the Revolutionary era, and of the church in early America, and Dixon R. Fox, editor and author of many books on the colonial era, for influencing him to undertake his lifelong studies of black life in colonial New England. At Columbia, he was introduced to various streams of historical thought, from colonial American history to European history. He was also challenged intellectually. In September 1928, he told Woodson that the first time he seriously doubted that he had passed an examination in history was in Dr. Evarts B. Greene's course in United States history.[55] During his brief career as a master's candidate at Columbia, despite his growing interest in blacks in New England and the fact that he wanted to become a historian for "the race," he was not necessarily dedicated to studying black history or, for that matter, even fond of its chief advocate.

One particular example best illustrates this. In 1925, during his first year at Columbia, Greene contacted Charles H. Wesley and asked him whether Wesley could help him with his "precarious financial situation." Greene's "favorite teacher" during his Howard days advised him to speak with Woodson about a possible job with the ASNLH. Greene contacted and met with Woodson, but at the time the Association did not have adequate funds to employ additional researchers. Woodson shared his philosophy of black history with Greene in a "stimulating two-hour conversation." At the time, the New

England native was not convinced by Woodson's dictum that black history needed to be told in order to rescue "the race" from oblivion and extinction. In fact, Greene pitied Woodson. Perhaps the Ivy League, elite environment of Columbia was going to Greene's head. Looking back on this meeting decades later, Greene described how he felt and confessed that he was indeed a victim of the miseducation he later campaigned against. "In my ignorance, I regarded Dr. Woodson as a dreamer, a visionary, albeit a brilliant scholar, wasting his time, trying to conjure up that which did not exist—Negro History." Greene thought that, instead, "he [Woodson] should be teaching at Harvard, Yale, Columbia, or some other ivy-league school."[56] Greene's skepticism did not last long. By the time he met Woodson again in 1928, he came to appreciate what Woodson was doing and in time developed into one of his most enthusiastic, dedicated, and unselfish co-workers.

During Greene's 1926–27 academic year, he took courses toward a PhD in history at Columbia. In his few personal memoirs, Greene did not elaborate on his years in New York; the most he said was that he was impressed with and challenged by the highly acclaimed professors in the Columbia University history department. From 1924 until Woodson offered him a job in February 1928, Greene's day-to-day life was most likely dominated by academic work and manual labor of some sort in order to earn money to pay for his room, books, supplies, and courses. He also made some lifetime friends in New York.

One of the best windows into Greene's mind, thought, and imagination during these several years comes again from his poetry. Between the time that he graduated from Howard and when he began working with the ASNLH, Greene wrote more than two dozen poems, all in keeping with the style of his early work at Howard. He employed conventional methods in rhyming and used a lofty language popular in earlier times. By far, the most prevalent theme of this body of work was love. Greene wrote about love as well as about the pain of of loving someone who no longer reciprocated the feeling. By March 1927, love, in Greene's experience, proved to be so powerful that in certain cases it could not be suppressed, ignored, or forgotten, no matter how hard he tried. Greene lamented:

If you have vowed—
  While tears of anguish rolled—
  That love's false sun eternally has set,
But from within
A voice, all knowing, speaks:
"Fool! Still you love and never can forget!"
Then you know tragic love.[57]

Essentially, Greene testified that one of man's greatest vulnerabilities was being in love.

Another topic Greene discussed several times while in New York was the meaning of death, how losing loved ones affected his state of mind. Sometime in January 1927, it appears that Beatrice, a friend of Greene's, died. He coped with her death through poetry. Though tears flowed from his soul, he wrote in a poetic eulogy that he believed that her spirit still "sits with us—the table's unseen guest." She still had the power to watch over her children, Greene asserted: to love her husband, encourage her mother, and laugh and cry with her friends. According to this poem, Greene believed in death only in physical terms. He shared with his African ancestry a belief that "human life does not terminate at the death of the individual, but," as John S. Mbiti argues, "continues beyond death."[58] Speaking as Beatrice, Greene wrote:

"Where'er you go, there too
Am I. O darling babes,
Dear mother, husband, friends,
Weep not for me, for Love
Has built a temple in
Your hearts and there I dwell;
I am part of you."[59]

A handful of poems written during Greene's years in New York stand out as being especially unique and intriguing since they do not philosophize on the illusive meaning of love or death. These poems run the gamut, from celebrating American aviator Charles A. Lindbergh to contemplating man's place in the universe to articulating the role of the New Negro.

On May 21, 1927, after thirty-three-and-a-half hours aloft, a twenty-five-year old Charles Augustus Lindbergh became the first man to make a nonstop transatlantic flight. It was one of the most monumental events in world history in the 1920s. Lindbergh had achieved what others thought impossible, and he became an "ultra American hero." The "Lindbergh phenomenon" is hard to pinpoint, but there is no doubt that Americans loved the young man with the "boyish grin" after he completed his meticulously planned, 3,614-mile flight. In the months after his achievement, Lindbergh received more than two million pieces of fan mail, five thousand poems, and honorary medals from different states and cities. The poetry on Lindbergh was featured in leading journals of the 1920s, such as *Literary Digest.* In 1927, a book of one hundred poems in honor of the so-called "incorruptible young man" was published. According to one scholar, Lindbergh inspired poets who were "attempting to resolve the duality of art and science." Lindbergh helped many of these poets validate their art in an increasingly technological era.[60]

Though his thoughts on Lindbergh were not featured in the *Literary Digest* or in *The Spirit of St. Louis: One Hundred Poems,* in November 1927, Greene wrote a poem commemorating Lindbergh's flight and expressing what this act meant to him. "To Lindberg" consists of two major methods. In two-line stanzas he stages a conversation between a young, fearless Lindbergh and elder "sirs" who try to convince him not to make his voyage. In a dynamic exchange, "grizzly grey-beards" attempt to convince Lindbergh to "renounce this fatal ride" for fear that, like the "two Frenchmen" before him, he would die. Lindbergh, in Greene's estimation, was a youthful, brave pioneer who knew of the dangers ahead but viewed his actions as being a major step for humankind and as an accomplishment in which all youths could especially take pride. After being warned by the older generation, Greene's Lindbergh replied with confidence:

> . . . I know the perils all,
> One thousand I'll fly before night falls.
> Youth must be served, and youth must lead the way,
> Bid me Godspeed, for I take off today.[61]

In Greene's estimation, Lindbergh's flight was one of the most significant events in world history. "Like him who sailed uncharted seas of old, the youth performed one forty times as bold." It was, more important, "youth's victory." Like the poets featured in *The Spirit of St. Louis: One Hundred Poems,* Greene may have also seen the similarities between himself and the young "ultra American hero." In simplest terms, both men seem to have shared the disposition of attempting to mesh values from two seemingly contradictory worldviews. A young Lindbergh was a simple, humble technological pioneer who also had spiritual and humane concerns. Similarly, Greene was among those black intellectuals born in the late 1800s who, consciously or unconsciously, sought to merge the social uplift philosophy of the "Old Negro" with that of the "New Negro."

Greene appears to have stood alone in the black intellectual community in praising Lindbergh. While the black popular press may have acknowledged this historical event, intellectual journals such as *The Crisis* focused on other events and issues. In May 1977, Greene sent a copy of his poem to the Missouri Historical Society, which was celebrating the fiftieth anniversary of Lindbergh's flight. He mentioned that Lindbergh's flight "inspired" him, and he suggested that his poem would help them "to ascertain how a young man reacted at the daring of another youth in the 'mad Twenties.'" It would be interesting to see how Greene's views of Lindbergh changed when the aviator began to speak of the superiority of whites over non-Caucasian people and attacked Jews during the era of World War II.[62]

During his Columbia years, Greene also wrote several poems in which he articulated his philosophical views of man's position in the universe. In a December 1926 poem entitled "Man," Greene mocked mankind, "a tiny speck" on earth, for thinking that he is the center of the universe, or even important in the broader scheme of things. He stressed the "infinitesimal" presence of man in the onward-moving, "incomprehensible" natural world and universe. In simplest terms, he noted that after an individual dies, tears may be shed, but soon enough his accomplishments would be surpassed by another and further lost in the forward-moving course of life. Greene advocated a belief in pre-destiny. He expressed that the course of this world "is set; it may not deviate—nor pause, but ever onward moves as heedless as before."[63]

As clearly demonstrated by his early life growing up in Ansonia and his life at Howard, Greene was no stranger to hard work. He carried this ethic into his graduate studies at Columbia. During his first year of doctoral work, he wrote a poem called "Exhortation," in which he stressed the need for people to work hard and persevere even when "you ever feel discouraged." During such times, Greene drew inspiration from "the rare old masters" who only "through years of toil" successfully climbed "life's ladder." Greene, who first truly gained national recognition as a scholar and historian nearly two decades after he first enrolled in Columbia, concluded that:

> Fame is not won overnight;
> Grit your teeth and keep on plodding
> You will win, if you but fight.[64]

❖ ❖ ❖

The years Greene spent in New York at Columbia corresponded with the climax of one of the most significant cultural and artistic movement's in black America's history, the Harlem Renaissance. While scholars have intensely debated the influence of Harlem Renaissance creative artists—their success and failures, their place in the broader context of American literary evolution, the rise and decline of the movement, the leading figures within the movement, and the focus and inner workings of the movement—practically all scholars agree that during the immediate post–World War I years until about the mid-1930s, many black intellectuals, especially creative artists based in Harlem, viewed themselves as turning a new page in black middle-class intellectual cultural consciousness, identity formation, and overall worldview. There was an unprecedented amount of diverse, creative, artistic activity taking place among African Americans. This New Negro was distinctly different from the older guard of black leadership and intellectual caretakers, especially black spokespersons prominent during the age of Booker T. Washington. Though they claimed otherwise, New Negroes, whose glory years were in the 1920s (before the economic downturn of 1929), were very much like their predecessors in that they advocated race pride, self-help, social justice, racial solidarity, the development of a black middle-class ethos, and, at times, integration and assimilation.

What made these self-proclaimed New Negroes different from their intellectual forebears was that through their various artistic vehicles they took pride in day-to-day black working-class and Southern folk culture, attempted to depict and explain black ghetto life, celebrated their ancestral African roots, and employed a (perhaps) more radical rhetoric and poetry than the previous generations. At the same time, their work was highly promoted by a range of white publishers: white patronage was essential to the success of the Harlem Renaissance's leaders. In retrospect, it seems quite ironic that these New Negroes viewed themselves as being so much more assertive and independent than their predecessors while they were, unlike most of their elders, accepted by the mainstream. The "New Negro" renaissance was not this simple and clear cut. There were many heated debates between various individuals and schools of thought.

The major debates concerned whether or not African American artists were distinct from their white counterparts and, therefore, whether or not they should produce "racial" or "universal" art, should cater to the white public and popular sentiments, or could continue vindicating the race with romantic and glorious images of black culture or strive to paint more balanced portraits of black life. Most black intellectuals naturally straddled these various positions. The major debates between black intellectuals during this era stemmed from generational differences. The older generation of "race men" like Du Bois, Harlem Renaissance promoter Alain L. Locke, and Marcus Garvey, whose movement thrived because of the new atmosphere ushered in (in part) by the creative artists, often opposed Harlem Renaissance writers' language use and celebration of black folk and urban culture, believing that it helped to fuel white prejudice and justify racial oppression.

Others, like Benjamin Brawley, believed that his younger counterparts lacked proper training, evidenced by their artificial, "free verse" poetry that paid no attention to the scholarly standards of the day.[65]

The debate between George Schuyler and Langston Hughes in the pages of the *Nation* in 1926 provides one of the best examples of the differences in opinions regarding the role of art in the black intellectual community. Schuyler initiated the debate when he declared that black culture was not unique and was instead essentially the same as white American culture: "The Aframerican is merely a lampblacked Anglo-Saxon," Schuyler said. "Aside from his color, which ranges from very dark brown to pink, your American Negro is just plain American. Negroes and whites from the same localities of this country talk, think, and act about the same." Schuyler reasoned that blacks were molded by the same economic and social forces that affected whites. He ignored prejudice, institutional racism, and the distinct lifestyle and culture of black people. He wanted his readers, primarily liberal whites, to recognize that there were no "racial differences" between blacks and whites, differences that had been used for so long to buttress racial discrimination. Schuyler also directly addressed black artists, telling them that historically their works were essentially "identical" to those white American artists. He could not understand why black artists would want to separate themselves from "the national artist's norm." He claimed that Harlem Renaissance cultural nationalists were lending "a helping hand" to Negrophobists.[66]

In an immediate, clever rebuttal, Langston Hughes challenged Schuyler's premise that blacks were culturally American and that they had generated and should continue to generate art that was the same as the art of white Americans. Hughes centered his argument around a promising young black poet who once said to him, "'I want to be a poet—not a Negro poet.'" Hughes interpreted this statement to mean that his friend wanted to be white. Hughes identified this African American middle-class aspiration—"the desire to pour racial individuality into the mold of American standardization, and to be as little Negro and as much American as possible"—as being the major factor stunting the growth of a "true Negro art in America." Employing some amusing anecdotes, Hughes argued that members of the "Nordicized Negro intelligentsia" and "colored near-intellectuals" like Schuyler had been reared and taught to be ashamed of their culture. Hughes called upon black artists to see the beauty in the culture of the "low-down folks." For him, the culture of the black masses provided the black artist with "an inexhaustible supply of themes" highlighting his or her people's racial distinctiveness. He advocated that the black artist produced art that was "racial in theme and treatment" and took overt pride in being black. Even though this task would prove to be a difficult one, and even though Hughes argued in favor of total artistic freedom, he sought to rally his contemporaries to simply be themselves regardless of what white America thought.[67]

Greene did not directly join in the publicized debates of the Harlem Renaissance. To be sure, he was aware of such heated debates inasmuch as they were featured in *The Crisis* from March until November 1926. Given the value he placed on education and rigorous study, Greene probably agreed with Brawley's observations on the so-called lack of the movement's academic credentials. He was too practical an intellectual to devote a significant part of his life merely to depicting the lives of the black "proletariat life." As he demonstrated throughout his life after joining forces with Woodson, Greene believed that scholarship needed to be used to solve problems and that black intellectuals had the responsibility to lend a helping hand to the masses, as he exemplified through the 1930s when he, without receiving a fee, spoke on black history to countless schoolchildren or worked tirelessly for low pay at a black college and struggled on behalf of oppressed southeast Missouri sharecroppers.

Looking back at Greene's poetry at Columbia as well as at his collection from 1921 until 1937, it appears that he probably took a stance somewhere between Hughes and Brawley. Only three of Greene's poems during his Columbia years address themes popular during the Harlem Renaissance, themes Hughes would have deemed "racial." The rest of the poems would have perhaps satisfied Brawley's focus on concrete scholarly standards, Alain Locke's quest for a pure aesthetic, and/or William Stanley Braithwaite's focus on writing "universal" poetry. Greene is best viewed within the ranks of the "Genteel School" of Harlem Renaissance writers—writers who sought to demonstrate to white America that they were equal to them and deserved to be recognized by their leading literary circles. Often, they advocated a "raceless literature" or wrote about universal themes. One of the leading advocates of this school, nationally renowned literary critic William S. Braithwaite (1878–1962), did not refer to race in his poetry. Though he did contribute a piece to *The New Negro,* he wrote and edited several books on nonblack subjects between 1906 and 1950. A handful of female poets, including Anne Spencer, Greene's friend Georgia Douglas Johnson, Angelina Grimké, and Jesse Fauset, also often wrote poems that did not focus on black subjects. Others, like Claude McKay, James Weldon Johnson, and Countee Cullen, produced both "racial" and "universal" writings at various points in their careers. Most of Greene's poetry addressed "raceless" themes, such as love, death, nature, and the vastness of the universe. His poetry, which was "racial in theme and treatment," existed, but it was not the norm.[68]

A year after the monumental anthology *The New Negro* appeared, Greene wrote three poems that stand out. Two of them depart from the classical, lofty, Shakespearean-style verse he had developed a taste for. Instead, he turned to a black, Southern dialect that young writers of the 1920s borrowed from turn-of-the-century African American poets like Paul L. Dunbar, transforming it into something new and dignified. In a poem entitled "The New Negro," Greene translated the significance of the new African-American worldview of the 1920s in religious terms. For him, an important aspect of black America's new identity rested on rejecting an "other worldly" religious orientation as well as a God constructed by whites in order to enslave blacks psychologically. Greene wrote:

> Ah used to heah de ole folks say:
> "Dis worl' ain't gwine to las'
> Dat eberthing down heah below
> Will fall wif Gabriel's blas'."
>
> I'se often heard dem in de church
> A shoutin: "Lawd twill please us,
> To let de white folks hab de worl',
> But gib us Massa Jesus."
>
> An' den ah laffs an' snickers so,
> Cause folks like me an' you,
> Knows dat de white folks got de worl',
> And Massa Jesus too.
>
> Ah don know what de futah holds,
> But sence I'se heah below,
> I'se gwine ter git some ob dis worl',
> An' let Mass' Jesus go.[69]

Taking control of "some ob dis worl'" and letting "Mass' Jesus go" echoes part of the philosophy espoused by Marcus Garvey—who stressed the need to see God in one's own image—and Greene's use of dialect in the first person is in one sense an act of giving agency to the black masses. Like black writers of the Harlem Renaissance era, Greene employed dialect in a manner much different from the manner of Dunbar, Washington, or even Mary McLeod Bethune.

In another 1927 poem, "Of God," Greene elaborates on the necessity for blacks to reevaluate their views of God and religion's role in their struggle. "Of God" is also narrated in the first person. The "Ah" (I) in this poem, evidently a black man who speaks in a nonconvoluted, to-the-point, simple language, says that he believes that "God must be white" because he listens to whites' prayers "but don't care nuttin 'tall 'bout our affairs." The speaker in Greene's poem has come to the conclusion that God could not be black because of how blacks suffer from racial violence. When Greene wrote this poem, more than three thousand blacks had been lynched since Booker T. Washington opened the doors of Tuskegee Institute. There had also been many race riots. Greene's subject did not believe that his people were God's chosen people who had to suffer before their salvation:

God sho' ain't black, cause den
He never could
Allow de whites to burn
Us up like wood.[70]

Greene's speaker's solution is not to turn to a white or a black God for guidance and protection. Instead, he gives up on praying to any God "beyond de skies." Greene continued:

An' when we calls dis white
God in our woe,
How can he heed de cries
He does not know?

So if our prayers upon
His deaf ears fall,
Le's break from him an' hab
No God at all.[71]

Greene was not an atheist. He was attempting to look at American society through the eyes of a people who were at the bottom of the economic, political, and social hierarchy. Like his New Negro contemporaries, he sought to explain, translate, and reinvent the thoughts of the black masses. In addition to these two poems written in dialect, Greene wrote another thought-provoking poem entitled "Jazz."

During the era of the Harlem Renaissance, jazz gained national recognition. While it was popular among working-class blacks, many members of the African American elite "recoiled in disgust from music as vulgarly explosive as the outlaw speakeasies and cathouses that spawned it." What some members of the Talented Tenth said about jazz and other indigenous black American musical expressions "sometimes verged on the unprintable." In his 1921 *The Negro in Art and Literature,* the prolific writer Benjamin Brawley (1882–1939) commented that jazz, "a strident form of music originating in Negro slums," emerged hand in hand with "a mood that was of the very essence of hedonism and paganism." Many young Harlem Renaissance artists rejected Brawley's sentiments and sought to celebrate this creation of black folk. The rhythm and content of Langston Hughes' poem "Jazzonia" celebrates the mood that jazz evoked. For Hughes, jazz was the essence of black America's soul and culture of resistance. Some New Negroes were ambivalent toward jazz. In *The New Negro,* J. A. Rogers celebrated jazz as being a distinctly black, working-class creation, "a revolt of the emotions against repression," which had a lot to offer American democratic culture. He also described it as being a primitive tendency with "vices and vulgarizations, . . . sex informalities," and a "morally anarchic spirit." Rogers believed that with "more wholesome growth in the future," jazz could work to help democratize America. He called upon the black intelligentsia to "lift and divert [jazz] into nobler channels."[72]

Viewed within this broader context, Greene's poem seems to portray jazz somewhere between Hughes's and Rogers's portrayals. In his poem "Jazz," Greene refers to this musical expression as being "mad music." "While the mad music played," Greene was seduced by a woman. He became "enraptured" by her "charms, . . . forgetful of the world," and "lost in the dizzy whirl." Jazz, in Greene's view, "woos the soul's desire." The Columbia graduate student could have meant many things here. Jazz for him could have been a positive force in stirring up deep emotions. Greene could have interpreted jazz, "the mad music," as corrupting man's senses, turning man into an intoxicated, defenseless pawn. It is also possible that he could simply have been using jazz as a metaphor for discussing his intimate feelings. Greene's ambiguous portrait of jazz might reflect his personal internal struggle with a music with which he was previously unfamiliar.[73]

Several years after writing "Jazz," Greene (living in Washington, D.C.) rushed home from work one day in hopes of listening to the opera "Aida" over the radio. When he arrived at his home, he was relieved to discover that it would be broadcast at 11:00 P.M. "And when that hour arrived," Greene wrote in his diary on November 11, 1929, "everyone who had a radio, much to my dismay, was tuning in on jazz. My love of *good* music will yet prompt me to purchase a radio." By his late twenties, he seemed to have had a fairly well-trained ear for such music. By the late 1940s he called himself "an ardent lover of music" whose favorite composers were not Ellington, Henderson, Armstrong, or Parker, but Beethoven, Tchaikovsky, Chopin, and Shostakovitch. Whatever the case may have been, Greene's poem "Jazz" reveals that he was affected by the cultural transformations of his times.[74] "The New Negro," "Of God," and "Jazz" appear to have been among the last poems Greene wrote before he began working with Woodson, and he appears to have put his poetry aside during the first several years of working with the Association. He focused his energies on maintaining a detailed diary and began writing poetry regularly again by 1932.

6 An Unselfish Worker for the ASNLH, 1928–33

IN FEBRUARY 1928, Lorenzo Johnston Greene "unexpectedly" received a telegram from Carter G. Woodson requesting that he meet him at the Hotel Dunn, "the outstanding Negro Hostelry in New York City on West 135th Street, just off 7th Avenue." Greene and the "great man" talked for a while in the hotel lobby, and then at about six o'clock they went to eat dinner at the YWCA around the corner. "Over a delightful meal Dr. Woodson finally got down to the business which had brought him to confer with me in New York," Greene remembered. Woodson informed Greene, who had just completed the thirty credits required for a master's degree in history from Columbia University, that the Association for the Study of Negro Life and History (ASNLH), in conjunction with the Institute of Social and Religious Research of New York City, was preparing to make a scientific survey of the black church. The goal of the project was to examine the effects that the black church, rural and urban, had on the intellectual, moral, recreational, economic, and social development of the black community. (In late April 1928, midway into the study, the goal became clearer: "It is hoped that this study of the Church will bring out the defects in that institution," Greene ascertained, "thereby impelling it to show greater concern for the community.")

Woodson told Greene that Charles H. Wesley was going to supervise the research. Catching Greene off guard, Woodson told him that he had been keeping up with his work at Columbia since they had first met three years earlier. He surprised Greene further by offering him a position as an ASNLH "field agent" working under Wesley. Several decades after Woodson died, Greene recalled this event: "He offered me the seemingly fabulous salary of

$1,800 a year, plus travel expenses. Penniless as I was, such an offer sounded like a gold mine. Noting my temporary silence, Dr. Woodson asked me whether I would accept his offer. I did so with alacrity fearful that he might withdraw it."[1]

Greene's decision was not one made in total desperation, however. In the late 1920s, John W. Davis, president of West Virginia Institute, offered Greene a position teaching English and German; in late March 1928, after Greene had already accepted Woodson's offer, Thomas Elsa Jones of Fisk University offered him a job teaching history for two thousand dollars a year as a substitute for Harvard-bound A. A. Taylor. Later, while working with Woodson, Greene was offered jobs teaching at Howard University and at North Carolina Agricultural and Technical College at Greensboro. Greene saw many benefits to working with Woodson. He viewed it as an opportunity to end his mother's "long years of washing, ironing and cooking for white folks." It also presented Greene with the chance to acquire some materials for a PhD dissertation, pay off some of his student loans at Columbia, and test the effectiveness of his training. In addition, Greene perceived this job as representing his initiation into the work of racial uplift. By late March 1928, Greene wrote in his diary, "I would not give up this work now for a teaching position. It is too fascinating." By accepting this position, Greene had initiated a change in his earlier perceptions of the "Father of Black History." The man whom he once pitied was now his boss and would soon drastically affect his early development as a scholar.[2]

The period from early March 1928 until early September 1933, when Greene accepted a job teaching at Lincoln University, "marked a crucial point" in Greene's life. In this brief period (subdivided into various phases), he worked as Wesley's assistant in the field exploring black churches and interviewing various folks in Baltimore, New York, and Suffolk, Virginia (March 1928 through June 1928); from July 1928 until February 1930 he served as Woodson's right-hand man, publishing his (Greene's) first scholarly article, proofreading Woodson's monographs, coauthoring several ASNLH studies, and serving as organizer for the Association in Washington, D.C.; and from June 1930 until the fall of 1933, Greene and four Howard University students traveled throughout the country on a bookselling campaign. Within each of these phases, separated by an important event of some sort, Greene generated different ideas and matured as an intellectual, scholar, and historian (many of his ideas, however, remained the same and overlapped in two or more of the periods). Any changes in Greene's ideas of ways of thinking were largely the product of the particular setting in which Greene operated at a particular time.

❖ ❖ ❖

"Today [March 15, 1928] marks one of the mile-posts of my life. For the first time in my life, I am assuming responsibility. Today I begin to draw upon the accumulation of seven years of collegiate and graduate training. Theory must be translated into practice," Greene recorded in his diary. "Words must be resolved into action; in short, Lorenzo J. Greene is on trial—on trial before a critical, unsympathetic public, that measures success or failure by the performance of, or the ability to discharge, the tasks it sets before him. God grant that I may summon every ounce of energy to vindicate my extended training! If I fail, I have studied, sacrificed, and labored in vain."[3] Greene clearly took his role in the ASNLH very seriously. In reality, he was not going to be under close public scrutiny. He was nervous and anxious because this was his first experience with hands-on research, sociological in nature and similar to Du Bois's *The Philadelphia Negro* (1899) and his groundbreaking studies with Atlanta University. Greene's assignment was to amass, organize, and interpret data and surveys collected from one hundred churches, one hundred youths, three hundred prominent Negro citizens, and two hundred whites in order to assess the role of the church in the black community.

Between March 16, when he began working in Baltimore, until late June 1928, when Woodson suddenly ended the Association's role in the study, Greene visited hundreds of churches in various communities in Baltimore and Virginia, where he interacted with church leaders and preachers, prominent whites and blacks, community youths, and the black working class. He stayed in Baltimore for about three weeks and in Virginia for slightly more than two weeks; he also briefly returned to New York and spent several weeks in Washington, D.C., making sense of the data he collected.

Greene experienced the difficulties of conducting field research in the black community: many preachers were quite reluctant to provide him with information because the project was funded by whites and because he was an outsider. In Virginia, he visited black homes with a "colored child-welfare nurse." He ventured into the black community of Saratoga, Virginia, and delivered presentations on black history to many high schools. He informed them about the nature of the ASNLH's work and inspired them to work toward uplifting their people and fellow man. Greene also scheduled speaking engagements for Wesley and Woodson. Traveling out of D.C. to Baltimore, and especially to Virginia, was an eye-opening experience for Greene. The black ghettos of Baltimore shocked him. Suffolk and Saratoga, Virginia, and the surrounding rural areas revealed even more to Greene, representing perhaps his first intimate contact with segregation in the South. He was shocked at the effects that this "insidious, vicious thing" had on blacks' educational levels, their living and working conditions, and their disposition toward whites. Greene constantly compared New England and Southern blacks' educational experiences, often downplaying the latter. Upon several occasions, he vowed to never live in the South. By 1933, he had changed his mind.

During his several months as a field investigator, Greene kept a meticulously detailed account of his day-to-day experiences, commenting on a range of experiences and contemporary issues. His diary served as an outlet for his most sincere and candid impressions and opinions about various people, life in general, and where he viewed himself in the greater scheme of the universe. His observations ranged widely, helping us reconstruct the consciousness, the early worldview, and the developing intellectual identity of a novice field researcher, social scientist, historian, and social reformer from New England. Among other things, he commented extensively upon the black masses, ministers, nationally recognized leaders, Woodson and Wesley, and the black professional class. He discussed his ideas of religion and history; he also provided a philosophy of some sort for African American advancement.

His perceptions of many ministers and of the black working-class culture in general revealed the effects of growing up in a small, isolated, northeastern town with an almost invisible black population, and of attending an elite, Ivy League college for several years. Greene definitely drew caste-determined lines between himself and his subjects. His diary abounds with humorous and critical descriptions of black ministers: he described a reverend of Shiloh Baptist Church in Baltimore as being a "sleek, greasy . . . interesting man, not well educated. Say[s] 'Ah' and 'Heah'; speaks very broadly and with a typically southern accent. Yet he was kind, affable, and obliging."[4] Greene harped on the fact that another (AME) evangelist was illiterate and that this somehow affected his character. Greene pitied uneducated preachers who had mail-order degrees and claimed to be healers. He also commented on the disorganization and lack of education of black ministers he met, yet he was not completely critical of illiterate preachers. In Baltimore, for example, a Reverend Brown, "illiterate though he was, blind man leading the blind," moved Greene with the "spontaneity of his words, which at times assumed a grandeur, similar to that of a Demosthenes or a Webster." Greene tended to speak very highly of ministers who were opposed to emotionalism. Still, he believed that, overall, the majority of black ministers were ignorant, lacking the training to "fight intelligently for the rights of the race."[5]

Greene's perceptions of the poor, working-class folk whom he encountered reflected his close affiliation with "social uplifters" of the late nineteenth and early twentieth centuries. Greene perceived East Baltimore, a black section, as "a sink of ignorance" where "most Negroes live in dilapidated houses. Brazen, leud, and unkempt women; sly, evil-looking men."[6] In Harlem he was disturbed by the daily behavior of ordinary people: "Train was full of Negroes who acted disgracefully. Embarrassed me, yelled, ran from coach to coach, laughing boisterously, drinking, fussing, and passing coarse jokes. Ought to have been in a cattle car. Were I a railroad executive, I'd segregate them myself," Greene said. "There are some Negroes who should be segregated, but it should not be made general. There are some intelligent, well dressed, and orderly. They should be given consideration, but there are some who are not fit to sit with hogs. The same applies to whites as well." Greene added whites to this discussion, perhaps because he wanted to make it clear that this behavior is a human condition, not one restricted to blacks. Greene was opposed to his people acting in this manner because he saw it affecting their opportunities. Like his predecessors who were very much preoccupied with etiquette, Greene believed that this type of behavior provided whites with more ammunition to justify their oppression of black Americans. Many of Greene's New Negro counterparts would have portrayed this type of behavior with openness—pride, even.[7] Greene's experiences in Suffolk seem to have exasperated a bourgeois attitude within him. "Morals: Very low, on the whole especially among the factory workers," Greene said in his assessment of Suffolk. "Both white and blacks exhibit sexual laxity." Echoing Booker T. Washington, Greene acknowledged that racial discrimination was a crime that drastically affected black America's destiny, but he also believed that blacks could do a lot to remedy their situation. A revolution in morals in his mind did not require the aid or sympathy of whites.[8]

Historically, highly educated black intellectuals and leaders have viewed themselves as cultural reformers, as the bearers of civilization and a refined culture for a culturally deprived black population. Religion has been one of the most important vehicles of this social uplift program. During the "golden age of black nationalism," black leaders, especially, perceived themselves as being the missionaries for the masses. Because of their often Puritan, Northern upbringing and quest to be recognized and accepted by white society, they frowned upon the cultural practices of the masses whom they were often not prepared or equipped to understand. In terms of religion (before thinkers of Greene's generation), this attitude is best demonstrated by Charlotte Forten (1838–1914) during Reconstruction and by Du Bois around the turn of the century. Forten, the granddaughter of the well-known Philadelphia abolitionist James Forten, was one of the many Northern teachers who ventured to Port Royal Island, South Carolina, to educate the newly freed population. While there, she was a keen observer and maintained a detailed diary. When she returned from South Carolina in 1864, she published her observations in the *Atlantic Monthly.* This Philadelphia native was extremely fearful of the African-rooted religious practices of the Sea Island blacks. She commented, "In the evenings, the children frequently came in to sing and shout for us. These 'shouts' are very strange,—in truth, almost indescribable . . . it is probable that they are the barbarous expressions of religion, handed down to them from their African ancestors, and destined to pass away under the influence of Christian teachings."[9] Nearly four decades later, Du Bois echoed Forten's observations in an essay entitled "The Religion of the American Negro" in *The New World.* Grounded in what Cornel West has called Du Bois's "Puritan New England origins and Enlightenment values," Du Bois, like Forten, feared this highly emotional brand of African-rooted religious practices. In *The Souls of Black Folk,* Du Bois described a church service in rural Tennessee, his first encounter with a "Southern Negro Revival":

> A sort of suppressed terror hung in the air and seemed to seize us,—a pythian madness, a demoniac possession, that lent terrible reality to song and word. The black and massive form of the preacher swayed and quivered as the words crowded to his lips and flew at us in singular eloquence. The people moaned and fluttered, and then the gaunt-cheeked brown woman beside me suddenly leaped straight into the air and shrieked like a lost soul, while round about came wail and groan and outcry, and a scene of human passion such as I had never conceived before. Those who have not thus witnessed the frenzy of a Negro revival in the untouched backwoods of the South can but dimly realize the religious feeling of the slave; as described, such scenes appear grotesque and funny, but as seen they are awful.[10]

Nearly three decades later, Greene echoed issues raised by his fellow New England native; he was equally as disturbed by the religious practices of the urban black masses. In May 1928, while he was in Washington, D.C., analyzing his data for the black church study, Greene paid a visit to his cousin Bertha Baylor. While he was waiting for her, his attention was drawn to a church service of the United House of Prayer for All People. Greene wrote of this occasion:

> What I beheld almost made me weep. Surely, I told myself, these people could not be civilized. A swirling, jumping, dancing, shouting mass of human beings filled the place to overflowing. Screams, laughter, songs, and groans broke from this gyrating, frenzied, perspiring throng. I looked on with amazement. . . . The stamping of the feet, the cries of "lard have mercy" and "Hallelujah," the wild shouts and mutterings of those people awoke in me a profound feeling of pity. This is their conception of Christianity. Empty "mouthings." Emotional frenzy and manifestations of barbaric dancing and primitive religions in the midst of civilization.[11]

The similarity between Forten's, Du Bois's, and Greene's observations are striking. Greene and Du Bois seemed to have been witnessing the same event. While Forten and Du Bois's observations were more in line with the thinking of many black leaders of the time, Greene's comments seem somewhat archaic and out of tune with the thought of many creative black intellectuals of his generation who were glorifying black folk culture and attempting to explain its significance. Greene argued about the meaning of religion with his cousin Bertha, who was a member of "Sweet Daddy" Grace's church. For Greene, "religion did not consist of loud mouthings, shouting, dancing, and epileptic fits." He simply defined Christ's doctrine as being love. He argued that "every man has in him a bit of God that guides him aright" and that religion was a "personal affair between man and his creator." He stressed that instead of professing and broadcasting one's faith or beliefs in the streets, one should concentrate on living a righteous life. "Unselfishness, utter lack of vindictiveness, and service to one's fellow men" were the keys to his religious ideology. Greene's "religious creed" was the Golden Rule: he was very much like Booker T. Washington and Woodson in that he believed that religion was a component of day-to-day life, something that needed to be made practical.[12]

During the three months of researching the function of the black church, Greene articulated a philosophy of race advancement. He did not write one comprehensive essay on how to solve what his immediate predecessors called the "Negro Problem." Instead, scattered throughout his diary are a range of comments, at times spontaneous and candid. Beyond the church's serving as a day-to-day mechanism to help blacks survive, Greene did not place a very high emphasis on the church or on religion in his philosophy for uplifting blacks. He did, however, believe that the church had to play a more active role in the community—as a nexus of reform: "Let the churches unite and found community centers, something to interest these workers in clean living and harmless amusements, rather than concentrate on sex," he urged.[13]

Greene also suggested that instead of building so many churches, blacks should be more like Jews and focus on founding businesses. Like those whom Harold Cruse accused of buying into the "myth of Negro Business," he believed that economic nationalism would lay the foundation for political strength. "I believe that if we develop businesses, we will of necessity develop politicians, who will have interests to be guarded and, in protecting their own, will be securing the rights of their co-entrepreneurs," Greene remarked.[14] Greene believed that African Americans suffered in part because they allowed the "white man to open the way" and then followed blindly behind him. The "white man" ruled the world, he reasoned, because blacks chose to follow their lead. "We are consumers, not producers," he lamented.[15]

Greene also used his diary as an outlet for scrutinizing prominent black intellectuals and leaders candidly. While he praised Wesley during the duration of their working together, Greene was critical of Woodson. It seems that the longer Greene worked for the ASNLH founder, the more candid and sharp his critiques of Woodson became. Most of the conflicts between the two revolved around personality differences and their varying perceptions about how certain Association tasks should be performed. Greene tended to agree with his employer on the problems facing black America and how they could best be remedied. Greene had little patience with one of Woodson's contemporaries, long-time Howard University professor Kelly Miller (1863–1939). In early April 1928, Greene attended one of Miller's lectures at Grace Presbyterian Church in Baltimore. While he agreed with his elder's characteristic political stance advocating that blacks should "uphold the constitution, . . . engage in politics to secure their civil rights," and encourage political participation among ministers, Greene vehemently disagreed with Miller's conviction that African Americans "had special genius for religion and that he should abjure the material realm and bend his every effort to the furtherance of the spiritual." He deemed Miller's philosophy archaic and passé, asserting that it catered to the beliefs of a largely ignorant congregation of ministers. Though he acted like African American progressive reformers, Greene drew a sharp line between himself and older leaders. "Kelly Miller's sun of leadership has set," Greene commented. "The philosophy of men of this kind belongs to an earlier day."[16]

Greene's alternative sounds strikingly similar to something Booker T. Washington proclaimed in *Up From Slavery* and other writings and speeches. Greene wrote, "In my opinion, the white man has everything that conduces progress. Not only that, he has religion too, probably a thousand fold more sincere and practical than that of the Negroes." "I would rather," he continued, "ape the white man than wallow in the slough of artificial fervor and unprogressiveness that Kelly Miller proposes to his followers." In this case, Greene synthesized several broader streams of African American thought. Like his New Negro counterparts, he challenged part of the "Old Negro" ideology. Greene also downplayed black America's cultural "genius" and individuality. At age twenty-eight, Greene was not extensively well versed in black America's past and advocated that black people draw inspiration from a seemingly successful white American civilization—not only to uplift themselves and integrate themselves into American society, but also to work ultimately toward black liberation.

❖ ❖ ❖

On April 28, 1928, Greene returned to Washington, D.C., and began to interrogate the data and surveys he had collected for the black church study. His most extensive analysis was on the black Suffolk community. He divided it into three groups for separate analysis: professional churchgoers, professional non-churchgoers, and the illiterate masses. By late May 1928, Greene presented Wesley with the first draft of roughly two hundred pages of findings. His mentor made few corrections; Woodson felt differently. On June 5, 1928, Woodson sent Wesley and Greene a telegram declaring that their report was "worthless." The Association's founder believed that they were doing too much "sermonizing." Wesley and Greene ignored Woodson and sent their study instead to the Institute of Social and Religious Research in New York City (ISRR) on June 5. Shortly after Woodson returned to the office on June 8, Greene could sense that his boss was upset. Greene and Wesley did not discuss the telegram with Woodson, beyond acknowledging that they had received it. They decided to ignore their "self-opinionated" boss once again and continued to work on the "Suffolk Report." On June 21, the day the report was completed and ready to be mailed to the ISRR, Woodson called Greene into the kitchen, "the private sanctum," and they talked for several hours. Woodson informed Greene that the study was over, because Wesley, by accepting the position of presiding elder of the AME Church, had broken his contract between the ASNLH and the ISRR. Unless Wesley resigned his eldership, Woodson considered the study over. Greene was "dumbfounded." Suddenly, the months of meticulous research seemed to have meant nothing. He was equally concerned about how such an incident would reflect on black scholars in general—that it would not only confirm stereotypes about the "unreliability" of and the lack of solidarity among blacks, but that it would also adversely affect future projects of this sort and his personal reputation as a scholar.[17]

Why Woodson suddenly decided to terminate the ASNLH's support to the project remains open to interpretation. Perhaps, as Greene suggested, Woodson was becoming jealous of Wesley, one of the only other black doctoral historians at the time. Or maybe he was upset that Wesley ignored his telegram. Wesley told Greene that Woodson had never so much as intimated to him that by holding an eldership Wesley would jeopardize his job. Greene disagreed with Woodson and stood by Wesley throughout the conflict. After discovering that Wesley had willingly resigned, Greene became depressed. Not only had Greene turned down a teaching position at Fisk, but in early June, Walter Dyson had also offered him a job teaching history at his alma mater. On June 25, shortly after Wesley and Woodson met with ISRR representatives, the ASNLH director offered his distraught employee a job paying the same as his previous salary doing the same type of fieldwork, this time to develop a study of "Negro occupations." After two days of thinking and praying, Greene told Woodson that he would work on a study of African American occupations for a salary of at least two thousand dollars. Woodson offered him $166.66 a month, and Greene agreed to the arrangement, as long as he had the liberty to accept other job offers. Woodson reluctantly agreed. Despite how Woodson had treated Wesley, Greene believed that he could get along with him.

For the next several years, Greene undertook his eye-opening apprenticeship under the "Father of Negro History." Greene had learned a lot during the first four months of working directly under Woodson. He recognized the variety of skills and means needed for conducting sociological field research. He further honed his writing and editing skills—and he encountered Woodson's peculiar character. While he disliked how Woodson treated his employees (including Greene, himself), he deeply respected his devotion and unwavering commitment to the Association and the black history movement it advocated. From late June 1928 until Negro History Week 1930, Greene remained in Washington, D.C., and worked with Woodson in many different capacities. It was during these two years that Greene matured intellectually and began discovering the many sides to the African American historian's craft.

❖ ❖ ❖

Woodson, interested in pinpointing the occupations in which the presence of black workers increased and decreased, and why these changes occurred, hired Greene to conduct a practical study on black occupations through the 1920s. Greene worked diligently on this project from July 11, 1928, until *The Negro Wage Earner* was published in 1930. He frequented the Library of

Congress, examined census reports and met with various representatives for the Bureau of the Census, tabulated figures and analyzed statistics, and explored various journals, magazines, and newspapers from the 1890s through the 1920s. Despite his background in mathematics during medical school, Greene disliked working with figures and statistics. His approach to research was thorough and comprehensive, gathering all the data that appeared to "throw any light upon" his topic and then appraising this body of information later. Greene performed many other duties in addition to researching blacks in occupations. He proofread the galleys for many of Woodson's books and *Journal of Negro History* articles, including *African Myths, The Negro in Our History,* "Negro Makers of History," and Rayford W. Logan's "The Operation of the Mandate System in Africa" (1928). He often took this type of work home with him. Woodson benefited greatly from Greene's excellent writing and editing skills; Greene also advised Woodson to simplify the language of his books written for children and for the masses. Indeed, Greene often suggested to Woodson that he should write more books at the level of children. Though this work was demanding, Greene liked it because he learned firsthand about the long publishing process.

From mid-1928 until mid-1930, Greene was Woodson's number-one staff investigator and personal assistant, replacing Alrutheus A. Taylor, who worked closely with Woodson from 1919 until 1926, when he accepted a teaching position at Fisk. When Woodson was out of town, he often placed Greene in charge of the ASNLH's headquarters, which meant opening and closing the office, making sure the bills were paid on time, and acting as a secretary and janitor. Greene played a role in Woodson's various research projects as well; in January 1929, for example, Woodson instructed Greene, who frequented used bookstores in the Washington, D.C., area, to begin collecting old manuscripts pertaining to African Americans. Greene also worked especially hard for Woodson in publicizing and organizing the Negro History Week celebration in Washington, D.C., in February 1930. He visited black churches in the District and Virginia, lecturing about black history and informing congregations about the celebration. He also rallied the support of the masses by advertising the week's events in movie theaters in the black community.

Greene's hard work on this project paid off. On February 10, 1930, he estimated that between five thousand and six thousand people attended the program held in Armstrong High School's auditorium in Washington D.C. The success of this program had a profound impact on a thirty-year-old Greene. "Negro History shall be my life's work. The Association is indelibly stamped upon me. It is my cause and shall transcend everything else, even my allegiance to Woodson," Greene wrote in his diary on the night of the celebration. "I knew I had found my life's vocation and that Dr. Woodson was my historical idol."[18]

These years were especially productive for Greene in terms of his development as a historian. While conducting cutting-edge research and working for Woodson, he read many different books pertaining to American, African, and African American history. Throughout his diary, he briefly reviewed these materials. Among his favorite books in this period were *A Tropical Dependency* (1906) by Lady Flora F. S. Lugard, and *The Negro in Pennsylvania* (1911) by Raymond E. Turner. Greene's philosophy of history during this time was derived from both Woodson and Wesley. Greene believed in "impersonal scientific history" void of emotionalism. He celebrated the fact that Woodson could write about "the horrors of peonage in the South . . . so objectively that the reader could not tell whether the author was white or black." He did not agree with Du Bois's philosophy of writing in order to propagandize black humanity. Greene called Du Bois's *The Negro* "a pretty fair work, although he lets his personality creep in from time to time." He made a similar critique of a *Journal* article by William Brewer about John Russworm.[19] Greene, like Benjamin Quarles and John Hope Franklin, wrote in an openly objective manner well into the second half of the twentieth century.

Greene respected the detached writing style of Woodson, Wesley, and others, and he strove to imitate it, adding his own twist. Greene did not completely frown upon using black history as propaganda or removing history from academic circles. As a lecturer, he called upon blacks to celebrate their glorious past and emancipate themselves from mental slavery. In Georgetown in December 1929, he told an audience of Baptists that all blacks suffered from "a disease more deadly than cancer or consumption—an inferiority complex." He proceeded to recount for them the monumental achievements of their African ancestors. Greene believed early on that black history should be written at the level of children "in order to inspire racial self-respect, a pride and a consciousness of being black, and to furnish the Negro a means for dispelling his inferiority complex."[20] Greene was very much like his mentor. He operated in a private, elite, academic setting as well as within a more accessible black community. His approach was multileveled, meshing various philosophies toward history. Like his Progressive Era predecessors, he believed in a modern, scientific history that "subordinated romantic values to a scientific spirit," emphasized impersonality and objectivity—however elusive, as Peter Novick has argued—and "tended toward a rigid factualism."[21] At the same time, he was wholeheartedly committed to using black history to build pride and self-esteem within black people.

Between 1928 and 1930, Greene published his first pieces of historical scholarship: *The Negro Wage Earner* and a long article in the *Journal of Negro History.* In mid-August 1928, Woodson told Greene that he would like to publish part of an essay, "Negro Slavery in New England," which Greene had written for a history seminar with Dixon Ryan Fox at Columbia in 1927. Greene was shocked at the proposal, not believing that he had the merits of a solid historian yet. Though Woodson suggested that the title be changed to "Slavery and Awakening in New England," he respected Greene's scholarship. After some hesitation, Greene accepted Woodson's suggestion and for the rest of the month revised the original manuscript, drawing greatly from the Library of Congress's repository. Greene's essay was published in the *Journal* in late 1928. "Slaveholding New England and Its Awakening," the final title, assessed slavery in colonial New England in eight sections: the colonial period, Puritan sanctions for slavery, status of slaves, conversion of the slaves, treatment of the slave, slave codes, the awakening, and legislative action.[22] Treating slavery in colonial New England with the objectivity of Earl E. Thorpe's "New School" of black historians, this essay laid the foundation for Greene's *The Negro in Colonial New England, 1620–1776* (1942).

By January 1930, after completing his comprehensive examinations at Columbia, Greene submitted to Woodson the final draft of his study on black occupations. Later that year, it was published as *The Negro Wage Earner* under the authorship of both Woodson and Greene. Woodson decided to add his name after advertisements in the *Journal* as late as July 1930 announced Greene as the sole author. In the introduction, Woodson claimed: "most of the data in this treatise were collected by Mr. Lorenzo J. Greene. These findings were then checked, corrected, and supplemented by the undersigned, who reduced the work to literal form."[23] Greene was irate with Woodson's actions. Along with others in the ASNLH office, he knew that he had done all of the hard work for this study, to the point of jeopardizing his health. Woodson offered some surface-level conclusions based on a careless reading of the manuscript. "There is not an idea of Woodson's in the entire book," Greene confided in his diary in December 1930. "Woodson never held a high place in my estimation, but now my regard for him in every respect, save scholarship, has sunk into its nadir."[24] A year later, Woodson even admitted that Greene was the major force behind *The Negro Wage Earner.* When the book was later criticized by the *New York Tribune* and by Ira De A. Reid in *Opportunity* for its "weak interpretations," Greene did not object, noting that Woodson carelessly drew shallow interpretations from a body of data Greene had collected and the Association director did not even fully comprehend.

Greene's study contains seventeen brief chapters and explores patterns in black occupations and employment since roughly 1850, focusing on patterns since 1890. Because sources were scarce, Greene's commentary on black employment before 1890 is fairly scant. He outlined primary distinctions between the opportunities available to the Northern and Southern slaves, explaining that blacks in the North were mostly domestics, whereas the bulk of their Southern counterparts served as agricultural workers. Greene elaborated on the subject of black laborers in the South, remarking that different manufacturers and industries such as railroads and shipping opened the door to many skilled black laborers. Following the Civil War, Southern blacks, according to Greene (and the census bureau), were relegated to three occupation areas: sharecropping, domestic work, and unskilled manufacturing labor. While he acknowledged the presence of independent and collectively operating black farmers, their existence was "relatively insignificant" to his study. Greene praised Hampton and Tuskegee Institutes for their attempts at scientifically enlarging this class of independent black tillers of the soil.[25]

In 1890, 1.1 percent of blacks were found in "the professions," and three-fifths of the African American wage earners were illiterate.[26] According to Greene, the industrial revolution in the South had little positive effect on blacks. Because they were not trained to do the skilled labor of whites, they did the same work as during the days of slavery. This era also saw a decrease in black managers and an increase of black tenant/cash renters, cash-share tenants, and share tenants, all of whom were exploited.[27] Greene spent a considerable amount of time exploring the ramifications of the Great Migration on the role of black women as domestics and black males' pursuits in transportation, manufacturing, mechanics, skilled trades, and a host of other industries.[28] A significant portion of his study revealed how some blacks found refuge in specific sectors, such as tinsmithing, automobile industries, the coal mines and railroads, the packing industry, tanning and curing, shoe factories, soap companies, vegetable and fruit canning, tobacco growing and harvesting, gasoline station work, and ship building.

In July 1931, the *Journal* positively reviewed the book: "*The Negro Wage Earner* will hardly be appreciated as much today as it will be a few decades hence when persons will cease to give most of their attention to the polemic aspects of history and economics and will approach these matters from the definitive point of view," the anonymous reviewer (most likely Woodson) wrote. "This book accomplishes an important task of summarizing what the Negroes have done in making a living in the various occupations. . . . We are often called upon to discuss the various aspects of the progress of Negroes and find ourselves drifting into unprofitable discussion because of the lack of adequate data as to what the Negroes have actually achieved in the various lines in which they have been employed. [The] need for such data has been supplied by this book."[29] The *New York Times* also positively reviewed it; the *Tribune* and *Opportunity* were more critical: their reviewers pointed out what they believed were inconsistencies in the data and the interpretations.

Criticisms aside, Greene worked extremely hard on *The Negro Wage Earner.* In his diary, he laments reading and recalculating "figures, figures, figures"—a testament to the difficulty involved in such a historically grounded statistical study. Such rigorous academic work, coupled with Woodson's high expectations, took its toll on Greene. By fall 1929, he became so sick with stomach problems that he thought that he was going to die.

❖ ❖ ❖

During the period of nearly two years while he worked for Woodson in the ASNLH headquarters, Greene recorded many significant observations in his diary. Not only did he closely follow current events, but he also continued to comment critically on black leadership, male and female, and to formulate an ideology for black social uplift. Between the summer of 1928 and the winter of 1930, Greene critiqued many black leaders for a variety of reasons. He agreed with Woodson's ideas that the NAACP and Du Bois were too preoccupied with propaganda and lacked "practicality" and "some cogent and systematic plan." He also agreed with the Association founder that the Urban League was not focused enough and that interracial struggles were flawed.[30]

Unlike Woodson, Greene dismissed many of his black women counterparts involved in the struggle. Before ever visiting out one of their meetings, Greene concluded that the Federation of Women's Clubs "are interested more in the social functions" connected with their annual sessions "than with any constructive program for racial amelioration." Certainly, Greene, like many men of his time, underestimated the influence of black female reformers. Less than a week later after he actually attended a session of the federation, however, he developed a different outlook. "The Negro male certainly has every reason to envy this organization composed of members of the so-called weaker sex," Greene wrote on August 3, 1928. He noted that the federation program was "forward moving" and even that women in general were more enthusiastic, zealous reformers.

Nevertheless, one need not overstate Greene's support of black female leadership: when describing black women leaders, he seemed to have focused more on their physical attributes than on their ideologies. In one instance, his comments reveal how he had perhaps internalized the "colorphobia" of the black community, something he later spoke out against in his diary. In his late twenties, Greene apparently supported the black bourgeoisie notion that lighter skin was more attractive, intellectually and physically. "Miss Burroughs is a woman of medium height and build, dark complexion, and not at all good looking . . . Miss Hunter resembles Miss Burroughs as to height and build. She, however, is a mulatto and is possessed of one of the most charming personalities. . . . She speaks softly and her words are accompanied by a smile that issues forth like soft and delightful music."[31] These observations were rooted in his personal taste for female companions rather than in his view of the black community in general.

Greene regarded black male leadership much more seriously, even though he criticized one of its leading spokesmen; he, like most African American intellectuals of the 1920s, was quite skeptical of Marcus Garvey's spiritual African return, deeming it "chimerical" at best. However, he did agree with the Jamaican hero's economic nationalist platform, his dream and plan of making blacks "economically self-sufficient." At one level, a young Greene's views on how best to solve black America's problems derived components from the preexisting and contemporary trends in black intellectual thought. He supported the growth of independent black businesses and championed blacks' abandoning impractical forms of religion.[32]

Working for the Negro History Week celebration in 1930 greatly influenced Greene's outlook. By February 1930, Greene articulated a multilayered vision of African Americans' place in U.S. society, a view that mirrored Du Bois's theory of "double consciousness" and cultural pluralism. He recognized blacks' unique contributions to American culture and researched and spoke about the injustices endured by blacks. At the same time, like Woodson, he was optimistic and hopeful about American race relations and the integration of black people into American society as equals. He wanted to employ black history as a means of bringing people together. Though during his late twenties he began to read many books on the glorious past of Africa, he took enormous pride in the fact that he was "an American and New Englander to boot." Further, while planning for the Negro History Week celebration in 1930, he protested vehemently against substituting James Weldon Johnson's "Lift Every Voice and Sing" for "The Star Spangled Banner." Greene argued passionately that African Americans were "first and foremost American citizens," and that adopting Johnson's anthem would "not only be tantamount to reunification of our citizenship, but a voluntary yielding up of those rights and privileges for which we have been so long and bitterly contending." Greene and Woodson optimistically believed that their symbolic support of a nation that, for roughly three centuries, had oppressed their ancestors would have helped them. At age thirty, in the midst of a cultural rejuvenation of the black intelligentsia, Greene held fast to an outdated yet understandable ideology for attaining black social justice. While employed as a professor at Lincoln University in Missouri, he recognized the limitations of such an outlook and reconfigured it accordingly.

❖ ❖ ❖

The early 1930s were particularly pivotal for Greene. In a span of roughly three years, he initiated a bookselling campaign for the ASNLH, "officially" entered the world of white academe, published two studies on black employment, wrote a brief essay on Southern blacks during the Depression, worked as a member of the Committee on Negro Housing of President Herbert Hoover's Conference on Home Building and Home Ownership, authored *Negro Housing* (1932) with Charles S. Johnson and some others, and lost his soulmate and "dearest treasure" to another man. Most important, by early September 1933 he ventured to Lincoln University in Jefferson City, Missouri.

The brief period from the summer of 1930 until the summer of 1931 represented a major phase in Greene's intellectual development. By the dawning of the Depression years, the sale of the ASNLH's books had dropped drastically. Nicely bound hardcover books were literally mildewing in the Association headquarters' basement. In mid-1930, Greene suggested to Woodson that they sell the books cheaply in order to salvage something from the situation. Greene, who had experience at selling magazine subscriptions in the summer of 1927, volunteered to travel across the country selling books and spreading the name of the Association. A skeptical Woodson agreed to sell the books for near wholesale prices. These books included Woodson's *The Negro in Our History, Negro Makers of History, History of the Negro Church,* and *African Myths;* Maurice Delafosse's *Negroes of Africa;* Kelly Miller's *Everlasting Stain;* Willis Richardson's *Plays and Pageants;* and *Negro Poets and Their Poems* by R. T. Kerlin. The Association also offered other special combinations for those interested in Africa, religion, economics, teaching, and history in general. On June 21, 1930, Greene and four Howard University students—John Wesley Poe, Noble Payton, James Cecil Wilkey, and Oliver LaGrone—piled into a used Model A Ford that Woodson had purchased, and they began their bookselling campaign. For Greene, the enterprise lasted for almost a year. He traveled through Virginia, Mississippi, Arkansas, Louisiana, Texas, Oklahoma, Missouri, Illinois, and Pennsylvania. The trip throughout the Jim Crow South had some dangerous implications with regard to personal safety, but surprisingly, the five men experienced very little racial hostility. While in Georgia they were called "niggers" by some "young white hoodlums" who were, Greene surmised, infuriated by the sight of five black men driving a car while the whites walked. Greene and his friends were never physically attacked in any manner.

Life for Greene and the others during this campaign was very hard in other aspects. Throughout 1930, they made very little money: whatever they did earn was dedicated to repairing the car, purchasing food, acquiring lodging, and washing their clothes. Greene routinely spoke of the awful food he had to eat. Unlike his traveling companions, he was not accustomed to eating in establishments run by poor, working-class folks. He could not stand the flies in restaurants and often went hungry or bought some fruit, milk, ice cream, or oatmeal. They stayed in a variety of places—YMCAs, boarding houses and cheap hotels, and in the homes of acquaintances and close friends. In one case, while seriously ill, Greene stayed in Chicago with James C. Wilkey's brother, who apparently rented a room in a whorehouse, a room that could be used by clients upon demand. The survival of these five African American men depended entirely on how many books they could sell. Yet, during the Depression, they nevertheless found a way to spend part of their meager income on entertaining women or playing golf.

The first four months of bookselling were very enlightening to Greene. He learned how to sell books, developed as a speaker, and experienced firsthand the state of blacks in the South. Greene was a tenacious salesman; upon arriving in a new city or town, he immediately identified the names, business addresses, and even home addresses of the black community's leading professionals, including lawyers, dentists, teachers, physicians, teachers, college presidents, and businessmen. He always contacted the ministers of leading churches and attempted to sell them a set of books relating to religion. He asked to speak at their churches about the ASNLH and the necessity of owning books about their past. He sold books to countless public schools and black colleges, including North Carolina College for Negroes, Winston-Salem Teachers College, Tuskegee Institute, Prairie View State College for Negroes, and Langston University. He established connections with leading businessmen and entrepreneurs, including C. C. Spaulding of the North Carolina Insurance Company, people at the offices of the *Chicago Defender* and the *Whip*, and members of Chicago's Urban League. During a full year of selling books, from June 1930 until September 1931, Greene made many contacts and sold many books. Though Woodson complained that many of the books he mailed out were returned, by March 1931 Greene maintained that he had, almost single-handedly, rescued the Association from bankruptcy.

❖ ❖ ❖

Overall, the bookselling campaigns were extremely significant in Greene's personal development, exposing him to the harsh realities of blacks' lives throughout the South. Greene was particularly struck by the conditions endured by unemployed black agricultural workers. He spoke to unemployed blacks and occasionally to some migrant white laborers. His experiences in Texas were especially enlightening: he had never seen so many blacks picking cotton for so little pay. "Men, women, and children of all ages were picking cotton," Greene commented on September 2, 1930. "Other men were filling the cart with the newly picked cotton. It was a novel sight to me—a New Englander."

Greene was shocked by the labor dynamics in Texas. He noticed that whites dominated the work in the gins, whereas blacks and Mexicans picked cotton. He observed that Mexicans, especially those in Waco, really hurt black laborers by always "underworking" them—accepting lower wages so that blacks had to accept lower wages as well. He was surprised that many blacks were not willing to submit to such low wages and instead migrated in search of more favorable conditions. He sympathized with them, yet he understood also why so many Mexicans had crossed the border.[33]

While Greene sold books and worked for the Association in the early 1930s, he continued to cultivate an ideology for improving the status of black America. He remained opposed to emotional, escapist brands of religion and believed that industrial education offered at black institutions were outdated, and that the only real solution along these lines was to transform such institutions into replicas of the Massachusetts Institute of Technology. He still believed strongly in the development of black-owned businesses, but at the 1930 ASNLH annual meeting in Cleveland (October 26–30) he emphasized that the black middle class "must develop a business or businesses that can attract the patronage of all groups." He also frowned upon protests that struck at the economic foundations of white supremacy. Boycotting was a dangerous tactic, in Greene's estimation: he believed that it "may slip from our grasp and crush the wielder."[34] Greene's opposition to the "Don't Buy Where You Can't Work" boycotts of the early 1930s was temporary. While working at Lincoln University during the end of the decade, Greene spearheaded a movement to help economically disenfranchised sharecroppers of southeast Missouri. He clearly underwent significant changes between 1930 and 1939.

At the root of Greene's social philosophy of black uplift was still the optimistic, Woodsonian belief that knowledge of and appreciation for the past was essential to improving blacks' status. In late January 1931, Greene once again reaffirmed and proclaimed his dedication to black history: "My life's purpose is to further the Negro's appreciation of himself, and all the petty chicaneries, petty treacheries, and dishonesty of Woodson could not deter me." Greene's philosophy of history was also still grounded in a rigorous, scholarly framework. In the early 1930s, he objected to the polemic columns Woodson wrote in various leading black papers. He embraced the belief that historians' writings should adhere to the U.S. historical profession's standards of modern scientific scholarship. Woodson's columns, Greene concluded, did not impart "historical information" but instead "denigrated" the Association's work into "muckraking." Ironically, Greene condemned Woodson for something he himself practiced in different settings.[35]

During the early 1930s, after the publication of *The Negro Wage Earner* in 1930, Greene continued to develop as a scholar. In late October 1930, he noted in his diary that he wanted to "write a pamphlet on Negro unemployment in the South, its causes, and remedies, and sell it." Woodson did not seem to accept Greene's idea and instead encouraged him to conduct a study of black unemployment in Washington, D.C. Though Greene never published his proposed pamphlet, sometime before March 1931 he wrote a revealing twenty-page article entitled "Sidelight on Economic Conditions among Negroes in the South during the Depression, 1930." This unpublished document represents Greene's most comprehensive analysis of the major problems facing the black American middle class and masses before the modern civil rights struggle. Though scholarly, it is written in a simple manner, digestible by those with rudimentary reading skills. The last six pages of the paper were clearly directed to both the black working class and middle class; indeed, Greene seems almost to be giving them orders. By the time he sat down to write this pamphlet, he was no longer skeptical of his scholarly capabilities.

For Greene, blacks in the South during the Depression faced "their greatest crisis since emancipation." Based largely on his own observations and interviews with black and white workers, he analyzed the displacement of the black agricultural workers, paying close attention to the entry of whites into positions previously dominated by blacks, the cheap-working Mexicans who migrated in large numbers to Texas, Oklahoma, Arkansas, and southern Louisiana, and to the widespread droughts during the Depression. Black independent farmers, Greene asserted, were disappearing because of the Depression, coupled with their inability to secure loans at reasonable rates. Greene noted that these former farmers left the rural areas for the cities in search of work. "Here they force the townspeople out of their already dwindling employment and also bring down their wages to a minimum," he observed. In other fields of work, such as domestic service, hotel work, barbering, common labor, factory labor, and skilled labor, Greene noted that blacks were being displaced by whites and Mexicans and by larger, technological transformations. In his sophisticated analysis, Greene noticed and articulated this complex web of interrelationships.[36]

Greene offered many remedies, calling on black workers to hold on to the jobs they had. In a Woodsonian fashion, he placed responsibility for the situation on the exploited black laborers themselves. He instructed them to be punctual, reliable, clean, tidy, neat, and honest; to stop "tattling on" their fellows "in order to curry favor with the boss"; to stop loafing, sulking on the job, asking for raises during times of economic hardships, and cutting down on work time if one received a raise; to train oneself, by attending night school if necessary, to hold a job; and to make oneself "indispensable on the job." Echoing Booker T. Washington, Greene said, "Do not tell that a job is due to you because you are a Negro, but because you are able to give your employer the largest return for his money."[37]

Job conservation was only one step in Greene's solution to black unemployment during the Depression. Although he said nothing about protesting for political and civil rights, he reinvoked a philosophy of self-help, self-determination, and pragmatic living. He first called upon blacks to "become producers instead of consumers." In order to better realize this, as Washington had counseled decades earlier, Greene urged blacks to flee from the vices of the cities and return to the "millions of acres" of land in the South in order to engage in trucking and raising poultry raising, fruit, and cattle. Greene posited that blacks in the South could maintain farms of six to ten acres and avoid the ills of sharecropping. He was not alone in advocating such a stance: during the 1920s and the Depression era, many black leaders advocated a "Back to the Farm" movement. The foundation for Greene's solution to black poverty, however, was the development of black businesses. He believed that the black masses and black middle class in the South possessed the common sense and the means to create and maintain businesses. Like Woodson in *The Mis-Education of the Negro,* Greene told his people to stop living above their means: "Instead of building or buying the most elaborate houses, riding in the most expensive limousines, and trying to outdo whites in dressing," Greene pointed out, "[the black businessman] should put this surplus money to work." He also told his middle-class colleagues to stop pouring money into useless fraternity lodges and buildings. He advocated that such money be invested in factories, in turn providing labor for the masses.[38]

The creation of black businesses was key to Greene's solutions. He counseled black ministers to stop building so many churches and instead called upon preachers to invest these "hundreds or thousands of dollars" in the development of black businesses. "Don't spend your cash with the white man and run to the Negro entrepreneur asking for credit as soon as you are broke," Greene outlined in his nationalist economic program. "Your patronage will mean a larger number of jobs for your sons and daughters." Greene's nationalism was mild in comparison to Garvey's, for Greene believed that blacks needed to establish a commercial relationship with white America. Like Father Divine, he told blacks to spend their dollars wherever they could earn them.[39] Greene's final plea fell in line with the tradition of post-Reconstruction black social thought: racial solidarity among a Talented Tenth. Greene ultimately believed that the changes he called for would be generated by the middle class. He described the laboring masses as being helpless and ignorant of the seriousness of the Depression. In his estimation, "school teachers, parent-teacher associations, the press, pulpit, lodges, clubs, and social welfare agencies" needed to wage an "intensive campaign . . . to awaken the Negroes in general from their apathy and stupor." Greene concluded his pamphlet with the following admonition: "Many of them, though jobless, are laughing, dancing, and kicking up their heels, while their very economic foundations are crumbling about them."[40]

Around the same time that Greene wrote this pamphlet, Woodson published *The Rural Negro* (1931), which assesses the conditions "among the peasants and persons living in centers of not more than two thousand inhabitants" in Southern locales. Woodson, admittedly, did not do all the legwork himself. "The investigators of the Association used the questionnaires largely to find clews to things more important than what was generally disclosed," the ASNLH founder said. "They went to the people's homes, approaching them indirectly as ordinary visitors, and after winning their confidence obtained facts which otherwise could not have been collected. In many cases these investigators collected written and printed materials to support what persons had to say about themselves and the communities in which they lived."[41] Along with Iva R. Marshall, Glenn C. Carrington, John T. McKinley, and Robert C. Woods, Greene was one of these nameless "investigators." Greene also helped Woodson with *The Negro Professional Man and the Community,* published a year after Greene went to Lincoln University.[42]

In 1932, two years following the appearance of *The Negro Wage Earner,* Greene produced a succinct survey entitled *The Employment of Negroes in the District of Columbia.*[43] This study explained and offered solutions to high black unemployment rates in Washington, D.C. The style and methodology was straightforward and reminiscent of *The Negro Wage Earner.* Greene distributed questionnaires to some 330 different firms in the District. The study itself is an analysis of the data. Using two key case studies—a newspaper plant and a laundry service—he explored the segregation of the workplace, the high black turnover rates, social welfare, the "alleged undesirable qualities of the Negro worker," racism in the workplace, blacks as unskilled laborers, as well as the effects of the Great Depression. In his "Summary and Conclusions," Greene made four recommendations. He suggested that blacks needed to attend only those vocational and industrial educational schools that were highly advanced. He championed the idea that black workers "should be taught the proper and wholesome attitudes toward their jobs and that they be encouraged to make efficiency rather than favoritism or sympathy the criterion for their employment."[44] He called for more social welfare programs. In the end, Greene invited more studies like his to facilitate positive race relations.

❖ ❖ ❖

By the early 1930s, Greene was gaining recognition as a promising scholar within the black community as well as within white academe. He was a well-recognized figure on the lecture circuit of black intellectuals and leaders, especially during Negro History Week celebrations. Between the summer of 1930 and the fall of 1931, he became a first-rate speaker in black communities throughout the country while also entering the elite lecture circuit of white academe. During his bookselling campaigns, Greene spoke at various churches, colleges, and elementary and high schools within the black community. Sometimes he was given between ten and fifteen minutes to plead his case. In other instances, as in Philadelphia in February 1931, he was allowed most of the hour-long church service to speak. In the fall of 1930 in Oklahoma, he delivered some of his best orations. He spoke at Langston University to a group of between five hundred and six hundred people, including professors, students, youths, and unemployed laborers. Greene was most satisfied with his interaction with schoolchildren. In an elementary school in Oklahoma, he was immensely pleased to speak to a class of ten-year-olds. He shared with his attentive listeners the history of Africa, recounting how "Africans discovered America hundreds of years before Columbus."[45] Greene commented, after speaking with these children, "Never have I been more gratified or more satisfied with three quarters of an hour's toil." Early in 1931, Greene also felt equally as gratified in speaking to Philadelphia schoolchildren about Africa's contribution to discovery, art, empire building, culture, and human civilization.

Not all of Greene's speeches to black audiences praised Africa's glorious past. Like Woodson, Greene was (whether he admitted it or not) a polemicist of sorts. In November 1930, Greene publicly critiqued the black church so much that on November 22, Woodson wrote to his understudy and told him to disassociate himself from the ASNLH. Woodson believed that Greene jeopardized the Association's status in the black community of ministers and churchgoers. Woodson was also probably upset that Greene had not consulted him before making such statements.

While nearly all of Greene's speeches were directed toward black audiences, one of his most important speeches was delivered to the senior class at Dartmouth College, where in February 1931 he was invited to speak on "Labor Relations in America." His honorarium was fifty dollars, and he was very pleased with this opportunity, interpreting it as recognition for his hard work on *The Negro Wage Earner* and as a step toward independence from Woodson. "This invitation from Dartmouth brings me just that much nearer my breaking point with [Woodson]. Just so much more able will I be able to stand alone," Greene recorded in his diary on February 7, 1931. "I desire only the scholarship from him. Then, if necessary, I shall be free to wash my hands."[46] March 18, 1931, the day Greene spoke to the Dartmouth senior class, marked his "debut—so to speak—in academic society." Greene apparently performed well at Dartmouth. After March 1931, many other opportunities opened up for him, including working with Herbert Hoover's Conference on Home Building and Home Ownership beginning in late April of the same year.

❖ ❖ ❖

Of course, Greene's life was not perfect. In September 1932, his soulmate and "dearest treasure," Lenora Pritchett, married another man. Greene was devastated and even proposed to her in a last-minute act of desperation. Financially, Greene was in dire straits as well. From the fall of 1931 until the fall of 1932, he worked toward completing his doctorate at Columbia. For part of 1932, he received no fellowship money from the ASNLH. According to Arvarh Strickland, he became "totally dependent upon income from selling books. Often this meant that he had to accept speaking engagements, with only his expenses covered, in order to have an opportunity to sell books after his speech."[47] Well into 1933, selling books continued to be his fundamental source of income. The spring and summer months of this year were extremely bitter and sweet. In June, Greene's mother died. Then, thanks to Woodson's advocacy, Charles W. Florence, president of Lincoln University in Missouri from 1931 until 1937, offered Greene a position as assistant professor in the department of political science and history, paying two hundred dollars per month for twelve months. Greene accepted the offer and embarked upon another new and important phase of his life.

7 Discovering His Mission at Lincoln University, 1933–44

ARRIVING AT LINCOLN ON SEPTEMBER 2, 1933, Lorenzo Johnston Greene opened a new chapter of his life. He made Jefferson City, Missouri, his home and Lincoln University his base of operation, teaching full time there from 1933 until 1972. During his tenure at Lincoln, Greene developed into a first-rate professor, continued to work for Carter G. Woodson's Association for the Study of Negro Life and History (ASNLH), spearheaded Lincoln University's interaction with victimized sharecroppers in southeast Missouri in 1939 and in 1940 married concert pianist Thomasina Talley, completed his dissertation and published it, embraced the "Double V" campaign during World War II, battled the Lincoln University administration under the presidency of Clifford G. Scruggs for a higher salary, and began editing a leading journal for scholarly research and creative writings. By his early fifties, Greene had clearly demonstrated that he possessed all the qualities of a well-balanced scholar-activist. He successfully operated within the isolated walls of black and white academe while maintaining an intimate relationship with the black masses. He cautioned blacks not to use scholarship as propaganda, yet he continued to inspire black youths and adults with his captivating lectures and embraced a radical political outlook in attempting to help his economically oppressed counterparts. Greene's vision from 1933 to 1950 was truly authentic. At Lincoln, Greene was on his own, free from Woodson's control. This autonomy did have a price, however; in the late 1930s and the early 1940s, Greene found it extremely difficult to secure funding and support for his study on blacks in colonial New England. Greene's first decade at Lincoln, from the closing years of the Depression through the era of World War II, was one of great growth for the black New Englander.

❖ ❖ ❖

In early September 1933, Greene arrived at Lincoln University. He was greeted to Missouri by raw, white racism. He could not get a taxicab from the train station and was denied service in a Jefferson City restaurant. "Racism was so pervasive, that on the first night, unable to find a place to eat or to lodge, I cried," Greene recounted forty years after first arriving in Missouri. He was so distraught that he contemplated leaving Lincoln after receiving his first paycheck: the job the National Urban League of New York City had offered him surveying black employment in two blocks of West 127th Street looked more appealing to him. Initially, Greene had intended to remain at Lincoln for only one year and then take the Urban League job. When classes began, though, he changed his mind. "I realized that my services were needed here," he recounted in his early eighties. Greene also took pride in the fact that Lincoln was an "all-black school" located in Missouri's capital and that it "held the distinction of being the only institution of higher learning formed by Northern soldiers who fought in the Union Army during the Civil War."[1]

He was pleased that there were so many leading black intellectuals at Lincoln, and with them he became determined to change the economic and social climate that oppressed Missouri's black population. Missouri has "an infamous tradition of lynching." From 1900 until several years before Greene arrived in Jefferson City, at least seventeen black men were lynched. In the same year Greene arrived at Lincoln, a man named Lloyd Warren was murdered and burned in St. Joseph, Missouri. Throughout the 1930s, there were several miniature race riots in the state as well.

The Depression also took its toll on black Missourians. By 1930, 43 percent of black workers in St. Louis were unemployed; by the time Greene arrived in Jefferson City, close to half of all black families in St. Louis were receiving some from of aid from the government. Black agricultural workers in Missouri were victimized even more. Throughout the 1930s, black workers found it difficult to unionize, and black sharecroppers found it especially hard to make ends meet. Some New Deal policies alleviated a portion of the economic hardships endured by a small sector of Missouri's African American population. Under the guidance of Mary McLeod Bethune, the National Youth Administration "enabled students and others, particularly at Lincoln University, to earn a college education or to learn trades." Overall, Greene's first several decades in Missouri coincided with an era of widespread segregation and racial discrimination.[2]

In other respects, Greene's years at Lincoln were positive. According to William Sherman Savage, Charles W. Florence, Lincoln University president from 1931 until 1937, initiated a host of highly significant changes at the school, improving the administration, school traditions, scholarship of students, college training, teaching methods, and extracurricular activities. Most notably, he established a debating society, a school paper (the *Clarion*), and a comprehensive exam process for seniors; he also encouraged professors to attend graduate school and inaugurated a High School Day. A year after Greene arrived at Lincoln, the university witnessed a 32 percent increase in students and was admitted to the North Central Association of Secondary Schools and Colleges.[3] The progress at Lincoln during Greene's early years at this original land-grant college for blacks not only coincided with a period of political tensions on campus but was also significantly shaped by Nathan B. Young's two presidencies. During his first term as president from 1923 until 1927, Young strove to make Lincoln an "accredited" undergraduate college for blacks, transforming it from a "secondary industrial school" to a respected liberal arts college. Though he blended "trade training and academic education," he focused on increasing Lincoln's academic status and reputation.[4]

Young increased the requirements for teachers and professors, shifted the curriculum to focus on rigorous academic training, and mobilized the community around the university's new image. By 1925 and 1926, the high school department and normal department, respectively, achieved significant accreditation. By 1927, when Young was first released, the academic reputation of Lincoln had significantly increased. Young served his second term as president of Lincoln for nineteen months between 1929 and 1931. His presidencies polarized Missouri's black community, the majority of whom seemed to have supported Young. In 1934—in part as a result of Young's efforts—Lincoln became fully accredited a year after Greene arrived on campus.[5]

According to Gary Kremer, Greene contributed immensely to Lincoln's becoming a "Black Culture Mecca of the Midwest." Under the presidency of Nathan B. Young, many leading African American scholars were recruited to Lincoln. When Greene arrived on campus, he was welcomed by a first-rate faculty, including historian William Sherman Savage, English professor Sterling Brown, artist James Dallas Parker, and short story writer Cecil Archibald Blue. In the 1930s, Greene teamed up with Blue and they called themselves "the color boys." They shared a place they called "the Monastery," which became "an off campus site for faculty-student interaction" and where they frequently hosted "all night discussions about Roosevelt's New Deal, international communism, and race relations." According to Greene's testimony five decades later, "the Monastery" had a respected reputation beyond the walls of Jefferson City.

In the 1930s, Greene became intensely involved with academic life at Lincoln. He was an active professor, served as secretary of the university debating team, and with other professors strove to make Lincoln "an academic replica of Amherst."[6] Unfortunately, Greene did not keep a diary of his Lincoln years. He wrote very little about his life and work there, although it was at Lincoln during the 1930s that he underwent significant transformations as a scholar-activist and intellectual. Between 1933 and 1940, Greene was a concerned teacher dedicated to social change; he continued working with Woodson, returned to writing poetry seriously again, and joined the ranks of prominent black activists by spearheading a campaign on behalf of southeast Missouri sharecroppers.

An investigation of the Papers of Lorenzo Johnston Greene reveals that he was a teacher who was deeply involved with his students inside and outside the classroom. He seems to have taken students' opinions seriously: after his courses were concluded, he had his students comment on the course. Most noted that he was a very demanding, knowledgeable professor. He was often praised for his ability to make the social sciences interesting, simple to comprehend, and relevant to the times. "I've gotten a broader vision and a greater desire and determination to help cure the 'ills of society,'" one student wrote. Another student said, "I have received more practical knowledge from your lectures than from any of my other courses." A few students, though, had some problems with Greene. One student believed that he took "certain students for granted," while another remarked that the workload was "unbearable." Greene strove to influence the actual life of his students. He took great pride when his students returned and told him that he "had some little influence on their success in life."

Greene's concern with Lincoln went beyond the student body.[7] He was determined to reform the segregated South. Along with a few professors from Lincoln and the University of Missouri, Greene worked hard, from the early 1930s on, at breaking down the walls that separated the two universities. When he first arrived in Missouri, meetings between blacks and whites could not be held on either campus. He challenged this and claimed that his and his cohorts' efforts resulted in four white professors at the University of Missouri losing their jobs.

In 1973, Greene recounted to a friend that he had inspired Lloyd Gaines to apply for admission to the law school at the University of Missouri in 1935. Gaines's application initiated a wave of major Supreme Court decisions (see *Gaines v. Canada et al.*), which, in Greene's estimation, "finally culminated in the landmark decision of the High Tribunal in May, 1954."[8]

In early 1936, Lincoln University's Board of Curators decided to conduct a serious study of the university in order to determine what specific changes were needed to improve the institution. On April 28, 1936, a committee of five convened and decided to elect Greene to conduct the survey beginning in the summer months. By late December, Greene had completed his report, totaling forty-six pages, and he was ready to present it to the board. In "The Needs of the Negro in Missouri in Respect to Higher Education," he offered more than ten recommendations to be instituted over a period of ten years.

He called for changes affecting the lives of both faculty and students, advising the board that they develop at Lincoln "strong" departments of business and commerce, mechanic arts, agriculture and veterinary science, sociology, physical education, kindergarten education, and fine arts. He argued that such changes would enable their graduates to enter into their respective communities and make valuable contributions. For professors, he recommended salary increases equal to those offered at the University of Missouri and suggested that "creative work be encouraged." Black professors and scholars found it very difficult to get support for their work on campus. While at Howard University, president Mordecai W. Johnson (1926–1960) denied funding to pioneering biologist Ernest Everett.[9] Greene, who was teaching a full load and trying to complete his dissertation at the time of the report, suggested that a faculty research fund and a research committee be established. "Leaves of absence with pay for the purpose of research and reduction of teaching load were some of the ways the school was to encourage creative work,"[10] Greene suggested. Greene's study was insightful, but he did not convince the survey committee and the university.

❖ ❖ ❖

While at Lincoln during the 1930s, Greene continued to work with Woodson. In February 1934, Greene remained dedicated to the ASNLH and the early black history movement. Between February 11 and February 18, he spoke at more than a dozen locations in Missouri and Kansas. "I am enclosing a check for $10.00 which the faculty of Sumner High School of Kansas City, Kansas, donated to me for expenses," Greene wrote to Woodson in 1934,

"Since my expenses have been paid to Kansas City Missouri and since I could not think of exploiting Negro History Week for my own benefit I had them make out the check to the Association." Woodson applauded Greene for his overarching "spirit of sacrifice" and for his intellectual contributions to the annual meetings. Greene remained faithful to Woodson and the Association even in the midst of controversy. Though he did not agree with the manner in which Woodson dismissed Rayford Logan in January 1937, Greene guaranteed Woodson that the Association was his cause célèbre. Unlike Logan, Greene "refused to have anything to do with the proposed *Stokes Encyclopedia.*" Greene seemed to be just as dedicated to Woodson and the Association in his late thirties as he was when he served as an investigator more than five years earlier. "Personally I shall deplore anything which shall cause a rift in the ranks of those who are so intimately bound to the Association as this person [Logan] and the rest of us. For me it is my first love; the thing to which I have dedicated my life and I should regret to see its work even momentarily retarded by something of this kind," Greene wrote to Woodson early in 1937.[11]

Throughout the rest of the decade, Greene continued to support Woodson and the ASNLH. He participated in the One Dollar Sustaining Membership, the *Negro History Bulletin,* and Negro History Week. He gave Woodson some key suggestions as to how the Association might survive the days of philanthropic drought and advised him to institute "a tag day, on which persons of every income bracket, no matter how small, might be given an opportunity to contribute to the work of the Association." Greene suggested that Woodson encourage the masses to purchase tags or buttons symbolic of their contributions. After he arrived at Lincoln, Greene also established the Negro History Week celebrations in Missouri and adjacent states. Under Greene's influence, Lincoln University became "a clearing house" for speakers during this week. Greene reported to Woodson that within a relatively brief period, more students and teachers began enrolling in black history courses, Missouri libraries began acquiring more books pertaining to black America, significant numbers of people frequently wrote to Lincoln asking for available information on black history, white high schools and colleges began writing to Lincoln asking for information about black America's past, and "school authorities" permitted the "teaching of Negro History in all of the Missouri public schools."[12]

While working closely with Woodson from the spring of 1928 until the summer months of 1933, Greene appears to have put his poetry to the side. During these years, he apparently wrote no more than ten poems, and nearly all of them reflected his romantic side. Several of the poems were composed as responses to his "soulmate" Lenora Pritchett's decision to marry another man in September 1932.[13] After arriving at Lincoln, Greene returned to writing poetry. This venture served as an essential outlet for Greene's deeper thoughts about life. Between the fall of 1933 and 1937, Greene wrote more than thirty poems. Nearly all of these poems were tributes to women and a substantial number of these were for Thomasina Talley, whom he married in December 1941. Out of this large group of writings, one stands out. "To a Brown Girl," written in 1936, is a lyrical poem written in a black, Southern dialect. The main character is a "pretty brown girl" who has, for whatever reason, experienced some great pain in her life. The narrator, who comforts the young woman, asks God to "shoo de pain away" and "make dis brown girl well."[14] When read aloud, the poem takes on the character of the jazz poetry made popular by Langston Hughes. The poem also takes on the character of a song by an amateur blues singer.

Greene appears to have written his last body of poetic works at Lincoln after only five years of working there. Why he apparently stopped typing out his poetry is hard to pinpoint. The most obvious explanation is that he became intensely involved with academic work and later with political activism. By the late 1930s, he began to focus increasingly on completing his dissertation, devoting much of his energies toward carefully marrying academic culture with a life of social and political activism.

❖ ❖ ❖

"Unforeseen events," Greene recalled in 1987, "often change the face of history." When Lincoln University President Dr. Sherman D. Scruggs asked Greene to fill in for him as a speaker at a high school in southeast Missouri in mid-March 1939, the enthusiastic history professor had no idea how much this experience would change his life, especially his perception of the role of the university-trained scholar. After Greene spoke to teachers, students, and townspeople at Charleston High School, he returned to his car and realized that he had locked his keys inside. By the time they were able to unlock the car, the teachers had convinced Greene that it was much too late for him to drive back to Jefferson City. They offered him a place to stay overnight and one said that in the morning he would take Greene to witness the hardships endured by a group of sharecroppers who had protested their ill treatment and walked off of the plantations. Before this point, Greene had heard of the sharecroppers' protest, but like others, he did not know the specific details of the case.[15]

The sharecroppers of southeast Missouri, 95 percent of whom were black, had begun their protest several months earlier. On January 9 and 10, 1939, "approximately 1,300 to 1,500" white and black sharecroppers were evicted or walked off the plantations where they worked and lived. Hundreds then "camped along the rights-of-way of U.S. Route 60 and 61, two major highways of the Bootheel in Southeast Missouri." Under the guidance of Reverend Owen H. Whitfield, a "charismatic" African American preacher, labor leader, member of the Southern Tenant Farmer's Union, and sharecropper, many of these sharecroppers protested against "unspeakable living conditions, wretched housing and lack of sanitation . . . unhealthy diet, starvation wages, poor educational facilities and maltreatment." The demands of these exploited workers were simple and radical. They called for the sharecropping and tenant farming system to be abolished, the formal organization of the farm workers, consistent wages, the right to raise their own animals and crops, "free pasturage," the "use of a team truck to haul produce to market," and some other modest rights. Because these fundamental rights were not met, the determined sharecroppers protested.[16] Arvarh Strickland has offered the following succinct summary of the events leading up to the sharecroppers' demonstration:

> This demonstration focused attention on several major economic issues that faced the nation's agricultural interests during the New Deal. The mechanization of agriculture, for example, led to the displacement of agricultural workers and the consolidation of holdings throughout the South. New Deal agricultural policies accelerated that process by paying farmers to reduce the production of certain crops. Large landowners, in turn, used the government payments to purchase tractors and other equipment. Increased mechanization meant that they had less need for tenants to cultivate and harvest their crops. Moreover, by requiring landowners to share the payments made for reducing production with their sharecroppers and tenants, the government made it more profitable to use day laborers.
>
> The mass release of sharecroppers and eviction of tenants were part of the results. Without homes or a means to make a living, thousands of sharecroppers soon faced starvation. With no political or economic power, they had little chance for relief. Consequently, they sought to dramatize their nearly hopeless plight in order to receive some form of governmental assistance until better times returned.[17]

The morning after Greene delivered his speech before Charleston High School, he visited the sharecroppers, witnessing firsthand their hardships.

He was "shocked and distressed" at what he saw. He could not believe that men, women, and children could be treated like that in the United States. He spoke "freely" with many of the sharecroppers and took photographs in order to raise the consciousness of his colleagues and students back in Jefferson City. During this initial visit, he also met Walter Johnson, a spokesman for one group of the sharecroppers, who underscored to the Lincoln University professor that his people did not need pity, but rather the basic necessities of life, "food, clothing, shelter, medicines, etc. . . ." Greene promised Johnson that he would help. After Greene returned to Lincoln, he shared his experiences with his eight o'clock American history class. He told them how the sharecroppers were being victimized by their landlords and how the federal, state, county, and local government had turned their backs on these working peoples' plight. Greene then chastised his students for being more concerned with their spring prom than with the basic human rights violations in their state. Later on that March day, on separate occasions, two of his students, Adele James, president of Lincoln's Delta Sigma Theta chapter, and Bernice Smith of Alpha Kappa Alpha, told professor Greene that they had decided to give all the money that they had saved for their prom to the sharecroppers of southeast Missouri. One other student, Cynthia Bolt, a senior history major and president of the Lincoln University Student Council, also met with Greene that day and informed him that the council had resolved to donate their entire treasury to the sharecroppers.[18]

According to Greene, after these initial events, "a whirlwind campaign" blossomed. President Scruggs called a "special convocation" and invited Greene to address the student body and faculty as a whole. He "emphasized their pressing need for shelter, food, clothing, medicine and the best approach for getting relief to them." After his testimony and plea, the campus developed into "a hive of activity." By April, students, teachers, and concerned citizens of Jefferson City donated, bought, and collected "nearly a truckload" of clothes and food. In addition, close to two hundred dollars was donated to the sharecroppers. On one occasion, Greene accompanied several of the female student leaders to the sharecroppers' makeshift homes in order to give them the provisions. He wrote, "I cautioned the girls . . . to be particularly careful of their attitude toward these people. In no way, I warned them, should they act . . . in a patronizing or condescending manner." Greene continued, "If anyone did so, I would take her back to the home where we were staying and leave her until we were ready to return to the university." Greene's students acted appropriately and were deeply affected by the sharecroppers' "malnutrition, poor sanitation, and inadequate health care."[19]

Throughout the spring and summer months of 1939, Greene maintained close connections with a group of the sharecroppers. He was determined to improve their status significantly. In order to build his case, he had the sharecroppers themselves articulate and document the reasons they left the plantations and how their lives were since then. Greene took these pleas very seriously. He saved them, and they constitute roughly two containers of the Papers of Lorenzo Johnston Greene. Greene also broadened the campaign beyond the walls of Jefferson City. He appealed to leading African American newspapers to publicize the sharecroppers' plight. Claude Barnett, editor of the Associated Negro Press, helped Greene tell middle-class black Americans and liberal whites about this victimized group. As a result, concerned people throughout the country learned about the southeast Missouri sharecroppers' plight; some sent money and clothing, and a handful offered their own sometimes far-reaching solutions.

Greene served as one of the main contact persons for the sharecroppers. He responded to many concerned citizens' inquiries. He also pressured the U.S. government. On May 21, 1939, he asked Henry A. Wallace, Secretary of Agriculture, for information about the sharecroppers, and he requested that the department help them. In early June 1939, John Fischer, Director of Information, responded to Greene's letter. He informed the Lincoln professor about the background of the southeast Missouri area and defended the Roosevelt administration, claiming that the Farm Security Administration had attempted to help "the 300 families who took part in the demonstration" by giving them grants (averaging less than twenty dollars per family), loaning twenty-six families some tents for shelter, and attempting "to carry our a permanent rehabilitation program."[20]

While Greene solicited the FSA, local leaders continued to fight other battles. In early June, two of Greene's students, Adele James and Marianne White, helped Reverend Whitfield raise the down payment necessary to purchase ninety acres of land for slightly more than three dollars an acre. After they purchased the land, other obstacles surfaced. Many whites proved to be hostile and attempted to prevent Whitfield and his people from settling on their newly purchased land. Additionally, the land was not suitable for raising crops, and whites did not hire black labor. Throughout the summer, Greene continued to involve Lincoln students in helping the sharecroppers. He did so at great personal risk and met much resistance. "Rumors circulated that if I continued my trips to Southeast Missouri," Greene recalled a year before his death, "I would not return alive." A friend of his even offered to arm and protect him. Greene continued to travel to southeast Missouri without a gun or a bodyguard.

The university also posed a threat to Greene's work. In mid-July 1939, President Scruggs told Greene that "state officials" would "reduce Lincoln's appropriations" if the university did not stop aiding the sharecroppers. Greene and other activists at the university ignored President Scruggs's warnings, and Scruggs, realizing he was outnumbered, did nothing to further hinder the university's activists from continuing their efforts. By the dawning of the next decade, Greene's and others' works bore some fruit. In 1940, the Farm Security Administration began constructing homes for the sharecroppers. A year later, the housing project was completed, and a total of ten villages—seven white and three black—were built. The homes were equipped with the basic necessities and could be paid off in easy installments totaling eight hundred dollars per family.

Thus in the late 1930s, Greene and his followers placed Lincoln University on the map as an educational institution concerned about the welfare of humanity, a black university with a vision of social activism linked with academic excellence. In 1987, Greene reflected on how students affected the lives of the sharecroppers. "Lincoln University students . . . acted as role models for some of the younger people," Greene noted. "Lincoln University, through its students and an accidentally involved teacher, played an active role in assisting the destitute sharecroppers of southeast Missouri, nearly a half century ago."[21]

❖ ❖ ❖

Had the Farm Security Administration not acted on behalf of the sharecroppers, it is very likely that Greene may have completed his dissertation at an even later date. Greene began working on his doctorate at Columbia after he received his master's degree in 1926. According to Greene, he first began "seriously" studying and researching blacks in colonial New England in 1931. The lapse in time between when he began doctoral research and when his dissertation appeared is best explained by the fact that Greene divided his time between various causes from the late 1920s through the early 1940s. He was a key figure in the black history movement spearheaded by Carter Woodson. He lectured at countless elementary and high schools, at colleges and universities, at churches, and at various black community functions. Greene was a dedicated social activist on Lincoln's campus, in Missouri, and even at the national level. He was also a committed and overworked teacher. Before the widespread integration of black intellectuals into the white academy in the 1960s and 1970s, black colleges and universities worked their professors to the point that many complained of not having enough time or resources to conduct the research necessary for establishing a reputation in their respective fields. From the late 1920s until 1942, Greene taught three to four classes during each semester and taught during the summers.

Between 1931 and 1941, Greene could have published some of his findings on blacks in New England as articles. He refrained from doing so because he feared that other scholars dealing with his subject would jump on it themselves or assign it to their graduate students. In retrospect, it is doubtful that his topic would have been something other historians would have been quick to take up. Most white historians did not believe that black history was legitimate; most established black historians of the time were close to Greene and probably would have respected his work. Black graduate students did not begin writing dissertations on black subject matters en masse until the civil rights era. In reality, more serious obstacles stood in Greene's path.

By May 1941, Greene had successfully completed all requirements for his doctorate at Columbia University, "with the sole exception" of publishing his dissertation. At that time at Columbia, before candidates actually received their degree, they were required to submit "a specified number of printed copies" to the university. In 1941, Greene did not possess the financial wherewithal to pay for such copies. His funds were "exhausted in developing the study." Like many black scholars several decades before World War II, Greene had received funding from a few white foundations. In 1934, the Julius Rosenwald Fund granted him four hundred dollars with which he has able to "collect indispensable data from libraries in Massachusetts, Rhode Island, and Connecticut." In 1935, the General Education Board granted him $810, which he used to conduct research in New York City libraries and to take classes at Columbia University and the New School for Social Research. In 1940, the Rosenwald Fund gave him a fellowship, which helped him complete the dissertation. He did not, however, have enough money to pay for the publication of the dissertation. He could have published his study with an obscure publisher for no more than $400, but concerns about the reception of his study led him to turn to a more reputable press. He wanted to join the ranks of leading scholars: in the early 1940s, Greene was a black historian in the prime of his career, with a truly groundbreaking study complete, who would nevertheless have great trouble rallying the support he needed and deserved.[22]

In late October 1941, in desperation, Greene wrote the American Council of Learned Societies of Washington, D.C., requesting financial support. He told the council's secretary for grants-in-aid, Donald Goodchild, that he needed between fifteen hundred and eighteen hundred dollars to publish his "valuable contribution" with Columbia University Press or another reputable publisher. Several months later, Goodchild told Greene that the council could not meet his request, supposedly because of the "large number of applications."[23]

Greene was therefore made painfully aware that publishing his work would depend on his own determination and effort. From the fall of 1941, he began actively advertising himself as a lecturer. He sent brief résumés and letters offering his services as a speaker on "Negro history or [on] some of the social and economic problems facing the Negro today" to many different colleges, universities, and organizations throughout the country. In November 1941, he politely asked John B. Eubanks of the National Council of the YMCA in Dallas, Texas, if he could help him raise money to publish his dissertation. "Thanks for your words relative to my completing the work for the doctorate degree. . . . It was quite a lengthy dissertation and I am now seeking to raise some $2,000.00 in order to publish it," Greene shared with Eubanks, "For this reason I have decided to schedule as many speaking engagements as possible during this school year. . . . I would consider it a great favor if you would pass my name on to other branches and schools and organizations which might have need of a speaker on some aspect of Negro history or the present day problems confronting the race."[24]

By late January 1942, Greene had not raised enough money to publish his dissertation. He wrote to the head of Columbia University's department of political science, George Braxton Pegram, asking "whether it would be possible for the Faculty of Political Science to waive temporarily the requirement for publishing the dissertation as a prerequisite for awarding the degree."[25] Having his PhD in hand would allow him to vie for a promotion at Lincoln or seek employment elsewhere—perhaps with the federal government, where he felt he could "do his bit" in a time of national emergency. He spoke also of wanting to become the head of the history department at an eastern college. In 1941, he applied for positions at several city colleges in New York. Though Greene enjoyed teaching and interacting with the Jefferson City black community, he had become disenchanted with Lincoln University, and he reasoned that in the East he could exploit "broader opportunities," such as libraries that contained sources pertaining to colonial New England. To his dismay, none of the eastern colleges replied to him, and Greene sensed that racism had played a part in this.

In February 1942, he shared his concerns with the outspoken pastor of New York's Abyssinia Baptist Church, Rev. Adam Clayton Powell. At the time, Powell was a member of the New York City Council and worked hard at getting "qualified Negro professors" on the faculties of New York's municipal colleges. Greene asked Powell if he could help him in his quest to desegregate the academy, to "break down this intellectual barrier against the Negro."[26] Powell's efforts apparently did not help.

Greene also showed early interest in at least one black college. In January 1942, he wrote to Dr. James E. Shepard, president of the North Carolina College for Negroes, seeking a position in their history department, saying that he was "eager to become associated with a dynamic institution" where he "might render a larger service than is possible at Lincoln University."[27] But whether Greene applied at a school in North Carolina or some "eastern school," the obstacle of applying for jobs with no diploma in his hands proved insurmountable.

Eventually, *The Negro in Colonial New England, 1620–1776* was published as one of the Columbia University Studies in History, Economics, and Public Law by Columbia University Press and in London by P. S. King and Staples sometime between August 1 and August 15, 1942.[28] The 494th dissertation in the series, Greene's study included 334 pages of text—404 pages with the bibliography, appendices, and index—and it was fairly expensive, retailing at $4.50. However arduous the path to publication was, Greene's problems at Columbia probably did not stem from racism. "Between 1930 and 1962, Columbia University awarded 144 doctoral degrees to graduates of black colleges—more than any other American institution."[29] Greene's class of 1942 did indeed have its share of black scholars who earned a doctorate from Columbia.

Greene was extremely thankful to many white professors and many of his black colleagues for making his study possible. He credited Emeritus Professor Evarts Greene with first suggesting that he conduct such a study. Greene, who retired in 1939, helped Greene shape his overall views of colonial history, proofread the manuscript, and helped him secure funding for conducting the necessary research. Other Columbia professors, including John A. Krout, Dixon Ryan Fox, Harry J. Carman, Samuel McKee Jr., Merle Curti, Aurthur W. McMahan, and Carter Goodrich, read the manuscript and offered "many helpful suggestions." Curti was perhaps the most qualified person of this group to review Greene's study. Before the World War II era, Curti was one of the few white scholars who tried to "integrate black history into the mainstream of American history." Curti affiliated himself with Woodson, included blacks in his *The Social Ideas of American Educators* (1935), and served as the advisor to Marion Thompson Wright, the first black woman historian in the United States to earn a doctorate in history (1940).[30]

Colleagues such as L. D. Reddick, Helen Boardman, Harold J. Jonas, and some Lincoln University faculty members also supported Greene. During Negro History Week of 1943, he wrote an extended thanks to Reddick for his help: "Certainly, your reading and criticizing of the manuscript, while in preparation, helped to make the printed opus a better work than it could have possibly been without it." His wife, Dr. Thomasina Talley Greene, checked references and read page proofs, and greatly supported her husband emotionally during an extremely stressful time for both of them. Woodson, for whom Greene had labored tirelessly for more than ten years, was not as supportive. In fact, the ASNLH founder seems to have discouraged Greene on at least one occasion. "When the Columbia University Press offered to subsidize publication of the NEGRO IN COLONIAL NEW ENGLAND, I considered it treason not to give first preference to the Association," Greene recalled. "Woodson took the manuscript, turned up his nose in characteristic 'Woodsonian' fashion, scornfully curled his lip and sarcastically asked, without even opening it, 'What do you have here? Nothing.' Punctuating it with a contemptuous snap of his fingers, he threw it on his desk." While he supported many younger, promising black historians, Woodson also, in Greene's words, "seemed to take pleasure in crushing any vestige of self-confidence" in his associates and assistants. Woodson's employees, especially his female secretaries, were often "constant objects of his sharp tongue." Woodson may have treated Greene in this manner because Green's study was conducted under the guidance of white professors, not Woodson.[31]

❖ ❖ ❖

Greene wrote, in the preface of *The Negro in Colonial New England, 1620–1776,* "Nowhere can a comprehensive treatment of the Negro in the Puritan colonies be found. The present study is an attempt to fill this gap in the literature of American colonial history." The book expanded on the ideas first presented in Greene's first scholarly article, "Slaveholding New England and Its Awakening" (1928). Greene began his study by exploring the origins of slavery and the lucrative slave trade in various New England colonies. He was a pioneer in examining advertisements for their references to blacks. According to Greene, New England whites, particularly from Massachusetts, made the slave trade profitable. He attested that New England did not have as many slaves as the Southern colonies and often received the more sickly slaves who were unfit for the hard labor of the Caribbean sugar colonies. Still, Greene challenged the prevailing myth of Puritan righteousness and rationality by investigating New England's tripartite justification of the peculiar institution: economic, legal, and spiritual. "Slavery was a part of the cultural pattern of the seventeenth and eighteenth century Massachusetts and of New England in general," Greene surmised.[32]

Greene faced many challenges in terms of sources. The first official census to include blacks was conducted in 1790, when slavery was under serious attack along many fronts. Greene conducted meticulous research in reconstructing colonial New England's black populations. He discovered that while Boston had many blacks, New Hampshire and Connecticut had very few, reflecting the influence of geographic conditions. One key finding was that by 1790, as many as 3,763 slaves were owned by 2,141 families.[33] In other words, the slave to slaveholder ratio was nearly 2:1. Greene also challenged the widely held presumption that blacks could only serve as domestics. Citing various advertisements, he found that blacks labored in sheep raising, stock farming, lumber industries, distilleries, fishing, trading, whaling, and other artisan-specific jobs. "Negro slaves were a valuable and essential part of New England's labor supply" in that they "unquestionably played a role in the commercial and industrial development of that section,"[34] he concluded.

According to Greene's findings, black New England slaves' day-to-day lives were regulated by a "mild" strategy of slave control. The laws were barely effective, and slaves managed to resist through stealing, "witchcraft," arson, murder, plots, and even suicide. This situation was further complicated because New England slaves "were considered both as property and as persons before the law." Such an "indefinite status" enabled some blacks to locate vestiges of free space in the courts and other institutions. Greene argued that despite such autonomy, black New Englanders were in many ways no different from whites culturally. "As members of the Puritan family, they assimilated the manners and customs of their masters," Greene pronounced. "The Negro was forced to revise the ideas, attitudes, and practices regarding marriage and sex relationships which he had brought form Africa, and to adopt those of the master class." In this case, Greene sided with his fellow Howard graduate and contemporary, E. Franklin Frazier, instead of with anthropologist Melville J. Herskovits.

Greene's views were complex. In exploring slaves' recreational activities, such as "training day," storytelling, and governors' elections, he asserted that the "most popular of all slave diversion . . . was dancing, an art which Negroes brought from Africa."[35] The last section of Greene's study is "The Free Negro," which did not exist in his earlier graduate school paper. While there is evidence of free blacks as early as 1646 in New England, he stressed that this freedom had restrictions. "Despite the handicaps under which they labored," he wrote, "the free Negroes of colonial New England were slowly shaping the foundation for the Negro families of the nineteenth and twentieth centuries. A number of them not only became leaders and spokesmen for their group but also received recognition from their former masters for demonstrating unusual abilities in their circumscribed condition."[36]

Greene's work was well accepted within the scholarly community, black and white. According to Woodson, who was earlier unsupportive of Greene's *Negro in Colonial New England*, "this work is another serious treatment of the history of the Negro . . . a new chapter in the history of the black man—a new chapter in the history of the United States." Woodson was impressed with how Greene employed "advanced scholarship" and "scientific method" to reveal the "truth" about a neglected aspect of New England history; he applauded Greene for debunking the myth of an antislavery heritage in New England. "While we must still feel ashamed of the South for its lingering medievalism inflicted upon the section by chattel slavery," Woodson concluded, "we must hold the Mayflower descendants responsible for accelerating that backward step into a darkness which still overshadows the land of cotton."

The other black scholar to review Greene's study was his long-time friend, Clarence A. Bacote. Before Bacote's review appeared, Greene told Ira De A. Reid, editor of *Phylon,* that he eagerly awaited Bacote's review, "especially since he does not see eye to eye with some of my conclusions." The review was not critical in terms of scholarly approach or content. For him, despite some typographical errors, Greene's study constituted a "major contribution to the literature of the slave period."[37]

While white reviewers praised Greene's study for its thoroughness and meticulous use of source materials, many defended their New England forebears. *The Negro in Colonial New England, 1620–1776* was reviewed in all of the leading American historical journals. "It is not probable that any significant additions will be made to the body of facts here presented by Dr. Greene," asserted Elizabeth Donnan. This well-known slave-trade scholar also claimed that Greene did not have the evidence to demonstrate the effects of the slave trade or the black presence on New England life. She concluded, "These effects were too slight to be discerned and measured." Historian Harvey Wish praised Greene's work: "The proslavery school of the ante-bellum South could have made profitable use of the facts that professor Greene has discovered regarding slavery in colonial New England." Wish added, "In view of the contradictory nature of the statistics upon which he has been forced to rely, he has displayed admirable caution in his conclusions." Wish, who published two articles in the *Journal of Negro History* before Greene's study appeared, also commended Greene for using the available sources with "ingenuity." Paul Lewinson of the National Archives agreed with his assessment, yet he criticized Greene for not examining his subject against the backdrop of blacks in Southern colonies. Harvard University's Oscar Handlin asserted that Greene did not have adequate knowledge "with some phases of Puritan ideas that sometimes leads to serious misinterpretation," especially when dealing with religion. Harry J. Walker of the *American Journal of Sociology* apparently had no problems with Greene's study.[38]

White reviewers tended to welcome Greene's study because of its impersonal commitment to historical factualism. Greene wrote *The Negro in Colonial New England, 1620–1776* in a scientific, non-emotional tone for many reasons. It was a dissertation completed at Columbia University during an era of scholarly conservatism and prevalent academic racism. In a note to L. D. Reddick in late January 1943, Greene noted that his professors did not object to any of his ideas, but instead only instructed him to "lessen some of the supporting evidence." Following Woodson's lead, Greene knew that there were many skeptics who would not easily swallow this pill. Greene showered his readers with solid evidence. This study was his first major publication and he wanted it to be taken seriously by the white academic community. Most important, at this point in his life Greene believed firmly that academic scholarship had to be scientific, objective, and rigorous in order to be legitimate. While he was certainly the prototype for the black scholar-activist, Greene drew careful lines between his scholarship and his political and social activism. Even throughout the turbulent 1960s, he remained firmly rooted in publishing objective scholarship. Despite his objectivity, Greene believed that he had written a radical-enough text to lose some friends. "If I still remain a 'persona grata' in New England now," Greene wrote to L. D. Reddick in January 1943, "I shall be very much surprised, since even some 'dark-complexioned Puritans' have already accused me of having traduced by section."[39]

About two decades after Greene's book first appeared, August Meier wrote to Greene telling him that he thought that *The Negro in Colonial New England, 1620–1776* was "one of the top half dozen monographs" in the field of black history. He asked Greene whether or not he could contact a publisher about reprinting it. Shortly thereafter, Meier contacted Arthur Wang in New York and strongly recommended that his press consider reprinting Greene's book. Hill and Wang, one of the various presses to begin publishing books on black history after the classic civil rights movement, did not express much interest in the plan. Under the general editorship of Meier in the late 1960s, Atheneum published some key studies in black history in paperback by Louis R. Harlan, Benjamin Quarles, Elliott M. Rudwick, Sterling D. Spero, and Abram L. Harris. Greene's book was the first for which Atheneum had acquired the rights, and it was one of the first volumes to be published in its "Studies in American Negro Life" series. Even though it was not first published by Atheneum until 1968, by 1966 Greene had received his advance royalty for one hundred dollars. In the preface to the Atheneum edition, Benjamin Quarles praised the study: "Of the many historical works that have been given second birth by the reprint revolution of our times, few are more worthy of serious attention than Lorenzo J. Greene's *The Negro in Colonial New England, 1620–1776.*"[40]

Since the late 1980s, a few more scholars have begun dealing with the issues raised by Greene more than fifty years ago. Building upon the theories of Melville J. Herskovits, in 1988 William D. Piersen published *Black Yankees.* He paid tribute to Greene and built upon his findings. His argument is, as time has allowed it to be, much more complex than his predecessor's. By exploring factors such as demographic patterns, the slave family, language, names, the role of elders, the enculturation and acculturation processes, Christianity and black folk religion, slave resistance, works habits, attire, the construction of homes, diet, games, music, humor, and Governors' Days, Piersen maintained that eighteenth-century black New Englanders consciously fused a "double identity"—"a folklore that may have looked Euro-American, but was instead a complex, intercontinental alloy." Piersen's study certainly would not have been possible without Greene's groundbreaking work. More recently, Joanne Pope Melish has also taken the historical discourse inaugurated by Greene to a new level.[41]

❖ ❖ ❖

By 1942, Greene was no longer known simply as the Lincoln University history professor who once worked closely with "The Father of Negro History." *The Negro in Colonial New England, 1620–1776,* particularly its meticulous, objective, and easy-to-read approach, clearly indicated that this former Howard University medical student took the historian's craft very seriously. His contributions to African American and colonial American history were heralded by black and white historians alike. Still, in the first several years of the book's circulation, Greene had to do a lot of self-promotion. Though Woodson spoke highly of *The Negro in Colonial New England, 1620–1776,* he did not go to any great lengths in promoting the book because it was not an Associated Publishers product. Woodson also realized that it was not the type of study suitable for the first- or second-time book buyer.[42]

Being the seasoned bookseller he was, Greene marketed and sold his own book throughout the 1940s. Whenever he gave lectures in Missouri and throughout the country, he attempted to make sales. Before speaking to a YWCA branch luncheon in Kansas City, Missouri, on February 20, 1943, Greene had Columbia University Press forward twenty-five prepaid copies of his book for display and sale. He also left copies with stores on consignment. In March 1943, the Missouri Book Store dedicated a section of a window to his book. The profits from these sales could not have been very important. He was primarily concerned with making a few dollars, getting his name into the discourse of the mainstream academy, and clearing the way for other black scholars. "I want to take advantage of as many opportunities to bring this publication before the public," Greene shared with Elsie M. Mountain of the YWCA. "Moreover, the Columbia University Press is especially anxious that books by Negro authors find as large an outlet among the reading public as possible; otherwise, the Columbia University Press and other large white publishers will remain hesitant about publishing books by Negroes."[43]

The sales manager of Columbia University Press in the early 1940s, Joseph Duffy, did not, however, work hard at promoting Greene's study. On several occasions Greene asked Duffy to promote his book in Connecticut bookstores and to make arrangements with salespeople and publishers like the General Subscription Agency at Mangum, Oklahoma, and The Crisis Book Shop in New York City. During the first half of the 1940s, Greene, with perhaps a little support from the sales managers at Columbia University Press, sold many copies of his book. Within a year and a half after *The Negro in Colonial New England, 1620–1776* first appeared, the first edition was "entirely sold out." The editor of the Columbia Studies told Greene that this was "a most unusual occurrence for a book of its nature"—even more noteworthy when one considers that Greene sold so many books during the war, when people were not buying too many books of this nature, and the government was campaigning to conserve paper. On February 15, 1945, the Publications Department of Columbia University Press notified Greene that they would reprint his book "as a commercial proposition . . . to meet the demand for orders." Columbia University Press bore "all expenses" and agreed to pay Greene one-third of the total net proceeds. The foreign agent was the prestigious London-based Oxford University Press.[44]

❖ ❖ ❖

Throughout the early 1940s, Greene's life was changed by factors beyond the publishing and promoting of his dissertation. In 1941, he married Thomasina Talley, "famous concert pianist of Nashville, Tennessee." Greene first met Talley in the early 1930s in Missouri. Talley came from a "musical family." Her father, a well-known chemistry professor at Fisk University, was a songwriter and celebrated basso with the second group of Fisk Jubilee Singers. Thomasina started taking piano lessons at age five; at age fifteen, she graduated from Fisk University with a major in music. After Fisk, she received scholarships to the prestigious Julliard School of Music in New York City, where she remained for three years, receiving her certificate in 1932. She then began teaching music at a black high school in Missouri. Greene met her soon after he arrived at Lincoln. Sometime in the 1930s, Talley left Missouri to teach in Texas. Then, in 1939, she received Rockefeller Fellowships to Columbia University. She and Greene "renewed their friendship, fell in love, and were married on December 19, 1941." She earned an EdD as well as a PhD in music and music education from Columbia in 1942, becoming the first black woman to accomplish such a feat. No doubt, she and Greene gave each other strength and motivation to finish their degrees.

During the 1940s, and beyond, Talley earned a living as a professional concert pianist, worked part time as teacher at Lincoln University, and gave individual lessons in her home. Like her husband, she was also active in social welfare societies, such as the Missouri Association for Social Welfare and the NAACP. Several years after being married to Talley, Greene expressed to his friend L. D. Reddick the joy of being married. "Married life is wonderful. Thomasina and I are inseparable. Had I known what married life was like, perhaps I should not have been so persistent in sacrificing everything for *The Negro in Colonial New England.* Verily, the ball and chain is of gold."[45]

Throughout the early 1940s, Greene continued to help Woodson and the ASNLH stay afloat. In October 1941, Woodson thanked Greene for his personal contribution of five dollars to the cause. "With the support of faithful workers like you we cannot fail," Woodson told his former assistant. In the early 1940s, Greene continued to work hard at placing Missouri on the map of the early black history movement. In mid-January 1942, he mailed out a letter to black schools in Missouri, asking them to make the Negro History Week 1942, "the greatest Negro History Week Celebration ever." He called upon his fellow workers to invite a speaker to talk about "some phase of Negro History" to the student body, present a play or pageant dealing with certain events "in the life of the race," and contribute to the ASNLH by obtaining subscriptions to the *Journal of Negro* and the *Negro History Bulletin* for three dollars and one dollar a year, respectively, and by securing a penny from each student and ten cents or more from each teacher. "Every meeting held, every penny raised, helps to forward this work so vital to our race!" Greene concluded.[46]

He was also well known throughout Missouri for his campaigning during Negro History Week and for working closely with different organizations. He had a close relationship with the Paseo Branch YWCA in Kansas City, Missouri, from the mid-1930s through the mid-1940s. He helped the organization, which he deemed "a tower of strength in disseminating the history and contributions of the Negro," with their annual Negro History Week Celebrations. In February 1944, he discussed the possibility of setting up a Negro History Institute in Kansas City that would host nine of his lectures covering the role of blacks "in the development of World Culture" from ancient times through the present. Greene suggested to the YWCA that the lectures be delivered over five weekends, with participants paying ten dollars to register.

By June, Greene and the executive secretary of the organization, Elsie M. Mountain, made formal arrangements for the lecture series. He gave her the choice of nine potential titles and subdivided the lectures under four major subjects: the African origins, "Black Builders of the New World," free blacks before the Civil War, and blacks in industrial America from 1860 until 1944. Greene's lecture, he outlined, would be accompanied by a recital by his wife. In total, they asked for $450: $200 for Greene's lectures and $250 for his wife's concert. Greene ended up delivering the lectures from November 8 until November 11, 1944, for the fee of $425 including his wife's recital. Each lecture lasted for about two hours. The turnout was "fine" in Greene's estimation, and he hailed the series a success. This probably meant that at least twenty-five folks attended each seminar. Since Executive Secretary Mountain was ill during the lectures, several weeks later Greene provided her with a four-page, single-spaced summary of their contents.[47]

Woodson was especially surprised by what his former employee was able to accomplish. "I am surprised to hear that anyone is Missouri is interested in the study of the Negro. . . . What have you done there to bring about the change?" Woodson sarcastically commented to Greene. "Missouri is generally black as far as supporting the Association for the Study of Negro Life and History is concerned. We receive more support from one school in Washington, D.C., than we do from the whole state of Missouri." Greene also impressed Woodson by mobilizing the faculty at Lincoln University. In mid-May 1943, Woodson thanked the faculty and employees of Lincoln for their contribution of nineteen dollars. While Woodson appreciated Greene's efforts at the grassroots level, he wished that his former employee could have been more active with the *Journal*. Early in 1944, Greene told Woodson that he was sorry that he had to sidestep "some of the things" he "desired very greatly to do" because of his "other duties." He nevertheless assured Woodson that he had "only the welfare of the *Journal* and the Association at heart" and that he would review books or would render "any other service" for the Association.[48]

One of the "other duties" about which Greene spoke was his concern with the role of blacks during World War II. In late 1941 and early 1942, Greene wrote a series of letters to William Henry Hastie, Assistant to the Secretary of War, asking him to send him all the available information regarding the overall status of blacks in the armed forces. He offered his services as a lecturer to black soldiers in the various segregated training camps throughout the country. The Secretary of War did not have any job openings for Greene, and Hastie was not too helpful in briefing him on blacks' conditions during the war. "The policy of the War Department has been that these units and the individual soldiers therein be accorded identical treatment with all other organization and soldiers," Hastie responded to Greene.[49]

Greene strongly supported the United States during World War II and volunteered his services elsewhere. In January 1942, he wrote to Dr. Ambrose Caliver, Senior Specialist in the Education of Negroes for the Office of Education, summarizing his credentials and offering his "services to the government in any capacity in which they may be utilized to the greatest advantage of the nation." About two weeks later, Caliver informed Greene that there were no available positions that suited his credentials. Greene did not end his quest to serve his country, however. In early March 1942, he applied to the Office of Facts and Figures as a possible spokesperson for the Liaison Bureau for Group Morale. Once again, he was denied a formal position because of "budgetary concerns." Sometime in late March, Greene met with Theodore Berry, liaison officer from the Office of Facts and Figures, but he was not offered a position within their office either. Greene continued his patriotic quest to serve his country. In late June he wrote Mary McLeod Bethune to ask if the National Youth Administration could use his services in any way. Though she could not employ him, Bethune was instrumental in opening some other doors for Greene. "The very mention of your name proved an 'open sesame' to everyone I approached," Greene told the elder clubwoman. Most important, Bethune referred him to George Barnes, Assistant to the Director of the Office of War Information.[50]

In early November 1942, Greene wrote a very important letter to Barnes. He told the assistant director that despite their "fine work," they were making "little impression upon most of the 12,000,000 Negroes in the country" because the department's representatives were not actively attempting to reach them. He informed Barnes that white morale-building speakers all too often alienated blacks with their racist presentations. He provided him with several examples he had witnessed firsthand in Missouri. Greene argued that black participation was at an all-time low, and he warned Barnes that if such speakers continued their work, blacks would "become fertile breeding grounds for Axis propaganda, as shown by a few disillusionary Negroes who have identified themselves with the Pacific movement." Greene's solution was that the Office of War Information should instigate an "all out" campaign "to build up sagging Negro moral and thereby secure their wholehearted support of the war effort." Greene sketched out a detailed job description for a black man—namely, Greene—who could help gain the widespread black support. Greene declared:

> I believe that the Office of War Information should have on its staff a Negro, possessing a broad background of the history of the Negro group, one who is conversant with their economic, social and political problems and who, through service to his people and through the various experiences gained from his identity with this minority, understands the psychology of the Negro. He must make the Negroes feel that they are part and parcel of the American people, that they have a stake in American Democracy which they helped to found and preserve. He must make them feel that their whole welfare is bound up with the ultimate victory of the United Nations, that life under Axis domination would be intolerable. He must be able to appeal to the Negroes' past, he must recall to them their loyalty and sacrifices whenever American has been at war, thus arousing in them enthusiastic determination to defend the priceless heritage which they have helped to create. Lastly he should convince them that although they have not received all of the benefits of American Democracy, the prospects of achieving this goal are brighter now than ever before in out History. . . . I think that I am well equipped to do this job by virtue of training, experience and contacts.[51]

Roughly a year later, Greene continued his enthusiastic support of America's role in World War II. On the morning of December 2, 1943, as the Air Raid Warden and the Chairman of the Committee on War Information at Lincoln, Greene spoke to Jefferson City blacks and whites over the local radio station, KWOS. He stressed that food was "vital to winning the war," and then he commended Americans, especially black and white citizens of Jefferson City, for planting "Victory Gardens" in order to help supply "our boys at the front" and America's allies during 1943. After mentioning some of those who did exceptional jobs in canning, drying, and salting "thousands of quarts of food from their gardens" on behalf of "Uncle Sam," he asked Jefferson City citizens to be active participants in helping to raise the proposed 380 million acres of food for 1944. "Let us remember that all of us, irrespective of race, creed, or color, have a vital stake in this conflict . . . Either we all win it, or we all lose it." In concluding his brief appeal, Greene said, "If food production and conservation can shorten the war, I assure you that Negro citizens of Jefferson City will be in there doing their utmost to put the 1944 food campaign over the top and thereby help to insure the total defeat of the Axis in 1944."[52]

World War II evoked a complex collection of feelings within Greene. Like black spokespersons since the Revolutionary War, he hoped and believed that if his people demonstrated their unyielding patriotism and dedication to American democracy, then white America would return the favor by granting black people equality. He joined the "Double V" campaign against fascism at home and abroad with great enthusiasm and optimism. Yet, as a critical, revisionist historian, he knew that blacks, after fighting for white Americans in the American Revolution, the War of 1812, the Civil War, the Spanish American War, and World War I, still were mired in institutional racism, racial violence, and everyday discrimination on American soil. Perhaps his analysis of the historical record suggested that this was the time when white Americans were finally going to acknowledge their humanity. He did not welcome the harsh realities of the war; indeed, in the immediate aftermath of the World War II, he became the pacifist he once was in the 1920s. "War . . . is, in most cases, inexcusable and always abominable. Peace must be considered the normal state of society," Greene wrote. "It must be striven for, prepared for with all the fervor that society from time to time immemorial has devoted to war."[53]

8 Life at Lincoln University, 1944–50

THE MID- TO LATE 1940S was an especially trying and busy time for Lorenzo Johnston Greene. In addition to completing his dissertation in 1942 and the death of Carter Woodson in 1950, he became increasingly disenchanted with Lincoln University; he not only sought employment elsewhere, but he also struggled with President Sherman Scruggs and a special committee over a salary increase. Despite this preoccupation and distraction, Greene continued to be active as a scholar, writing a handful of published and unpublished articles and book reviews, working hard to make a trilogy out of his work on colonial New England, and serving as the editor for Lincoln's short-lived yet impressive *Midwest Journal.*

Shortly before completing his dissertation, Greene applied for positions at several different colleges in New York. The teaching load was heavy at Lincoln, and he wanted to gain more recognition. Furthermore, he was searching for a more thriving intellectual atmosphere. Being located in the East would have given him easy access to explore documents dealing with colonial New England. None of the white colleges where he applied responded to him. Greene also showed interest in teaching at Tennessee A&I State College; he and his wife taught there during the summer of 1944. Shortly thereafter, Greene wrote the school's president, Dr. Walter S. Davis, and indicated that both he and his wife would be interested in working there if they could join the faculty in June 1945, if Mrs. Greene could receive $250 per month for ten months, if Greene could receive a salary comparable to his current income at Lincoln, and if he could become head of the History Department.[1] Greene's plan did not materialize.

Despite his dissatisfaction with Lincoln University, by the mid-1940s, Greene had moved slowly up its academic ladder. During the 1943–44 academic year, he served as the acting head of the history department; by 1945, the department consisted of no more than three members, including Greene. It was while he was in this position that he challenged the university for a higher salary. In the spring of 1944, Greene first recommended to Lincoln's Dean Dawson that his salary be made equal to that of the regular department head, $360 per month—for him, a raise of about $40 per month. On April 7, 1944, Dawson brought Greene's request to President Scruggs, but he did not recommend that his salary be increased. Toward the end of the month, the dean informed Greene that he did not believe that he deserved a raise. Several weeks later, Greene wrote back to the dean and requested "that a faculty committee be appointed to pass upon the merits of my request and to show cause, if necessary, why I should not be paid a salary equal to that of a department head."

During the summer of 1944, Greene, Dawson, William Sherman Savage, and Scruggs met to work out Greene's case. On September 9, Scruggs informed Greene that he had decided to award him a salary increase from $310 to $335 monthly, effective September 1. Still unsatisfied, Greene wrote a letter to Scruggs on September 15 outlining his case. He thanked Scruggs and members of the board of curators for the small raise, but he added that he still wanted to be accorded the "extra compensation" given to department heads based on his training and services to Lincoln, which "are equal to, or, in some cases, even surpass those of department heads." Greene believed that his case was an example of the inequalities scarring Lincoln. In closing, he assured Scruggs that as long as he was connected with Lincoln, he would continue to work hard toward building the "highest type of educational institution." A raise in his salary, he added, would facilitate achieving this goal at a much quicker pace.[2]

Greene had believed that in the spring of 1945 "a settlement" and "proper adjustment" would be made. In early March 1945, Greene wrote to Scruggs with confidence, reminding him that he hoped his salary demands would be met.[3] Scruggs, however, informed Greene that he had misunderstood the conclusions reached at the conference. According to Scruggs, he never promised to meet Greene's demands. He told Greene that he had appointed a special committee to deal with his case and to consider—based upon "the views that Professor Greene holds . . . , the supporting data which he presents," and "all available sources"—whether or not he deserved the salary increase he proposed. Scruggs assured Greene that this investigation would not have any negative consequences, like demotion or dismissal. He also told Greene that he could supply the committee with "any materials" to be considered, and that Greene had the right to appear before the committee "before or anytime after it begins its work."[4]

Scruggs's special committee included W. R. Ralbot, U. S. Maxwell, W. W. Dowdy, G. R. Cotton, and O. A. Fuller. Serving as an outside consultant and advisor to the committee was C. F. Littell, a professor of history and political science at Cornell College, Mt. Vernon, Iowa. Scruggs expected a report from the committee by May 1, 1945.[5] Several days later, Greene challenged the investigation procedure, pointedly critiquing the criteria for promotion in rank and salary as they appeared in Lincoln's handbook. He wanted to be judged based on his training and preparation for his job, teaching effectiveness, scholarship and professional standing, research, personal character, as well as his various community service activities. "I seek no special consideration. Neither do I expect that the Committee will establish new standards for my appraisal which are not in harmony with the criteria already adopted by the University for such purposes," Greene said, concluding, "I merely hold that a comparative evaluation of my services to the University, using the above criteria as a yardstick, should enable me to receive compensation equal to that of any other professor in the College of Liberal Arts."[6]

Throughout March and part of April 1945, it appears that the committee met and began investigating Greene's case. On April 25, Greene presented his case in person and in the form of a letter. His presentation included fifteen pages of text and several exhibits of evidence that, though brief, served as a useful window into Greene's scholarship, teaching, and social activism from the mid-1920s through the mid-1940s. He discussed his training since his days at Howard, highlighting his work with the Association for the Study of Negro Life and History (ASNLH). In order to demonstrate the effectiveness of his teaching, he wrote, at random, to fifteen students whom he had taught between 1933 and 1943. He asked them to assess his teaching. Ten students responded, representing in his estimation "several points of view." Greene also submitted many informal statements from students, which he noted were collected months before the formal investigation began.[7]

The strongest part of Greene's claim rested in his history of community service. He divided this work into three categories: "(a) services to the school community, (b) services to the community in which the school is located and (c) services outside the community in which the school is located." As an active professor on campus, Greene noted that he had been a member of many committees since 1933, spoke to faculty and students "on innumerable occasions," had been appointed in 1936 by the board of curators to help evaluate Lincoln, and strove to break down the social barriers separating students and faculty. He mentioned that after he was married in 1941, he often held his classes at his home and "constantly" advised students on various issues. He even "frequently" gave students "material assistance." In terms of off-campus community service, Greene highlighted that he had spoken at various venues about a range of issues—education, black history, civil rights, World War II, and race relations. He highlighted his role in reforming segregated education, helping destitute sharecroppers in southeast Missouri, and in spearheading an antilynching campaign.[8]

Greene's professional work seemed equally as impressive. He listed five journal articles, five newspaper articles, and five books he had authored or co-authored. He noted that he was working on three articles and two books complementing *The Negro in Colonial New England, 1620–1776*. He explained that the paucity in his publications while at Lincoln could be best explained by the fact that he strategically chose not to publish the findings of his dissertation as articles or the text of any of his countless speeches. He maintained that his professional standing could be determined by his membership in professional societies, his honors, and the publication and public reception of his dissertation and other publications under the auspices of the ASNLH. According to Greene's evidence, he was a well-known historian who belonged to ten professional societies and who had significantly contributed to the American historical profession. Greene ended his plea thanking the committee for their consideration; he also asked that if he were denied his request, then the committee should "show cause" why he "should not receive a salary equal to that of the higher paid professors in the Liberal Arts College."[9]

On December 7, 1945, under the leadership of Chairman Walter R. Talbot, the special committee laid out its final responses to Greene's claims, challenging Greene on each of the criteria by which he was judged. They opened their consideration of the case by indicating that they did not agree with Greene that it was their duty to "show cause" with regard to why he should not be granted the salary he desired. They stressed that their decision would be based largely upon the evidence Greene supplied them with, therefore placing the burden on him. Their response ran nearly fifty pages.[10]

The committee believed that Greene had training that met all of the requirements of the university, yet they questioned the fact that most of his nonacademic experience was acquired before he joined Lincoln's staff. They disagreed with Greene's method of ascertaining his teaching effectiveness and thought that the letters he solicited from students were not objective, implying that Greene may have been "suggestive" in seeking these evaluations. On November 12, the committee therefore asked the history department head about Greene's teaching methods. According to the committee, he responded that Greene worked better with graduate students than with undergraduates mainly because he was known to give his students demanding assignments of "great length."

The biggest blow the committee delivered to Greene was their dismissal of his community service. They said that merely belonging to a committee on campus or to an organization did not mean anything. They added that in the 1943–44 school year, Dean Dawson told the president that Greene "had not rendered his services to the various committees of the faculty as he is capable of doing." While they acknowledged that he was an active speaker, they pointed out that he did not adequately describe the nature of his speeches. They challenged his assertion that his 1936 "Needs of the Negroes of Missouri in Respect to Higher Education" was a significant document. The committee credited Greene somewhat for interacting with students outside the classroom and for fostering better faculty-student relationships. However, they claimed that as president of the Faculty Club, Greene was quite ineffective and was even opposed by other faculty members.

The committee recognized that Greene was a committed activist, but for the purposes of their review they decided not to consider activities "which did not have their origins at some time prior to the 1944–45 school year." They claimed that while he provided an impressive list of speaking engagements, the public relations office at the university did not list Greene as a highly sought-after speaker. They implied that since he was only requested to speak outside the walls of Lincoln twice, he was not as effective as he had implied in his report of April 25. The committee ignored the fact that as a grassroots lecturer, Greene spoke before audiences without making formal arrangements through the university. Greene did his own advertising and arranged his speeches himself. He also served as manager for his wife in her music career.[11]

The final and perhaps most painful criticism the committee delivered to Greene concerned his scholarship. They said that after arriving at Lincoln, Greene's small list of publications was "hardly suggestive of a prolific writer or even an energetic worker." Though they had no choice except to admit that his *The Negro in Colonial New England* was widely praised, they belittled it by positing that its acclaim was "due in part to the fact that the field and subject are intelligible to the ordinary man." Other, more technical dissertations, they continued, received much less attention. This group of nonhistorians implied that Greene's work was not a piece of scientific scholarship.

The special committee concluded that Greene did not offer evidence of "extraordinary strength" and, therefore, did not demonstrate that he deserved a higher salary. In their estimation, he still needed to furnish proof and data indicating that he was of great worth to Lincoln. They concluded that he should only be granted a raise in salary that equaled the average size of salary increases granted by the university. They then said that Greene could determine further raises based upon his publication record. "As Dr. Greene increases his scholarly production while at Lincoln and as he increases his contributions to the school, his salary should be increased just as any professor who might do more scholarly work and fulfill all his duties within the school should expect increases in salary," the committee concluded.[12]

This incident helps shed some light on obstacles faced by black scholars during the era of segregation at historically black colleges and universities. Greene's peers dismissed and belittled his case. On December 10, 1945, the committee gave Greene a copy of their preliminary report so that he could make some corrections. One can clearly sense Greene's anger with the committee members in his insightful, critical margin notes. At one point, when the committee accused him of following an "improper procedure" and implied that his report was "courageous or foolhardy," Greene penciled in that "such statements are liable for slander!"[13] Greene's case revealed other things and had other consequences. He was a pioneer in many ways. He was one of the first professors to challenge the Lincoln administration in this manner, as evidenced by the many subsequent general recommendations proposed by the special committee—that the university adopt policies concerning the role of department heads and acting heads; revise its methods for evaluating appointment, promotion, and salary increases; keep better records; and keep faculty up to date with all regulations concerning cases like Greene's.

The final corrected copy of the special committee's examination of Greene's case was presented to President Scruggs on July 5, 1946, more than a year after Greene initiated his request. They considered the case finished. Theirs, however, was not the final word. "You will recall that the Special Committee, headed by the great G. Robert Cotton, sought to deny my request for equality of compensation, only to have a University of Chicago man grant my claim," Greene shared with a friend in April 1948.[14]

❖ ❖ ❖

Greene did not stop his efforts at reforming Lincoln's treatment of its faculty. Sometime in the late 1940s, he and some other concerned faculty members wrote to the president and the board of curators concerning "the problem of implementing the salary equalization principle." As early as May 1942, the board indicated that it would "strive continuously" to increase the salaries of Lincoln University faculty members until the compensation was equal to that of professors at the University of Missouri. The average salary differential from 1942 until 1948 between the highest-paid full professors at Lincoln and the University of Missouri amounted to $3,398, in favor of the University of Missouri professors. When Greene made his complaint during the 1944–45 academic year, his colleagues were especially underpaid: the highest-paid professor at the University of Missouri commanded $7,635, while his counterpart at Lincoln only made $3,600.[15]

The representatives of Lincoln's instructional faculty challenged the board of curators to raise the standards of Lincoln with respect to its fundamental physical environment and intellectual atmosphere. They stressed, as Greene had years earlier, that better salaries were "the necessary first step" in bridging the gap between salaries at Lincoln and the University of Missouri. The faculty further informed the board that Lincoln had fallen behind other black colleges and universities, pointing out that many leading professors left Lincoln for much better salaries elsewhere and that even some high school teachers with lower qualifications were making more money than some Lincoln professors.

Greene also vented his anger against Lincoln to his close friends, commenting that Lincoln seemed to be preoccupied with the "external trappings" rather than with "the real and worthwhile things." He lamented that teachers were not funded to attend professional meetings and that for about six months they did not even have toilet paper for the students. He also remarked that "inter-faculty division" was at an all-time high since department heads were seeking to increase salaries, an attempt "to revive the same old evil against which I fought for three years."[16]

Despite the struggles Greene waged with administrators, he continued to be an active scholar throughout the 1940s. *The Negro in Colonial New England, 1620–1776* was his most significant historical publication and certainly earned him fame as a published historian. His two major articles in this period were published in 1944 in the *Journal of Negro History* and *Phylon*. In "The New England Negro As Seen in Advertisements for Runaway Slaves," Greene called for a more creative approach to studying slavery. He considered this research a "relatively untouched phase of American Negro

Slavery." In surveying sixty-two New England newspaper advertisements from 1718 until 1784, he sought to shed some light on slaves' personalities. He touched upon slaves' employment, birthplaces, names, ages, sex, physical characteristics, peculiar personal traits, attire, and personal possessions. "For this reason," he said, "advertisements for runaway slaves are a mine of invaluable information—information which, when collected, analyzed and synthesized, afford an otherwise unobtainable picture of the slave personality." According to Greene, for example, slaves carefully calculated their flights during the "desirable season," late summer and early fall. Not only could they more easily acquire basic provisions, but they also avoided flight during the long, cold winter. In Greene's estimation, the advertisements also revealed aspects of the master class's personality.[17]

In the same year, Greene published a refreshing article on eighteenth century slave mutinies during the Middle Passage aboard New England vessels. He reasoned that such a study was necessary because leading scholars of slave revolts, including Herbert Aptheker, Joseph C. Carroll, and Harvey Wish, had not addressed one of the first acts "in the tragic drama of the Negro's continuous struggle for freedom." According to Greene, his ancestors "seized every opportunity to escape enslavement or to end their suffering." Attempting to kill the crew and return to African was a frequent tactic. Though the captured Africans did not have the weapons or the organizational structure of the crews, they did, Greene stressed, have numbers and an "insatiable desire for liberty."[18] Based on a careful examination of firsthand accounts from Elizabeth Donnan's four-volume catalog of primary sources and other slave traders' journals, Greene described many of the slave revolts aboard New England slave ships, concluding that there were probably more unsuccessful revolts than successful ones, that Rhode Island slavers had the most rebellions, and that even though the American Revolution paved the way for the abolition of the slave trade in major New England states by the 1780s, Puritan merchants maintained an illegal slave trade, and uprisings continued to take place on these vessels. Greene concluded his brief article in a tone that would be echoed decades later by Vincent Harding in his classic, *There Is a River:*

> The foregoing insurrections portray but a single scene in the first act of a mighty drama for freedom, in which African slaves were the principal actors and the New England slave ships the stage. To complete the act, it is necessary to set forth similar struggles aboard other American vessels and ships of all the other nationalities which participated in the trade. Thus would be

> told the epic tragedy of battles for freedom fought by millions of blacks, on thousands of ships over a span of three and a half centuries. Such a work, especially for American slave ships, would make an heroic prelude for the second act in the drama—the Negro's struggle for liberty on American soil—. . . and overthrow completely the fiction that the Negro tamely submitted to enslavement.[19]

Several years after he completed his dissertation, Greene began publishing articles that were more emotional. He meshed meticulous scientific research with some emotional outpourings. Du Bois's *Phylon* was a perfect forum for such efforts.

❖ ❖ ❖

Throughout the 1940s, Woodson solicited Greene's help as a book reviewer for the *Journal.* At no point in his career was Greene the prolific book reviewer Woodson was. This was unfortunate, because Greene was a very critical thinker who had the ability to find the most intricate oversights and problems with books. In 1948, he reviewed John Hope Franklin's *From Slavery to Freedom* (1947) in the *Journal of Negro Education.* Like most reviewers, Greene welcomed Franklin's work, deeming it "the most authoritative as well as the most readable synthesis of the Negro in America that exists in print." Yet, in the tradition of Woodson, he pointed out in detail the "few minor imperfections" and "occasional lapses from the general high standard maintained throughout the work." His most profound criticism concerned the title. Greene believed that a more accurate title would have been *From Freedom to Slavery.* He asserted that during the last five hundred years, African Americans had been waging a struggle to regain their freedom. Before slavery and the slave trade, Greene noted that blacks in Africa "had built up independent states of their own with relatively high civilizations."[20]

After *The Negro in Colonial New England, 1620–1776* was published, Greene worked on many articles dealing with New England and struggled to make his work part of a trilogy. Late in 1945, Greene asked President Scruggs if he could take a leave of absence at half salary from February until September 1946 so that he could conduct research at libraries in New England, New York, and Washington, D.C., in order to complete a study entitled *The Abolition of Slavery in New England, 1638–1784.* This monograph, the last of a proposed trilogy, would address the origins, evolution, and significance of antislavery in seventeenth- and eighteenth-century New England. Greene planned to explore the effects of humanitarianism and the "equalitarian philosophy" of the

Revolutionary era on antislavery sentiments and abolition in New England. He pronounced that his study would be especially unique because he planned to explore "abolition efforts by the slaves themselves." While Columbia University Press expressed interest in Greene's work in October 1945, he still needed to raise about forty-eight hundred dollars in order to complete the study. Greene told Scruggs that the General Board of Education had already agreed to grant him three thousand dollars and that his study was going to fill a great gap in American social history.[21] Scruggs granted Greene's request.

Between February and September 1946, Greene made significant progress. He had collected "a large amount of data" from the Library of Congress, the New York Historical Society, the State Library of Massachusetts, the Yale University Library, and the Connecticut Historical Society and the State Library. He carefully sifted through various troves of primary documents "for the precious nuggets which they occasionally yielded." He collected data that was previously unknown to researchers. He also spoke with descendants of people related to many New England abolitionists. In mid-October 1946, Greene asked President Scruggs if he would give him another leave of absence from February 1 until September 15, 1947, at half salary so that he could complete the study. He explained that he still needed to visit some "key repositories," and that collecting primary documents and securing photostats had been difficult. He also needed to expand the time frame of the study through 1800. Several months later, Scruggs informed Greene that a special leave of absence with a stipend of $1,912.50 from February 1 until August 31, 1947 was approved. About a month earlier, the General Board of Education agreed (after some deliberation and after Scruggs had written to them several times) to contribute two thousand dollars toward Greene's work, to be distributed from February until October 1947.[22]

After another nine months, Greene did not complete his study. In late December 1947 he informed Scruggs that he had assembled "virtually all the data for the study" (much of which is currently in his personal papers housed at the Library of Congress). Greene had not yet completed the study because he was still busy filing the data and beginning the actual writing processes. Teaching "and its incidental duties" took up a great deal of his energy; he was probably teaching at least three separate courses, each requiring unique preparation. Greene told Scruggs that if the university supplied him with a stenographer and reduced his teaching load, he would be able to finish the study "sometime in the ensuing year." Though Greene never published the study, he made some important findings previously unknown to American historians.

❖ ❖ ❖

In the late 1940s, Greene called for an analysis of slave resistance. He shared the views of his contemporaries like Joseph C. Carroll, author of *Slave Insurrections in the United States, 1800–1865* (1938); Raymond and Alice Bauer, who published a groundbreaking article on the intricacies of slave resistance in the *Journal of Negro History* (1942); and Herbert Aptheker, who published *American Negro Slave Revolts* in 1943. Greene also posited that the military history of New England during the American Revolution needed to be "largely rewritten," taking into consideration the role of blacks in the war. He also contemplated publishing a book of primary sources on New England blacks.

During this period, Greene became the editor of the *Lincoln University Research Journal,* renamed the *Lincoln University Journal* and then, by 1949, the *Midwest Journal.* In the 1930s and 1940s, several black colleges founded and subsidized their own scholarly magazines, the most popular being the *Journal of Negro Education,* founded at Howard University in 1932 by Charles H. Thompson, and *Phylon* of Atlanta University, established in 1940. In 1946, Lincoln joined the ranks of these historically black universities when the school's legislative faculty voted to create a scholarly magazine through which its faculty could publish their research and findings. The name of the journal was the *Lincoln University Bulletin;* its first issue appeared during the summer of 1947.

On November 21, 1947, Sidney J. Reedy and Cecil Blue met at Greene's home in order to draw up some "concrete suggestions" for the editorial committee and staff of the *Lincoln University Bulletin.* The main thrust of the meeting was Greene's suggestion that a plan for a new magazine with a new name, set of policies, agenda, and program be presented to the faculty. At this meeting, Greene defined the new magazine, which he proposed be named the *Midwest Journal,* the *Midwest Review,* or the *Midwest Record,* as being "a vehicle of expression for creative writing (including fiction, poetry, drama, literary criticism, etc.) and for writing of a scholarly nature." Greene welcomed all subject matter, except "highly specialized" studies that would only be understood by a select group of scholars. He wanted to establish a wide readership. The length of the articles was set at about five thousand words. Greene suggested that the journal have three departments—articles, documents, and book reviews—and that it be published as an annual. He reasoned that it could be published more frequently if there was interest.

At this initial meeting, he said that he wanted to have the first volume published on May 15. He proposed that the first deadline for submission be March 15. There were many things essential to the new journal. Greene suggested that they put forth requests for "necessary office space, equipment, materials, secretarial help, etc."[23]

On January 21, 1948, "the Legislative Faculty of the University approved the recommendation of the Editorial Board, authorizing an enlargement in scope of the *Lincoln University Research Journal,* thereby making the magazine to be devoted to both research and creative writing." In mid-March 1948, Greene described the journal to his colleagues as being one that sought to stimulate research and creative writing among Lincoln's faculty. Throughout March 1948, Greene solicited articles from many important historians and intellectuals, including Rayford W. Logan, Luther Porter Jackson, C. Eric Williams, Marion Thompson Wright, Herbert Aptheker, Sterling Brown, Benjamin Quarles, Georgia Douglas Johnson, and Lois Mailou Jones. Greene struggled to get contributors and was under great pressure. "I am appealing to you in my 'hour of extremity' . . . . Will you send us a contribution for this number? The subject we shall gladly leave to you," Greene inquired of both Sterling Brown and Benjamin Quarles. He extended the same type of invitation to many other colleagues, although he was a little more frank with his friend Luther P. Jackson: "Will you do me a big favor? Lincoln University has decided to publish a magazine . . . I have had the 'misfortune' to be appointed Editor. You can guess the rest. In short, I need your help." While everyone he contacted supported his efforts, many were simply too busy to contribute anything at such short notice. Greene and his associates were perhaps a bit overly optimistic in thinking that they would be able to bring the first issue out even by June 15, 1948, only a few months after they were really becoming established and organized.[24]

In August 1948, Greene sent out a letter to his Lincoln colleagues informing them to be patient, that the *Midwest Journal* would "see the light of day" very shortly—by the early fall, he hoped. "Fact is, we've been afflicted with 'beginner's woe.' Remember, we're starting from scratch; building from the ground up. We've had trouble getting our Staff officially set up so that we could function with maximum efficiently; trouble getting regular, efficient secretarial help," Greene confessed. "The task of editing has been . . . heavy . . . and in addition to this responsibility, the Editor carried a full teaching schedule the summer." The editors and staff also spent a great deal of energy debating the function and nature of the journal. They debated whether the magazine should be interracial in its scope or whether it should be devoted to black Americans. None of the editors had any experience in publishing a magazine and they were not prepared for all of the problems that came with the territory.[25]

The first issue of the journal appeared in March 1949. Roughly six hundred copies were printed and "widely distributed" throughout the United States and abroad. Free copies were sent to members of the Lincoln University faculty and staff, "outstanding officials of the state and nation," leading scholars, and various libraries, public and private, including the United Nations Library. Greene also sent a copy to President Truman. "It is not a perfect job by any means," Greene humbly told L. D. Reddick in late March.[26] Greene was most disturbed by the printing job, which was done at Lincoln. Others, however, did not seem to be bothered by what the editor critiqued. The first volume featured scholarship of many prominent scholars such as Herbert Aptheker, John Hope Franklin, Greene himself, Rayford Logan, Benjamin Quarles, and Melvin B. Tolson. Tolson's poem, "The Negro Scholar," was one of the most widely praised pieces. This professor of English at Langston University in Langston, Oklahoma, told Greene that his poem was "the first attempt to set forth the tenets of the Negro scholar in poetry." Tolson hailed the black scholar as being a "genealogist" of his people, a steady-handed surgeon who removed lies infecting "the truth of race." Tolson outlined the role of the black scholar in a similar manner to Woodson and Greene:

> The Negro scholar must uproot the lies
> Of ermine classes, puncture sophistries,
> Break through dilemmas, rip the fallacies
> Between his people and the Bill of Rights.
>
> The Negro scholar is prophecy,
> A Cloud by day, a pillar of fire by night,
> Seen by black slaves upon the auction block,
> Seen by black rebels with the grapes of wrath.
>
> The Negro scholar is a Daniel Boone
> Blazing a trail for Black America[27]

Famous black intellectuals also featured their scholarship in the pages of the *Midwest Journal* before 1950, including Langston Hughes and W. E. B. Du Bois.

The first volume of the journal was universally praised. In early August 1949, Greene showed his colleagues more than twenty positive reviews by leading black and white scholars. "The journal is exerting an influence toward increasing the academic prestige of Lincoln University throughout the country," Greene assured his co-workers. "As such, it can be an important factor in the development of more desirable public relations for the university." By summer 1949, the editors were receiving unsolicited subscriptions from individuals, scholars, libraries, and even from subscription agencies. Greene was fairly optimistic, believing that at least part of the cost of publication could be paid off by subscriptions.[28]

❖ ❖ ❖

While Greene clearly used the *Midwest Journal* as a vehicle for research and creative writing as well as for a strong public relations tool for Lincoln University, he also employed it as a forum for radical politics. When the Communist Party USA (CPUSA) was founded in 1917, anti-Communist thought in America escalated. The Red Scare or "Palmer Raids" of 1919–1920 gave rise to an American anti-Communist ideology. Beginning in the 1940s, organizations such as the FBI, the Chamber of Commerce, the American Civil Liberties Union, and the House Un-American Activities Committee formed an informal network for opposing Communists.

In the post–World War II era, anti-Communist thought reached a peak. Hoover proclaimed that American Communists were espionage agents following orders from the Soviet Union. In the late 1940s, the CPUSA was the target for the government's anti-Communist beliefs. Sparked by Senator Eugene McCarthy's report of July 1950, the McCarthy era became the most anti-Communist period in American history. As the lives of W. E. B. Du Bois and Paul Robeson demonstrate—and as Gerald Horne has demonstrated in his studies on Ben Chavis, William Patterson, and the Civil Rights Congress—for African Americans to align themselves with Communism during the post–World War II period was especially dangerous.[29]

In the midst of this wave of anti-Communism, Greene published two highly controversial articles, leading the government to identify him as a Communist. In "Role of Students in China's Struggle," published in the *Midwest Journal* in the summer of 1949, Shu-yi Yang celebrated Chinese Communists as the emancipating force in China. Then, in the winter of 1949, Du Bois published an article in the journal entitled "The Freedom to Learn." He suggested that Americans needed to introduce a "free and open" system of education by which students could study Marx and Communism. According to Gary R. Kremer, shortly after Du Bois's essay was published, one Saturday while Greene was working in his office at Lincoln, a federal agent visited him and asked him questions about his political agenda and that of the journal. In 1986, by means of the Freedom of Information Act, Kremer obtained documents from the Justice Department that indicated the government had a detailed file on the *Midwest Journal*.[30]

Roughly a year after the first issue of the *Midwest Journal* appeared, four major figures in the black struggle for social justice and equality died: Charles Drew (1904–1950), Charles Hamilton Houston (1895–1950), Luther Porter Jackson (1892–1950), and Carter G. Woodson (1875–1950). The ASNLH founder's sudden death on April 3, 1950, shocked his co-workers. Shortly after Woodson's funeral, Greene, Wesley, and other Woodson "Boys"—"Franklin, Reddick, Jackson, et al."—met at the Association's office "to decide whether the Association would continue." Woodson's associates and especially the Association's executive council realized that their deceased leader truly *was* the ASNLH. They also discovered that the Association's financial status was in shambles. The first dilemma facing the organization was selecting a new director-editor, a competent successor to the man of "Spartan-like existence."

Woodson left behind a will, drawn up in the 1930s. It empowered the heads of the history departments at Atlanta, Fisk, and Howard Universities with "some authority in selecting the editor." Due to the sudden nature of Woodson's death, the Association's executive council was unprepared. In this state of emergency, about a month after Woodson's death, the Association's president, Mary McLeod Bethune, appointed Rayford W. Logan to succeed Woodson as director-editor.[31]

This choice was an interesting and controversial one. According to one of Woodson's close colleagues, Woodson "despised and loathed" Logan ever since he sided with Anson Phelps Stokes and Thomas Jones in working on a rival encyclopedia on Africa in 1936. Luther Porter Jackson would probably have succeeded Woodson had he not died in the same month and year. Other potential successors included Greene, Reddick, and Franklin. Nonetheless, on June 24 and October 28, the executive council supported Bethune's decision. According to Kenneth Janken, Logan's "eighteen-month stewardship was, like many of his endeavors, tempestuous yet productive." Logan expanded the *Journal of Negro History* to include articles on "anything that touched the lives of African Americans." He also sought to repair the perilous financial status of the Association and change its business management system. He even brought in an outside auditor to assess the situation. William Brewer and Louis R. Mehlinger, among others, were vehemently opposed to Logan's new tactics. They were fiercely pro-Woodson and could not accept that a "traducer," in their words, could succeed their beloved friend.

On December 18, 1951, Logan sent a letter of resignation to Charles H. Wesley: the Howard University history professor could not stand working under the constant challenges of Brewer, Mehlinger, and others any longer.[32] The functions of the director-editor in matters of policymaking were taken over by then-president Charles H. Wesley. Brewer replaced Logan as the editor of the *Journal* from 1952 until his sudden death in October 1970.

During Logan's brief reign as director-editor, Woodson's other associates and disciples decided to carry on the torch in their own manner. Some of those who met at the Association office after Woodson's funeral established a committee to draw up new constitution for the ASNLH; Greene was elected the committee's chair, a position he did not seek out. During the fall of 1950, Greene worked on drafting a new constitution for the Association so that "never again will the organization be thrown in a state of chaos because of the death or defection of any one individual." Some of his initial thoughts were first articulated in September 1950. "We must make changes," he told Reddick: "In my opinion, the Director, Business Manager, Editor of publications, and so forth, must have separate and distinct responsibilities. I agree too, that new blood should appear on the Council."

In early October, Greene sent a copy of a constitution that he had been working on to Reddick and Brewer for constructive criticism. Brewer offered Greene many pointers. He instructed Greene that he needed to clarify the functions of the various officials, especially the editor of the *Journal* and the director of the ASNLH. He pointed out that he needed to include a detailed description of a secretary-treasurer and a business manager. Brewer warned Greene against placing too great a burden on the director, since he seriously doubted if anyone could be as devoted to the cause as Woodson was. He sent Greene a copy of the constitution of the American Historical Association "for whatever light which it may afford." Brewer also suggested that Greene, with the help of others, establish a program committee so that the director would not have all the power. In closing, Brewer stressed to Greene that in order for the ASNLH to continue, "Dr. Woodson's loyal disciples" would have to "rally to almost any reasonable sacrifice."[33]

Several weeks later, Greene responded to Brewer's criticisms and suggestions, and clarified his vision of the new constitution. Greene envisioned that, unlike during Woodson's reign, the director and the editor would be two different people with two distinctly different job descriptions. Greene thought that the directorship would be best filled by "a comparatively young man" trained in history. The job would be "largely a promotional one," that is, the director would devote a lot of his time to "promoting the welfare of the Association, and raising funds for the same." In Greene's vision, the editors of both the *Journal* and the *Bulletin* would not be paid for their services. They would take charge of the journals as volunteers to the cause. Greene placed all of the financial and business matters of the ASNLH and the Associated Publishers within the hands of a business manager. He agreed with Brewer's suggestion for establishing a program committee and initiating some fundraisers.[34]

Men dominated Greene's vision of the Association's leadership. While he may have respected Bethune as president of the ASNLH, apparently he did not believe that there were any black women historians qualified to serve as director or editor. He did not consider empowering a black female scholar in a leadership position in the ASNLH until several decades later. In the mid-1980s, Greene supported electing Darlene Clark Hine, then vice provost and a professor of history at Purdue University, to the Association presidency. "It is time the ASALH had a woman scholar as President," Greene wrote to Hine. "I am in your corner."[35] Greene was not as progressive as Woodson in how he viewed black women's roles in history or contemporary leadership positions.

A week after Greene responded to Brewer's comments, on October 28 and 29, 1950, during the ASNLH's thirty-fifth annual meeting held in Atlanta at several of the black colleges in the area, the executive council held "special" business meetings to discuss the future of the Association. Greene's ideas for a new constitution were presented to the council in his absence (he was at home resting at the advice of his physician), but they were pushed aside "without careful consideration" because article 6 of the constitution at the time forbade "any changes unless previously approved by the Executive Council." After hearing this from his Lincoln colleague, William Sherman Savage, Greene said that he would "have yielded on this technical point." He agreed, based upon the vote of the majority, that postponing such action was legitimate.

L. D. Reddick, however, refused to sit back and let his friend's "practical" suggestions go unnoticed. On November 1, 1950, he submitted a letter of resignation from the executive council and essentially severed "all official connections" he had to the ASNLH. He was deeply disturbed with the manner in which two members of the administration, Logan and Wesley, handled the business session of the Atlanta convention. He was opposed to the "brushing aside" of Greene's constitutional revisions. Like Greene, he strongly believed that the director-editor position needed to be abolished. He championed the idea that the *Journal* and the *Bulletin* be edited by one or two people and that the director be fully dedicated to his position. He did not feel that Logan could perform adequately while still holding a full-time job at Howard University. He also disagreed with how Logan dismissed his proposition to compile a book of essays in memory of Woodson, and he took issue with the fact that Logan and others did not follow Woodson's will concerning the selection of editorial personnel. Reddick concluded his letter with a direct attack on Logan and Wesley, proclaiming that they were not living up to Woodson's ideals and even working counter to the Association's best interests: "I no longer have confidence in two key members of the present administration of the Association. I would suspect them. I would watch for their subtle moves. I would scrutinize the circle of friends within which honor and power would be passed . . . Please understand, I am not saying that Dr. Logan and Dr. Wesley would behave in this manner. But I know that I would suspect them of doing so. I would stand guard against their every move and might then become an obstructionist."[36]

After this incident, Greene found himself caught in the middle of a heated feud. He was close to both Logan and Reddick and saw validity in each man's position. He even told them that he supported parts of their respective positions. While Greene agreed with his intentions and goals, he did not agree with Reddick's tactics. Greene believed that Woodson's successors should have been more concerned with remaining unified, strengthening the organization, and tolerating each other's views. In early November, Greene assured Logan that he understood his stance and that he would try to change Reddick's mind. Greene then wrote to Reddick telling him that he agreed with him on the specific constitutional changes he championed. However, Greene suggested to his friend that resigning was not the solution. He asked Reddick to follow his example: "The way to make the Association the instrument of Negro uplift, in my opinion, is not to resign when defeated on an issue, but to stay in there and keep fighting. The Association needs your point of view," Greene consoled his close friend. "It needs your enthusiasm. It needs someone like you. . . . I too shared your disappointment, but I am determined to stay in and fight for the set-up best calculated to strengthen the Association." Not surprisingly, Logan did not see Reddick's critique in the same light as Greene saw it. In mid-November, he sent a lengthy, point-by-point rejoinder to Reddick's letter to Greene and to the members of the Executive Council. Ultimately, Logan believed that his disappointed colleague's letter was a "flagrant attempt to sow distrust and to arouse dissension within the Association."[37]

Despite the problems dividing the Association and the taxing role Greene assumed as one of the key advisors to various parties, the *Midwest Journal* under Greene's guidance continued to blossom in the early 1950s. Some time between May and August 1952, the three editors of the journal informed President Scruggs of the progress they had made within the past four years: the journal was published semiannually at six hundred copies per printing, distributed throughout the world, and "men and women of all races" were contributors. Greene told Scruggs that as of May 1952, subscriptions totaled 130, "going mainly to libraries, . . . learned societies, educators, and laymen." The journal was also exchanged with about forty magazines from all over the United States and the world. Still, Greene and the other editors recognized that they had a host of obstacles standing in their path. They shared with Scruggs the great struggles in getting more participation from Lincoln faculty members and in making the journal a self-sustaining venture. Scruggs appears to have supported Greene's and his associates' efforts, at least on paper. In early August 1952, he sent copies of the twelve-page progress report to Lincoln faculty members, praising the work of the editorial staff and asking the faculty to read the journal's pages "with a growing desire to encourage its wide dissemination among readers like yourself."[38]

So the early 1950s seemed to forecast a promising future for the *Midwest Journal.* This bright future, however, turned cloudy in the middle of the decade. On June 20, 1955, the board of curators decided that the *Midwest Journal* would operate for the last time from the fiscal year beginning July 1, 1955, and ending June 30, 1956, with funding amounting to merely $1,750. On June 30, 1955, Scruggs informed Greene of this decision: "I am sorry that we do not have the money to carry on this publication. . . . As you know, publication is an expensive thing." As the end of the fiscal year approached, Greene asked Acting President Earl E. Dawson whether or not the *Midwest Journal* could have an extended life. On June 9, 1956, Dawson informed Greene that there were not adequate funds to support the journal after June 30. Greene "hated to see" the journal "cut off" since it had established such a wide readership, helped the university, and existed on a small printing budget. Greene voiced his disappointed:

> I realize that in your position the responsibility is yours to convince the curators how the aims and purposes of the University might he best advanced. Since the *Journal* is not considered essential to that program, I can understand your reluctance to continue to support the *Journal* since, in your opinion, to do so would impair other services to the University. I trust, however, that the elimination of the *Journal* at this time will not adversely affect the tendency of members of the staff to engage in research presently stimulated

in part by the knowledge that a vehicle was at hand for the publication of their findings.[39]

In its short existence of roughly eight years, the *Midwest Journal* under Greene's editorship accomplished a great deal. Not only did it bring attention and recognition to Lincoln University, but it also served as an important outlet for various scholars' creative research. August Meier was among the scholars who used the journal as a place to develop his earliest theories of black nationalism. Looking back on Greene's *Midwest Journal* more than three decades later, Meier commented that it was a well-edited, scholarly journal equal in caliber to the *Journal of Negro History*. Editing the *Midwest Journal* was a great learning experience for Greene. He got a taste of what his mentor did almost single-handedly for more than three decades. The cancellation of the journal may have been a blessing in disguise. It allowed Greene to take the vocation of being a scholar-activist to yet another level.

❖ ❖ ❖

From 1957 until 1972, Greene was a member of the Missouri Advisory Committee to the United States Civil Rights Commission. In 1959, as the chairman of the Subcommittee on Education, he completed a thorough survey entitled *The Desegregation of Public Schools in Missouri, 1954–1959*. As a veteran black historian, Greene was clearly still concerned with making history pragmatic and directly linked to sociological and statistical analyses, the same brand of research he conducted in *The Negro Wage Earner* (1930) and *The Employment of Negroes in the District of Columbia* (1932).

Based on questionnaires returned by one hundred district superintendents and eleven higher-learning institutions, *The Desegregation of Public Schools in Missouri, 1954–1959* reflected how Greene and his co-workers sought to determine and measure "the extent to which desegregation has been carried out in Missouri schools through April, 1959."[40] The Subcommittee on Education under Greene's leadership was concerned with a host of factors, including how individual communities implemented and reacted to desegregation, the actual processes involved, the impact of desegregation on black teachers, and the issues involved in interpreting the available data.

Greene's study is expansive, couched in a historical analysis of Missouri's segregationist culture, black population, and general evolution as a border state. Prior to *Brown v. Board of Education* in 1954, Greene emphasized that Missouri's black population, largely working-class "urban dwellers" relegated to the ghettos, faced "widespread discrimination." Segregation, its institutions and ideologies, flourished in pre-*Brown* Missouri. For Greene, "human relations" in Missouri between blacks and whites did not make significant improvements until the decade between 1949 and 1959. Yet blacks in Missouri, even after 1954, faced their greatest challenges, in Greene's estimation, with regard to housing and employment. These factors directly limited the realization of desegregation. The overall tone of Greene's study rings of both optimism and pessimism. Throughout the report, he praises Missouri's immediate compliance, at the state and local community levels, with the Supreme Court's monumental decision. "Desegregation has experienced a checkered career, varying in most states," Greene commented. "Missouri's experience has been a happy one," proceeding with "remarkable smoothness." Greene added that there was very limited opposition to desegregation in Missouri's educational institutions.[41]

At the same time, Greene noted that the statistics, percentages, and returned questionnaires needed to be scrutinized. Not only did Greene point out that by 1959, most black Missourians were poor urbanites still suffering from widespread segregation and very limited employment opportunities, but he stressed that "desegregated situations" and whites' verbal acceptance of desegregation did not eliminate expressions of de facto segregation, even in the schools. The "percentage of 'desegregated situations' bears no direct correlation to the number of Negroes actually attending schools with white children," Greene observed. "The majority of Negro pupils are still attending segregated schools" mainly because of residential segregation. Greene mentioned similar dilemmas at the college level. By 1959, blacks "represented only 0.38 per cent of the students" in Missouri's public colleges and universities.[42] Greene concluded his study of educational desegregation in Missouri with a detailed summary and the Subcommittee on Education's list of recommendations essentially calling for a stronger commitment to desegregation in Missouri. Echoing the sociological approaches pioneered by Du Bois's 1899 classic, *The Philadelphia Negro,* Greene stressed that there was a wide variety of factors leading to the continued separation of blacks and whites in Missouri.

By the middle of the twentieth century and at the midpoint of his life, Greene had accomplished what many black intellectual-activists today only dream of. He worked intimately with "The Father of Black History" for five years, taught at a historically black college for about twenty years, received a master's and doctorate degree from one of the most prestigious universities in the country, published a groundbreaking monograph, established his own family, and busied himself with a range of activities outside the walls of academe that sought to empower black America, particularly the poor working class. One of the most remarkable features of Greene's personality was his desire and ability to develop continuously as an individual. More important, he insisted that his personal evolution be closely intertwined with—and essentially dependent on—helping those in need and reforming American society and culture for the better.

Conclusion

THOUGH CARTER G. WOODSON and Lorenzo Johnston Greene were separated by a twenty-five-year generation gap and grew up in different parts of the country under distinguishable conditions and circumstances, their upbringings and early years were similar in important ways. They both came from poor, working-class families and as children and young adults contributed directly to the economic survival of their families' households. Their capacities to endure demanding physical labor beginning in childhood certainly contributed to their abilities as scholars to work long hours and take on the heavy tasks of producing rigorous scholarship during an era long before the age of advanced information technology. It is virtually impossible to compare the early scholarship of Woodson and Greene with that of black scholars who came of age after the Black Power era (1966–1975), especially those of us belonging to "the hip-hop generation," a group born between about 1965 and 1984 that relies greatly upon the recent and unprecedented advance of information technology.[1]

Both Woodson and Greene were born into the "nadir" of the black experience, and though Greene died in 1988, both lived their formative years during the era of Jim Crow segregation. They did not enjoy the space, opportunities, and privileges that their counterparts coming of age during the post–classic civil rights era did. Nonetheless, they envisioned an ideal America in which blacks could participate as equals, and they worked persistently to gain access to mainstream institutions as representatives for all African Americans. Woodson, Greene, and their colleagues—black women to a much greater degree—had to prove themselves during the era of segregation to be capable beyond any doubt. Even their greatest accomplishments did not secure their respect in American academe or equal treatment in U.S. society. African Americans have historically existed in oppressive conditions, challenging them to persevere in nontraditional, unorthodox ways, and to fashion cultures of survival. Black history is characterized by constant battles for survival in the face of great adversity and oppression that at times verges on genocide. Roughly half a century after the passage of the Thirteenth Amendment, Woodson and Greene contributed to what Na'im Akbar termed blacks' sense of "human resilience."[2]

Beyond overcoming similar obstacles, Woodson and Greene possessed analogous approaches and ideologies. In his diary throughout the late 1920s and the early 1930s, Greene critiqued Woodson's and his contemporaries' ideas of what it meant to be a black scholar and historian as well as aspects of their views of black social uplift. These criticisms did not prevent Greene from sharing many of his elder's philosophies. Woodson and Greene had similar experiences in becoming professionally trained scholars, which in turn influenced their overlapping worldviews. They belonged to a large group of black scholars who earned their doctorates from elite, prestigious universities yet were relegated to teaching at historically black colleges and universities. Woodson and Greene both studied under leading, often racist, white academic authorities; engaged in similar battles to meet the requirements for earning their degrees; and experienced brands of academic racism. They also possessed a great deal of hands-on experience and maturity before earning their doctorates, which probably helped them persevere. Woodson was age thirty-eight when he received his doctorate; and Greene was forty-two. Both men were productive and prolific scholars who published groundbreaking scholarship for their times. Greene's *The Negro in Colonial New England, 1620–1776* and facets of many of Woodson's studies have not been superseded to this day. For many historians, their scholarship remains logical—even mandatory—starting points.

Equally important, they shared a pragmatic philosophy of black history. Greene agreed wholeheartedly with his one-time "idol" that black history needed to be studied vigorously, written in an objective, scientific manner, and made practical. Both men very much enjoyed speaking to children and laypeople about their pasts while also investing serious efforts in legitimizing African American history in the mainstream academy. This delicate balancing act made them unique during and beyond their times. Black studies scholars are still struggling with "the tension between theory and practice" and the challenges of responding "to the needs of two masters, the academy on the one hand, and the black community on the other."[3] Woodson and Greene possessed a common social vision that dictated they make their craft relevant and practical by not only generating ideas and scholarship that spoke directly to the psychological needs of their people, but also by engaging in political and social activism. Both viewed their endeavor to promote and validate black history as being, in Woodson's words, a "life-and-death struggle." Though molded by their times, as all human beings are, they created an additional state of urgency for themselves. They seemed to have been driven by the dictum that every day was an important day, an opportunity to generate positive change and reflective thought.

In terms of their philosophies for black uplift, Woodson and Greene are comparable in provocative ways. They shared a similar ideology of black economic nationalism and religious pragmatism, believing that blacks should support productive black business ventures and that their religious orientations should be "this worldly." They were both Progressive Era "race men" in terms of their strategies for black uplift, maintaining their nineteenth-century predecessors' beliefs that the black masses needed to be saved by the race's exceptional men. They preserved and kept alive Du Bois's Talented Tenth notion at a time when leading African American intellectuals, especially self-proclaimed New Negroes, were attempting to revise such thought patterns. Woodson and his protégé routinely frowned upon the cultural mores and traditions of the black masses, especially Southerners, fearing that their behavior would endanger the entire race's chances of integrating into American society as equals.[4] Like their Progressive Era predecessors, they were genuinely concerned about the black masses' welfare and reached out to them, fostering interaction between various classes within the diverse African American community. At their core, despite their cultural chauvinism, they shared a belief that the black laboring class would play an important role in the struggle for black advancement.

Notwithstanding their noteworthy similarities, Woodson and Greene were distinguishable in meaningful ways. While Woodson was an institution builder and a leader of a movement, like many black intellectuals and scholars of his time, Greene used a black university as his base of operations. Unlike Woodson, who created his own autonomous institutional frameworks, Greene tapped into a vital, preexisting black institution, challenging its administrators and students to fulfill their potential as agents of social change. Devoting his services to a black college also limited Greene's abilities to be as prolific as his elder, since "teaching was the main activity expected and supported by these institutions."[5]

Woodson and Greene were also different types of leaders. Woodson was a nationally recognized spokesperson for black Americans. He published books that were read by scholars and laypeople alike, and he was called upon to share his ideas about blacks' status in leading, widely read and circulated black newspapers. In 1926, the NAACP awarded him the prestigious Spingarn Medal for outstanding achievement, and he routinely interacted with widely recognized black leaders of his time. Woodson was nationally accepted as "The Father of Negro History." Greene *was* the black history movement at Lincoln University and throughout the state of Missouri. In the early 1970s, Lincoln University instituted "Lorenzo J. Greene Week" and "Lorenzo J. Greene Day." Several days following his death on January 27, 1988, the state of Missouri adopted Senate Resolution No. 531 in honor of Greene's contributions. Woodson and Greene were clearly effective within their own contexts and spheres of influence.

Like Woodson, Greene was very much concerned with disseminating black history to the black masses. He lectured to countless and varied black and white audiences about black history. Greene, however, published very little material for mass consumption. Nor did he publish a general black history text, a task historically undertaken by leading black historians at one point or another in their lives, and he published only a handful of articles in the *Bulletin*. Woodson and Greene approached the task of writing differently as well. Greene, who wrote about one hundred poems between 1921 and the late 1930s, routinely expressed his innermost feelings in poetry and personal correspondences. He was very much like his contemporary Zora Neale Hurston in this regard. Woodson usually wrote very depersonalized, brief letters to his colleagues, employees, and dearest friends. Greene, who proofread many of Woodson's manuscripts, had mastered the stylistic mechanics of writing more than his mentor did. Woodson was more concerned about not allowing blacks to become "a negligible factor in the thought of the world" than he was with pleasant-sounding prose.

Woodson and Greene shared a belief that black scholars and intellectuals had a responsibility to work for *and* on behalf of the masses of their people, articulating this philosophy in divergent ways. Woodson was an outspoken, harsh critic of "highly educated Negroes" who were not directly involved "the cause." He belittled them in public arenas and discourse, as evidenced by *The Mis-Education of the Negro* and countless of his articles in black weeklies and the *Bulletin*. Greene refrained from dictating his ideology of black scholars' and professionals' social responsibilities in published, public testimonies.

He spoke with his actions and limited his critiques to his direct, personal interactions with middle-class, professional blacks, including students who were in the process of attaining such a status at Lincoln.

The current advanced state of African American history and Black studies owes a great debt to the efforts of Woodson, Greene, and other members of black history's formative years. The lives, work, and scholarship of Woodson and Greene challenge us to revisit the purpose of African American history and the role of the black historian. During the Black Power era, longtime professor of history at Morgan State University Benjamin Quarles (1904–96) wrote an important essay, "Black History's Diversified Clientele," which provides a useful framework for further assessing Woodson's, Greene's, and other black historians' conceptualizations of African American history. Productive during both the early black history movement and the post–civil rights era, Quarles offered a nuanced approach to African American history's multileveled functions. As Wilson J. Moses has suggested, Quarles's historical ideologies have "become part of our collective consciousness and we take many of his presuppositions for granted."[6] This has been the fate of many black historians, especially those active before the 1960s and 1970s—Woodson and Greene included, John Hope Franklin being a major exception.[7] Reflections on Quarles's ideas about black history are also useful in a discussion of Woodson and Greene because, despite their differences, these three scholars' approaches overlapped in various ways.

Though a contemporary of Greene's, Quarles did not work closely with Woodson. According to August Meier, there were "no direct connections between Quarles and Woodson," and Quarles avoided Woodson's rhetoric of explicit racial pride. Still, Quarles "regarded Woodson as the great pioneer and recognized that he and Woodson were similar in important ways."[8] Like Woodson and Greene, he came of age as a scholar during the age of Jim Crow segregation. As a historian, Quarles, like Woodson and Greene, was a "late bloomer" and "his achievement was accomplished under considerable odds."[9] Like Greene, Quarles was committed to teaching at a historically black university for more than a few decades. Woodson, Greene, Quarles, and other early black history movement historians all shared a common commitment to what Moses has called "contributionism," a concern "with demonstrating that African Americans have made useful contributions to the arts, sciences, and economy of the United States," and "messianism," "the doctrine that African Americans stand at the center of the American mission and destiny and that the African American presence has defined American democracy in ways that are singularly beneficial to American society and to the world."[10] They shared a commitment to researching and writing history in a quest for the truth and a more accurate representation of the past.

Quarles's fundamental approach to writing black history was quite similar to that of Woodson and Greene. In varying degrees, all three embraced an objective, narrative approach. Quarles wrote several books for a broad popular readership and authored important studies in social history that were well ahead of their times. Many of Quarles's works, like those of Woodson and Greene, continue to serve as key reference points for exploring monumental themes in African American history.[11]

In "Black History's Diversified Clientele," Quarles offered a general framework for viewing how diverse groups perceived and employed black history. He argued that black history was "being called upon to serve an increasing variety of publics." He focused on four broad and non–mutually exclusive groups: "the black rank and file, the black revolutionary nationalists, the black academicians, and the white world, both scholarly and lay."[12] For Quarles, the "black rank and file" relied largely on a glorified, popular version of black history to serve as "good therapy" and help support "an improved self-image." Today's hip-hop generation turns to black history in a manner similar to Quarles's rank and file, especially in terms of popular culture, the mass media, and cultural celebrations such as Kwanzaa, Martin Luther King Jr. Day, and Black History Month. Greene and especially Woodson acknowledged the rank and file in how they wrote and framed their speeches and lectures.

The second group in Quarles' analysis, "black revolutionary nationalists," employed black history mainly as "grievance collecting," focusing on black victimization.[13] Though there has been a significant decline in black nationalist thought since the end of the Black Power era, this body of thought and perspective still exists and actively draws upon black history. Cultural nationalists, afrocentric thinkers, organizations such as the Nation of Islam, and many outspoken reparations activists echo some of these philosophies. Woodson produced scholarship that has been appreciated by "revolutionary nationalists," especially *The Mis-Education of the Negro.*

Quarles's third group, "black academicians," viewed history as "a discipline, an attempt to recapture and mirror the past as accurately as possible" while correcting anti-black scholarship and generating new ideas. For Quarles, this group, like the "rank and file" and "revolutionary nationalists," "read black history with pride," highlighting the contributions of African Americans to American culture. At the same time, "black academicians" also addressed the "less glorious aspects of the black past" in search of what Woodson often called "the truth."[14] Quarles highlighted the dilemma that black historians and scholars like Woodson, Greene, and many others encountered, a challenge that still exists today. Quarles observed:

> The codes of his discipline bring the black academician face to face with one of the major problems confronting every social scientist, namely, whether his citizen role should overshadow his professional role, whether he should give priority to social action or to scientific inquiry. Should an academician strive for competence in his discipline or should he seek primarily to become personally involved and relevant? To the black academician this dilemma takes on an unusual urgency inasmuch as he is fully aware of the longstanding discriminations against black people in the American social order.[15]

Woodson and Greene developed malleable strategies that allowed them to simultaneously play the role of rigorous scientific scholar and social activist. At times, their lives as professional historians and activists overlapped, and at other times they practiced their different approaches exclusively within distinct spheres. Given the myriad problems facing modern black America, African American academicians and historians still face a quandary similar to that identified by Quarles.

The last group in Quarles's discussion is "the white community." "Whites need to know black history," Quarles asserted. Black history demonstrates "the centrality of the black American in our national experience," he said, and "would enable whites to more realistically appraise some of our country's boasted achievements and some of its acclaimed public figures."[16] Woodson and Greene were committed to the struggle of integrating African American history into the standard American historical narratives of their times. Like Quarles, they also addressed the wide range of historical relationships between blacks and whites. Woodson wrote African Americans into American history and Africans into world history, strove to integrate the study of African Americans and African peoples into American educational institutions, and etched out a viable space for African American history in popular American culture. Greene, on the other hand, focused his scholarly energies on incorporating the history of African Americans in colonial New England historiography and educating African American university students. Today, African American history can function in a similar way within the white community, as Quarles outlined and Woodson and Greene envisioned.

Woodson's and Greene's fundamental goals were important in shaping how African American history has been conceptualized for more than half a century. They sought to demonstrate to American society and to African Americans the crucial roles that Africans, African descendants, and especially African Americans played in the development of American culture and world civilization. Ultimately, they wanted African American history to become a widely recognized feature and enduring characteristic of American history in the U.S. academy and in all educational institutions throughout the nation. Equally important, Woodson and Greene believed that the once-hidden and ignored truths of African Americans' past could serve as great inspiration to black youths. The future of African American history and historiography will certainly build upon and reflect, directly and subtly, the noteworthy contributions of Carter G. Woodson, Lorenzo Johnston Greene, and other members of the early black history movement.

NOTES

Introduction

1. John Hope Franklin, "On the Evolution of Scholarship in Afro-American History," in *The State of Afro-American History: Past, Present, and Future,* ed. Darlene Clark Hine, 14–17 (Baton Rouge: Louisiana State University Press, 1986).

2. For in-depth discussions about the discrimination black scholars faced before the civil rights movement, see August Meier and Elliott Rudwick, *Black History and the Historical Profession, 1915–1980* (Urbana: University of Illinois Press, 1986), 75–159; Michael R. Winston, "Through the Back Door: Academic Racism and the Negro Scholar in Historical Perspective," *Daedalus* 100 (Summer 1971): 678–719; and Benjamin P. Bowser and Louis Kushnick, eds., *Against the Odds: Scholars Who Challenged Racism in the Twentieth Century* (Amherst: University of Massachusetts Press, 2002).

3. Several scholars have addressed the shift in patterns of racial uplift strategies during the late nineteenth century and early 1900s. See, for instance, Wilson Jeremiah Moses, *The Golden Age of Black Nationalism, 1850–1925* (New York: Oxford University Press, 1978), 5–12, 15–31; Deborah Gray White, *Too Heavy a Load: Black Women in Defense of Themselves, 1894–1994* (New York: Norton, 1999), 21–141; and Kevin K. Gaines, *Uplift the Race: Black Leadership, Politics, and Culture in the Twentieth Century* (Chapel Hill: University of North Carolina Press, 1996).

4. W. E. B. Du Bois, *The Souls of Black Folk* (New York: Dover, 1994), 2.

5. Alain Leroy Locke, "The New Negro," in *The New Negro,* ed. Alain Leroy Locke, 7 (New York: Atheneum, 1992).

6. Dia N. R. Sekayi, *African American Intellectual-Activists: Legacies in the Struggle* (New York: Garland, 1997), 4, 7; and Zak Kondo, *The Black Student's Guide to Positive Education* (Washington, D.C.: Nubia, 1987), 65.

7. Jonathan Scott Holloway, *Confronting the Veil: Abram Harris, Jr., E. Franklin Frazier, and Ralph Bunche, 1919–1941* (Chapel Hill: University of North Carolina Press, 2002), 32.

8. Darlene Clark Hine, *Speak Truth to Power: Black Professional Class in United States History* (New York: Carlson, 1996), xiii, xvii, xxiii.

9. Lorenzo Johnston Greene, "Dr. Woodson Prepares for Negro History Week, 1930," *Negro History Bulletin* [hereafter *NHB*] 28 (Summer 1965): 195. For similar assessments of Woodson's dedication to the study and promotion of black history, see Charles H. Wesley, "Carter G. Woodson—As Scholar," *Journal of Negro History* [hereafter *JNH*] 36 (1951): 12–24; Mary McLeod Bethune, "True Leadership is Timeless," *NHB* 13 (May 1950), 173; John Hope Franklin, "The Place of Carter G. Woodson in American Historiography," *NHB* 13 (May 1950): 174–76; L. D. Reddick, "Twenty-Five Negro History Weeks," *NHB* 13 (May 1950): 178–79; Arnett G. Lindsay, "Dr. Woodson as a Teacher," *NHB* 13 (May 1950): 183, 191; Alrutheus A. Taylor, "Dr. Carter G. Woodson: Inspirer and Benefactor of Young Scholars," *NHB* 13 (May 1950): 186, 189; Langston Hughes, "When I Worked for Dr. Woodson," *NHB* 13 (May 1950): 188; L. D. Reddick, "Carter G. Woodson (1875–1950): An Appreciation," *Phylon* 11 (2nd Quarter 1950): 177–79.

10. Darlene Clark Hine, "Black Professionals and Race Consciousness: Origins of the Civil Rights Movement, 1890–1950," *Journal of American History* 89 (March 2003): 1279; Darlene Clark Hine, "Carter G. Woodson: White Philanthropy and Negro Historiography," in Darlene Clark Hine, *HineSight: Black Women and the Re-Construction of American History,* 204 (New York: Carlson, 1994).

11. For a discussion of these scholars' roles as Harlem Renaissance promoters, see Cary D. Wintz, *Black Culture and the Harlem Renaissance* (Houston: Rice University Press, 1988), 102–29.

12. Rayford W. Logan, "Phylon Profile VI: Carter G. Woodson," *Phylon* 6 (4th Quarter 1945), 321; Taylor, "Woodson," 186.

13. Woodson's "Boys"—as they referred to themselves as late as the 1980s—were born in the 1890s and educated at some of the most prestigious graduate history departments in the country. Their doctoral dissertations concerned race relations, African American history, and, in the case of Logan, Africans in the diaspora. They all became involved in some form of social and/or political activism, and they all published important monographs. See Meier and Rudwick, *Black History,* 75–95.

14. Carter G. Woodson to Lorenzo Johnston Greene, 23 March 1945, Papers of Lorenzo Johnston Greene [hereafter Papers of LJG], container 74, folder 8, Manuscript Division, Library of Congress.

15. Recent studies that owe a great debt to Greene's scholarship include William D. Piersen, *Black Yankees: The Development of an Afro-American Subculture in Eighteenth-Century New England* (Amherst: University of Massachusetts Press, 1988); and Joanne Pope Melish, *Disowning Slavery: Gradual Emancipation and "Race" in New England, 1780–1860* (Ithaca, N.Y.: Cornell University Press, 1998).

16. Scholarship on Greene's life and work is scant. See Arvarh E. Strickland, ed., *Working with Carter G. Woodson, the Father of Black History: A Diary, 1928–1930, Lorenzo J. Greene* (Baton Rouge: Louisiana State University Press, 1989); Arvarh E. Strickland, ed., *Selling Black History for Carter G. Woodson: A Diary, 1930–1933, by Lorenzo J. Greene* (Columbia: University of Missouri Press, 1996); Meier and Rudwick, *Black History,* 19, 51, 62, 74, 79–83, 240, 281; Gary R. Kremer, "Lincoln University, Black Culture Mecca of the Midwest, 1921–1955," in *Black Heartland: African American Life, the Middle West, and the Meaning of American Regionalism,* ed. Gerald Early, 37–49

(St. Louis: Washington University, 1997); and Thorpe, *Black Historians: A Critique* (New York: Morrow, 1971), 110, 126, 176–77, 196, 222. Only one major book-length study currently exists about one of Woodson's disciples: see Kenneth Robert Janken, *Rayford W. Logan and the Dilemma of the African-American Intellectual* (Amherst: University of Massachusetts Press, 1993).

17. See Strickland, *Working;* Strickland, *Selling;* Lorenzo Johnston Greene, "Dr. Carter G. Woodson: The Man as I Knew Him," Papers of LJG, Container 92, Folder 1. This unpublished paper on Woodson exists in several different drafts between 1965 and the 1980s.

18. Lorenzo Johnston Greene to Patricia W. Romero, 15 March 1984, Papers of LJG, container 70, folder 8.

19. Bazel E. Allen and Ernest J. Wilson III, foreword to *The Crisis of the Negro Intellectual,* by Harold Cruse (New York: Quill, 1984), i–vi.

20. W. E. B. Du Bois, "The Talented Tenth," in *The Negro Problem: A Series of Articles by Representative American Negroes of To-Day,* ed. Booker T. Washington et al., 33 (New York: James Pott and Co., 1903).

21. Strickland, *Working,* 464.

Chapter 1: Representations of "The Father of Negro History"

1. See "Dr. Carter G. Woodson Project Proposal," (2002), http://www.cartergwoodson.com/ (accessed March 6, 2003).

2. See Kelly Miller, *An Estimate of Carter G. Woodson and His Work in Connection with the Association for the Study of Negro Life and History, Inc.* (Washington, D.C.: Association for the Study of Negro Life and History [ASNLH], 1926).

3. For an overview of how Woodson is treated in these widely circulated reference books, see Sister Anthony Scally, *Carter G. Woodson: A Bio-Bibliography* (Westport, Conn.: Greenwood, 1985), 146–47.

4. See Joseph Grimes, "A Study of the Negro Historian," (master's thesis, University of Iowa, 1935).

5. Langston Hughes, *The Big Sea* (New York: Knopf, 1940), 211.

6. Reddick to Greene, 26 February 1940, Papers of LJG, container 75, folder 3.

7. Greene to Reddick and others, 1 March 1940, Papers of LJG, container 75, folder 3.

8. Greene to Reddick, 16 March 1940, and Reddick to Greene, 18 March 1940, Papers of LJG, container 75, folder 3; Woodson to Greene, 1 May 1940, Papers of LJG, container 74, folder 8.

9. Greene to Reddick, 1 May 1940, Papers of LJG, container 75, folder 3; Reddick to "Fellows," 2 October 1950, Papers of LJG, container 73, folder 12.

10. Rayford W. Logan, "Phylon Profile VI: Carter G. Woodson," *Phylon* 6 (4th Quarter 1945): 315, 318, 321. To understand why Logan was upset with Embree, see Edwin Embree, *Thirteen against the Odds* (New York: Viking, 1944). William M. Brewer to Greene, 30 June 1950, Papers of LJG, container 72, folder 8.

11. For the most in-depth treatment of Logan and his relationship with Woodson, see Kenneth Robert Janken, *Rayford W. Logan and the Dilemma of the African-American Intellectual* (Amherst: University of Massachusetts Press, 1993).

12. J. A. Rogers, *World's Great Men of Color* (New York: Rogers, 1947), vol. 2, 668–71; Carter G. Woodson, "Book Reviews," *JNH* 28 (January 1943): 91–92.

13. Johnson to Greene, 16 March 1950, Papers of LJG, container 57, folder 14 and container 54, folder 7.

14. Romero to Greene, 7 July 1978, Papers of LJG, container 70, folder 8.

15. "News and Announcements," *American Sociological Review* 15 (June 1950): 441.

16. "Historical News and Notices," *Journal of Southern History* 16 (August 1950): 412–13.

17. Charles H. Wesley, "Carter G. Woodson—As Scholar," *JNH* 36 (January 1951): 12–24.

18. Mary McLeod Bethune, "True Leadership is Timeless," *NHB* 13 (May 1950), 173; August Meier and Elliot Rudwick, *Black History and the Historical Profession, 1915–1980* (Urbana: University of Illinois Press, 1986), 103–4; John Hope Franklin, "The Place of Carter G. Woodson in American Historiography," *NHB* 13 (May 1950): 174–76; L. D. Reddick, "Twenty-Five Negro History Weeks," *NHB* 13 (May 1950): 178–79; Arnett G. Lindsay, "Dr. Woodson as a Teacher," *NHB* 13 (May 1950): 183, 191; Alrutheus A. Taylor, "Dr. Carter G. Woodson: Inspirer and Benefactor of Young Scholars," *NHB* 13 (May 1950): 186, 189; and Langston Hughes, "When I Worked for Dr. Woodson," *NHB* 13 (May 1950): 188.

19. "A Great American," *NHB* 13 (May 1950): 180; Patricia Fletcher, "Dr. Woodson," *NHB* 13 (May 1950): 181.

20. W. E. B. Du Bois, "A Portrait of Carter G. Woodson," *Masses and Mainstream* 3 (June 1950): 19, 21, 23, 24; and Brewer to Greene, 30 June 1950, Papers of LJG, container 72, folder 8.

21. Jacqueline Goggin, "Carter G. Woodson and the Movement to Promote Black History" (PhD diss., University of Rochester, 1983), 317–18.

22. The debates between Woodson and Du Bois were recently reintroduced into scholarly discourse: see "Henry Louis Gates, Jr., on Carter G. Woodson: An Open Letter to Dr. Henry Louis Gates, Jr., Harvard University from the Executive Council, the Association for the Study of African American Life and History, 25 March 2003," *Journal of African American History* 88 (Spring 2003): 221–22.

23. See L. D. Reddick, "Carter G. Woodson (1875–1950): An Appreciation," *Phylon* 11 (2nd Quarter 1950): 177–79.

24. L. D. Reddick, "As I Remember Woodson," *NHB* 17 (November 1953): 36.

25. John Hope Franklin, "The New Negro History," *JNH* 43 (April 1957): 90, 91, 93, 94. The original article first appeared as "The New Negro History," *The Crisis* 64 (February 1957): 69–75. *The Crisis* did not even acknowledge Woodson's death, so in one sense this article represents the NAACP's first and perhaps most elaborate portrait of Woodson.

26. Earl E. Thorpe, *Negro Historians in the United States* (Baton Rouge: Fraternal, 1958), 55.

27. Thorpe, *Negro Historians,* 95.

28. Thorpe, *Negro Historians,* 99.

29. Thorpe, *Negro Historians,* 106.

30. Ulysees Lee, "The ASLNH, *The Journal of Negro History,* and American Schol-

arly Interest in Africa," in *Africa Seen by American Negroes: Africa from the Point of View of American Negro Scholars*, ed. John A. Davis, 413–14 (Paris: Presence Africaine, 1958).

31. One of the first scholars to carefully comb through the articles of the *Journal* as a whole was Ella Gaines Yates. See her "Annotated, Cumulative Index to *The Journal of Negro History* from January, 1916, through October, 1940" (master's thesis, Atlanta University, 1951).

32. Woodson's contributions were touched upon in several books, a few journal articles, and he was featured in one master's thesis. See Sister Anthony Scally, *Carter G. Woodson*, 147–60 and 191–92. Included among these sources is Noreen Hale, "Carter G. Woodson: Historian of the Negro American" (master's thesis, University of San Francisco, 1969). In addition, in the late 1970s Earl E. Thorpe reissued several of his writings on black history and Woodson. See, for example, "The Father of Negro History," in Earl E. Thorpe, *The Central Theme of Black History*, 49–75 (Westport, Conn.: Greenwood Press, 1979).

33. Charles H. Wesley, "Our Fiftieth Year: Our Golden Anniversary, 1965," *NHB* 28 (Summer 1965): 173.

34. Wesley, "Our Fiftieth Year," 195.

35. Jessie H. Roy, "Some Personal Recollections of Dr. Woodson," *NHB* 28 (Summer 1965): 186.

36. Lorenzo Johnston Greene, "Dr. Woodson Prepares for Negro History Week, 1930," *NHB* 28 (Summer 1965): 195.

37. Greene to Romero, March 15, 1984, Papers of LJG, Container 70, Folder 8.

38. Lorenzo Johnston Greene, "Dr. Carter G. Woodson: The Man as I Knew Him," Papers of LJG, Container 92, Folder 1.

39. Greene, "Dr. Carter G. Woodson," 34.

40. Greene to Romero, 15 March 1984, Papers of LJG, container 70, folder 8.

41. "Fiftieth Anniversary of the Journal of Negro History," *JNH* 51 (April 1966): 79.

42. Sterling Stuckey, "Black Americans and African Consciousness: Du Bois, Woodson, and the Spell of Africa," in Sterling Stuckey, *Going through the Storm: The Influence of African American Art in History*, 124 (New York: Oxford University Press, 1994).

43. Noreen Hale, "Carter G. Woodson: Historian of the Negro American" (master's thesis, University of San Francisco, 1969), 31; and Meier and Rudwick, *Black History*, 280–81.

44. See Richard A. Thomas, "Carter G. Woodson: A Critical Study of His Contribution to Black Historiography" (master's thesis, Michigan State University, 1971); Patricia Watkins Romero, "Carter G. Woodson: A Biography" (PhD diss., Ohio State University, 1971); and Thorpe, *Black Historians*.

45. Romero, "Carter G. Woodson," 95, 138, 185.

46. Rayford W. Logan, "Carter G. Woodson: Mirror and Molder of His Time, 1875–1950," *JNH* 58 (January 1973): 2.

47. For example, see Michael R. Winston, "Carter Godwin Woodson: Prophet of a Black Tradition," *JNH* 60 (October 1975): 459–63; M. Sammy Miller, "Letters from Dr. Carter G. Woodson to Mrs. Mary Church Terrell," *JNH* 61 (January 1976): 1–6;

and Otey M. Scruggs, "Carter G. Woodson, the Negro History Movement, and Africa," *Pan-African Journal* 7 (Spring 1974): 39–50. Alfred Young also completed a dissertation dealing with Woodson: see his "The Educational Philosophies of Booker T. Washington and Carter G. Woodson: A Liberating Praxis" (PhD diss., Syracuse University, 1977). For a sampling of the more popular writings on Woodson during this decade, see "Black Studies and History Week," *NHB* 35 (February 1972): 28–29; and W. Montague Cobb, "Carter Godwin Woodson," *NHB* 36 (November 1973): 151–55.

48. Scally was born in Baltimore, Maryland, in 1905. From 1940 until 1953, she was the director of the library at Mt. St. Agnes College, Baltimore. Her first major publication was *Catholic Negro Writers, A Bio-Bibliography* (1945). From 1958 until 1969, she was based in Pensacola, Florida, and served as the secretary of an interracial human relations organization called John XXIII Human Relations Council; she was also a youth counselor for the NAACP. From 1969 to 1970, she worked in the Cook County Jail in Chicago and taught black history to some of the inmates there. In 1973, she moved to Washington, D.C., and began getting interested in Woodson and started working with the ASALH. In the 1970s, she contributed many articles to a fairly obscure journal called *Community.*

49. Sister Anthony Scally, "Woodson and the Genesis of ASALH," *NHB* 40 (January–February 1977): 653–55.

50. For more information on this, see Irma Watkins-Owens, *Blood Relations: Caribbean Immigrants and the Harlem Community, 1900–1930* (Bloomington: Indiana University Press, 1996).

51. Tony Martin, "Carter G. Woodson and Marcus Garvey," *NHB* 40 (November–December 1977): 774–77.

52. See Joe Johnson, "Carter G. Woodson: Father of the Study of Black History," *The Crisis* 94 (February 1987): 35–37 (an article which deemed Woodson a self-made man, but unsurprisingly measured him by Du Bois's standards); Sister Anthony Scally, "The Philippine Challenge," *NHB* 44 (1981): 16–18; and M. A. Scally, *Walking Proud: The Story of Dr. Carter G. Woodson* (Washington, D.C.: Associated Publishers, 1983).

53. Papers of LJG, container 70, folder 14.

54. Sister Anthony Scally, *Carter G. Woodson.*

55. See August Meier and Elliot Rudwick, *Black History,* 1–71; Goggin, "Carter G. Woodson."

56. Goggin (b. 1953) began doing serious research on Woodson as a graduate student at the University of Rochester. After publishing her dissertation, she produced several articles on Woodson, including "Countering White Racist Scholarship: Carter G. Woodson and the Journal of Negro History," *JNH* (Fall 1983): 355–75, and "Carter G. Woodson and the Collection of Source Materials for Afro-American History," *American Archivist* 48 (Summer 1985): 261–71. The latter article is especially informative: Goggin traced how Woodson built up a collection of primary sources in the Library of Congress with the help of J. Franklin Jameson (1859–1937). From 1968, when Woodson's papers were finally processed and made accessible to scholars, until 1977, the Woodson collection was used extensively. Throughout the decade and into the 1990s, Goggin presented several papers on Woodson in various venues.

57. Greene to Goggin, 15 March 1984; and Goggin to Greene, 16 April 1984, Papers of LJG, container 69, folder 12,

58. Goggin, "Carter G. Woodson."

59. Greene to Goggin, 15 March 1984, Papers of LJG, container 69, folder 12.

60. Greene to Romero, 25 April 1984, Papers of LJG, container 27, folder 3; Greene to Romero, 15 March 1984, Papers of LJG, container 70, folder 8.

61. John Hope Franklin, "On the Evolution of Scholarship in Afro-American History," in *The State of Afro-American History: Past, Present, and Future,* ed. Darlene Clark Hine, 14–17 (Baton Rouge: Louisiana State University Press, 1986).

62. Darlene Clark Hine, "Carter G. Woodson: White Philanthropy and Negro Historiography," in Darlene Clark Hine, *HineSight: Black Women and the Re-Construction of American History* (New York: Carlson Publishing, 1994), 204, 206.

63. Meier and Rudwick, *Black History,* 1.

64. Meier and Rudwick, *Black History,* 42.

65. Meier and Rudwick, *Black History,* 71.

66. Meier and Rudwick, *Black History,* 280–81. For example, see Robert L. Harris "Review Article: The Flowering of Afro American History," *American Historical Review* 92 (December 1987): 1150–61. Earl E. Thorpe was very critical of the "elitist" nature of their study. See Earl E. Thorpe, "Book Reviews," *JNH* 78 (Spring 1993): 123–27.

67. Jacqueline Goggin, *Carter G. Woodson: A Life in Black History* (Baton Rouge: Louisiana State University Press, 1993), 1–94.

68. Goggin, *Carter G. Woodson,* 140–207.

69. See John David Smith, "Black Intellectuals As Activists in the Age of Jim Crow," *Reviews in American History* 22 (June 1994): 328–34; David Levering Lewis, "Book Reviews," *Journal of American History* 81 (September 1994): 760–61; Francille Rusan Wilson, "Book Reviews," *Journal of Southern History* 60 (November 1994): 832–34; and Alfred Moss Jr., "Reviews of Books," *American Historical Review* 100 (February 1995): 246–47.

70. University Publications of America, *Papers of Carter G. Woodson and the Association for the Study of Negro Life and History, 1915–1950,* (Bethesda, Md.: author, n.d.), brochure.

71. The volumes appearing in 1950 did not mention Woodson's death at all. In fact, only one or two articles mentioned Woodson, but none took note of his death. See Theophilus E. McKinney Jr., "A Need for More Knowledge of the Part Played by Negroes in the Development of Civilization," *Quarterly Review of Higher Education among Negroes* [hereafter *QRHEAN*] 18 (July 1950): 113–15. For the memoirs to fallen black leaders, see "Editorial Comment, Dr. Mary McLeod Bethune," *QRHEAN* 23 (July 1955): 131; and "Editorial Comment—In Memoriam," *QRHEAN* 24 (October 1956): 170–74.

72. "Newest Member of Hall of Fame: Honor Goes to Historian Carter G. Woodson," *Ebony,* February 1958, 27. The article also features a nice full-page picture of Woodson in his library holding a book in his hand.

73. Du Bois, "Portrait," 24.

74. See *Pittsburgh Courier* 41, April 8, 1950; and "Carter Woodson, Dr. Drew Rites Held in Capitol," *Pittsburgh Courier* 41, April 15, 1950, 3.

75. "Dr. Carter G. Woodson, Historian, Found Dead," *Chicago Defender,* April 8, 1950, 1; "Impressive Rites for Dr. Woodson in Washington," *Chicago Defender,* April 15, 1950, 4; "Dr. Carter G. Woodson, Noted Historian, Dies in Washington," *Norfolk Journal and Guide,* April 8, 1950, 1; "Father of History Week, Dr. Woodson Found Dead," *Afro-American,* April 8, 1950, 1–2; "Historian Held High Example," *Afro-American,* April 15, 1950, 7.

76. Recently, the ASALH has announced that they plan to produce a two-part documentary on Woodson, chronicling his life as well as his battles with the Phelps-Stokes Fund and Du Bois. The ASALH asserts that it hopes to "pull Dr. Carter G. Woodson's American experience from the cracks of history and expose the world to its importance." See "Dr. Carter G. Woodson Project Proposal," (2002), www.cartergwoodson.com (accessed March 6, 2003).

77. J. Rupert Picott, "National Shrine Carter G. Woodson House Restored to Original Beauty and Utility," *NHB* 44 (April/May/June 1981): 27. For the recent movement to restore Woodson's home, see Felix M. Armfield, "Saving a National Treasure: The Home of Dr. Carter G. Woodson," August 2002, www.oah.org/pubs/n1/2002aug/woodson.html.

Chapter 2: A Pioneer in Black Studies and History

1. For discussions of "race vindication" as a black intellectual tradition, see V. P. Franklin, *Living Our Stories, Telling Our Truths: Autobiography and the Making of the African-American Intellectual Tradition* (New York: Scribner, 1995), 15; V. P. Franklin and Bettye Collier-Thomas, "Biography, Race Vindication, and African-American Intellectuals: Introductory Essay," *JNH* 81 (Winter–Autumn 1996): 1, 14; and "Vindicating the Race: Contributions to African-American Intellectual History," 80th Anniversary Year, *JNH* 81 (Winter–Autumn 1996).

2. For a further discussion of Woodson's early years, see Jacqueline Goggin, *Carter G. Woodson: A Life in Black History* (Baton Rouge: Louisiana State University Press, 1993), 1–31; August Meier and Elliott Rudwick, *Black History and the Historical Profession, 1915–1980* (Urbana: University of Illinois Press, 1986), 42, 93; and Carter G. Woodson, "My Recollections of Veterans of the Civil War," *NHB* 7 (February 1944): 103–4, 115–18.

3. Meier and Rudwick, *Black History,* 71.

4. "Notes," *JNH* 4 (October 1919): 474.

5. Sterling A. Brown, "The Negro Author and His Publisher," *QRHEAN* 9 (July 1941): 145–46.

6. Arvarh E. Strickland, ed., *Selling Black History for Carter G. Woodson: A Diary, 1930–1933, by Lorenzo J. Greene* (Columbia: University of Missouri Press, 1996).

7. Patricia Watkins Romero, "Carter G. Woodson: A Biography" (PhD diss., Ohio State University, 1971), 121.

8. L. D. Reddick, "As I Remember Woodson," *NHB* 17 (November 1953): 36.

9. "Notes," *JNH* 4 (April 1919): 237; and "Notes," *JNH* 4 (July 1919): 347.

10. "Notes," *JNH* 4 (April 1919): 237; and "Annual Report of the Director," *JNH* 9 (October 1924): 580.

11. "Notes," *JNH* 9 (April 1924): 239.

12. Several historians seem to agree that the concept of Negro History Week originated in 1920. In that year, Woodson delivered a speech entitled "Democracy and the Man Far Down" to members of the Omega Psi Phi fraternity in Nashville, Tennessee. During the presentation Woodson commented that these fraternity members needed to become more active in promoting the study of black life and history. This Omega chapter responded by devoting one week out of every year to the study of black history. They called their celebration "Negro History and Literature Week." Their efforts continued until 1925. Woodson did not acknowledge the Association's Negro History Week as an extension of the Omegas' efforts. For a discussion of the origins of Negro History Week, see Romero; also, see Carter G. Woodson, "Negro History Week," *JNH* 11 (April 1926): 238–42.

13. Woodson, "Negro History Week," 238–41.

14. Michael R. Olneck, "The Recurring Dream: Symbolism and Ideology in Intercultural and Multicultural Education," *American Journal of Education* 98 (February 1990), 149.

15. Carter G. Woodson, *The Mis-Education of the Negro* (New Jersey: African World Press, 1990); and "How Shall We Celebrate Negro History Week?" *NHB* 8 (January 1945): 91. For a provocative discussion of Woodson's relationship with white philanthropists, see Darlene Clark Hine, "Carter G. Woodson: White Philanthropy and Negro Historiography," in Darlene Clark Hine, *HineSight: Black Women and the Re-Construction of American History* (New York: Carlson, 1994).

16. "Starting Right," *NHB* 1 (February 1938): 12; and "Renew Your Subscription," *NHB* 9 (May 1946): 188.

17. "The Annual Report of the Director," *JNH* 11 (October 1926): 551.

18. For a brief discussion of some typical Negro History Week events, see Goggin, *Carter G. Woodson,* 84–85, 119–20.

19. Every year after the founding of Negro History Week in 1926, Woodson reviewed the status of the celebration. See, for instance, "Negro History Week the Fourth Year," *JNH* 14 (April 1929): 109–15; "Negro History Week the Eight Year," *JNH* 18 (April 1933): 107–13; and "Negro History Week the Eleventh Year," *JNH* (April 1936): 105–10.

20. "Negro History Week," *JNH* (April 1936): 106–7.

21. Carter G. Woodson, "Start Now on Negro History Year in Order to Have a Negro History Week," *NHB* 5 (October 1941): 24.

22. Carter G. Woodson, "Supplementing Nothing," *NHB* 8 (March 1945): 144.

23. "Negro History Week Nation-Wide," *NHB* 12 (March 1949): 135.

24. Carter G. Woodson, "What Children Should Do in Observing Negro History Week," *NHB* 1 (February 1938): 12.

25. "Negro History Week the Eighth Year," *JNH* 18 (April 1933): 107–13.

26. L. D. Reddick, "Twenty-Five Negro History Weeks," *NHB* 13 (May 1950): 178–88; and "Annual Report of the Director," *JNH* 18 (October 1933): 362.

27. "Negro History Week Nationwide," *NHB* 12 (March 1949): 136; and "Jewish History Week," *NHB* 12 (June 1949): 194.

28. Carter G. Woodson, *Home Study Department of the Extension Division of the ASNLH, Inc.: Bulletin of General Information* (ASNLH: Washington, D.C., n.d.). For

a discussion of Tuskegee's Movable School or Jesup Agricultural Wagon, see Virginia Lantz Denton, *Booker T. Washington and the Adult Education Movement* (Gainesville: University Press of Florida, 1993).

29. Woodson, *Home Study.*

30. Woodson, *Home Study;* and "Annual Report of the Director," *JNH* 15 (October 1930): 396.

31. W. H. Crogman to Carter G. Woodson, 4 April 1927, Papers of Carter G. Woodson, reel 3, containers 5–6.

32. See *NHB* 1 (October 1937); and *NHB* 13 (May 1950): 170.

33. Lillian M. Rhoades to Carter G. Woodson, 14 November 1940, Papers of Carter G. Woodson and the Association for the Study of Negro Life and History, reel 1.

34. See "The Saturday Morning Art Class," *NHB* 5 (April 1942): 158; and Romare Bearden and Harry Henderson, *A History of African-American Artists* (New York: Pantheon Books, 1993), 381–88.

35. Carter G. Woodson, "Timely Suggestions for Negro History Week," *NHB* 1 (February 1938): 11.

36. Carter G. Woodson, "The Heritage of the Negro," *NHB* 3 (February 1940): 79.

37. Carter G. Woodson, "Suggestion for Improving the Negro Church," *NHB* 3 (1939): 9.

38. Carter G. Woodson, "Suggestions for Improvements in the Education of the Negro," *NHB* 3 (November 1939): 29–31.

39. Carter G. Woodson, "Mis-Representing the Negro," *NHB* 7 (March 1944): 144.

40. Carter G. Woodson, "Negroes Not United for Democracy," *NHB* 6 (May 1943): 170, 177; and Carter G. Woodson, "In Spite of No Leaders the Negroes' Hope for Democracy Lingers," *NHB* 6 (June 1943): 194, 213.

41. Carter G. Woodson, "How Foreign Merchants Exploit the Negro," *NHB* 3 (January 1940): 56–58.

42. Francille Rusan Wilson, "Racial Consciousness and Black Scholarship: Charles H. Wesley and the Construction of *Negro Labor in the United States,*" *JNH* 82 (Autumn 1997), 72–88; Franklin, *Living Our Stories,* 142.

43. Carter G. Woodson, "The Negro Looks for Democracy," *NHB* 7 (December 1943): 72; and Carter G. Woodson, "Why Negroes Fight in this War," *NHB* 7 (May 1944): 170.

44. John Hope Franklin, "The Place of Carter G. Woodson in American Historiography," *NHB* 13 (May 1950): 176.

Chapter 3: The Progenitor of a Twentieth-Century African American Iconoclastic Tradition

1. Since January 2002, countless articles have been published on the controversy surrounding the October 2001 meeting between Summers and West. The *New York Times* covered this event in great detail. For some examples, see Pam Belluck, "Black Scholar Looks beyond Mended Fence and Harvard," *New York Times,* January 10, 2002, sec. A; Kate Zernike, "Ideas and Trends: Can Crying Race Be Crying Wolf?"

New York Times, January 13, 2002, sec. 4; Marjorie Coeyman, "Harvard's President in the Hot Seat," *Christian Science Monitor,* January 8, 2002, 13; Richard Chait, "Why Shouldn't Harvard's President Ask Tough Questions?" *Chronicle of Higher Education,* February 1, 2002, 20; James Sullivan, "Can Hip-Hop Play in Academia?" *San Francisco Chronicle,* February 3, 2002, 74; Ronald Roach, "The Great 'Misunderstanding' at Harvard," *Black Issues in Higher Education,* February 14, 2002, 10–11; letter to the editor, "Is Harvard's President Unfairly Singling Out Black-Studies Professors for Scrutiny?" *Chronicle of Higher Education,* February 15, 2002, 4; Robert S. Boynton, "Black Studies Today: Out of Africa, and Back," *New York Times,* April 14, 2002, sec. 4A; Patrick Healy, "West Cites Reason for Quitting," *Boston Globe,* April 14, 2002, B3; James Bone, "Second Leading Black Scholar Defects from Harvard's Dream Team," *Times* (London), April 15, 2002, Overseas News; Martin Van Der Werf, "Lawrence Summers and His Tough Questions," *Chronicle of Higher Education,* April 26, 2002, 29; Rohan Preston, "Public Intellectual No. 1, and Cornel West's Recent Decision to Leave Harvard for Princeton Landed the Outspoken Thinker in the Headlines—Again," *Star Tribune,* May 22, 2002, 1E.

2. Danny Goldberg, "Harvard Raps West," *Nation,* February 4, 2002, 8; John McWhorter, *Wall Street Journal,* April 16, 2002, A20; Thulani Davis, "Spinning Race at Harvard," *Village Voice,* January 22, 2002, 39–41; and Ronald Roach, "Great 'Misunderstanding,'" 10–11.

3. Pam Belluck with Jacques Steinberg, "Defector Indignant at President of Harvard," *New York Times,* April 16, 2002, sec. A; Adolph Reed, "What Are the Drums Saying, Booker? The Current Crisis of the Black Intellectual," *Village Voice,* April 11, 1995, 33–36; and Tatsha Robertson, "Harvard Exodus," *The Crisis* (May/June 2002): 23–27.

4. For a discussion of these "iconoclastic" writings, see Bazel E. Allen and Ernest J. Wilson III, foreword to *The Crisis of the Negro Intellectual,* by Harold Cruse (New York: Quill, 1984), i–vi.

5. Allen and Wilson, foreword, i.

6. Alain Locke and other New Negro advocates also challenged parts of Du Bois's Talented Tenth notion. See Alain Leroy Locke, "The New Negro," in *The New Negro,* ed. Alain Leroy Locke, 3–18 (New York: Atheneum, 1992).

7. W. E. B. Du Bois, "The Talented Tenth," in *The Negro Problem: A Series of Articles by Representative American Negroes of To-Day,* ed. Booker T. Washington et al., 33 (New York: Pott, 1903).

8. W. E. B. Du Bois, "The Negro Bourgeoisie," in *W. E. B. Du Bois: A Reader,* ed. Meyer Weinberg, 56 (New York: Harper, 1970).

9. W. E. B. Du Bois, "Talented Tenth: Memorial Address," in *Writings by Du Bois in Periodicals Edited by Others,* ed. Herbert Aptheker, 78–88 (New York: Kraus Thompson, 1982).

10. Booker T. Washington, *My Larger Education: Being Chapters from My Experience* (New York: Doubleday, 1911), 114, 118, 120.

11. Carter G. Woodson, *The Negro in Our History* (Washington, D.C.: Associated, 1922), 274–79.

12. Carter G. Woodson, "Honor to Booker T. Washington," *NHB* 10 (March 1947): 126–28.

13. "Notes," *JNH* 18 (July 1933): 341.

14. Jacqueline Goggin, *Carter G. Woodson: A Life in Black History* (Baton Rouge: Louisiana State University Press, 1993), 3. In his monographs published before 1933, one can see traces of his iconoclastic character breaking through. In the final chapter of *A Century of Negro Migration,* Woodson makes many observations about how blacks have been victimized in America. In the last pages of *The History of the Negro Church,* he also offers a solution to blacks' dilemma. For Lorenzo Johnston Greene's discussion of Woodson, see his "Dr. Carter G. Woodson: The Man as I Knew Him," Papers of LJG, Container 92, Folder 1.

15. "Annual Report of the Director," *JNH* 16 (October 1931): 349–58.

16. Carter G. Woodson, *The Mis-Education of the Negro* (New Jersey: African World Press, 1990).

17. Woodson, *Mis-Education,* 9–37.

18. Woodson, *Mis-Education,* 26, 15, 23, 34.

19. Woodson, *Mis-Education,* 35.

20. Woodson, *Mis-Education,* 56, 65, 176.

21. Woodson, *Mis-Education,* 44, 131.

22. Woodson, *Mis-Education,* 144–72.

23. Woodson, *Mis-Education,* 56.

24. Woodson, *Mis-Education,* 122.

25. Alain Locke, "Black Zionism," *Survey* 69 (October 1933): 363–64.

26. See Anthony M. Platt, *E. Franklin Frazier Reconsidered* (New Brunswick, N.J.: Rutgers University Press, 1991).

27. E. Franklin Frazier, *Black Bourgeoisie* (New York: Free Press, 1957), 23–26.

28. Frazier, *Black Bourgeoisie,* 24.

29. Frazier, *Black Bourgeoisie,* 26.

30. See E. Franklin Frazier, *The Negro Family in the United States* (Chicago: University of Chicago Press, 1939); and Melville J. Herskovits, *The Myth of the Negro Past* (Boston: Beacon, 1958).

31. Frazier, *Negro Family,* 42.

32. Frazier, *Negro Family,* 153–63.

33. Frazier, *Negro Family,* 174–94.

34. Frazier, *Negro Family,* 195–212. Frazier's detailed emphasis on conspicuous consumption is reminiscent of Thornstein Veblen's *The Theory of the Leisure Class,* first published in 1899. Though Frazier did not acknowledge Veblen as one of his intellectual forebears, the similarities between their analyses are striking. Veblen meticulously explores the evolution of leisure class values and spirituality from inception through the modern industrial era. Like Frazier's black bourgeoisie who sought integration based upon accumulation of material goods, people excluded from Veblen's small "legitimate" or "subsidiary" leisure class segment (with their "conventional standards") actively attempted to assimilate their attitudes. Due to their economic inadequacies, the black bourgeoisie often adopted the spirituality of the leisure class in more symbolic, noneconomically determined manners. Like Frazier's case studies, they spent the small income they had on leisure class "paraphernalia" of all sorts. See Thornstein Veblen, *The Theory of the Leisure Class* (New York: Dover, 1994).

35. E. Franklin Frazier, "The Failure of the Negro Intellectual," in *The Death of White Sociology,* ed. Joyce A. Ladner, 58, 60, 65 (New York: Vintage, 1973).

36. The biographical information about Cruse was provided to the author by one of Cruse's former students, Janice Rowley Cooper, in the form of various unpublished biographical sketches and curriculum vitae.

37. Cooper, unpublished.

38. Frazier, *Black Bourgeoisie,* 26; and Cruse, *Crisis of the Negro Intellectual,* 454.

39. Cruse, *Crisis,* 71.

40. Cruse, *Crisis,* 565.

41. Cruse, *Crisis,* 11–63, 52, 57.

42. Cruse, *Crisis,* 65.

43. Cruse, *Crisis,* 327–28.

44. One of the outspoken advocates for deromanticizing the writing of African American history is Clarence E. Walker; see his *Deromanticizing Black History: Critical Essays and Reappraisals* (Knoxville: University of Tennessee Press, 1991); and his *We Can't Go Home: An Argument about Afrocentrism* (New York: Oxford University Press, 2001).

45. Robert L. Allen, *Black Awakening in Capitalist America: An Analytic History* (New York: Anchor Books, 1970), 168–71.

46. For Cruse's solutions, see *Crisis,* 83–95.

47. Cruse, *Crisis,* 541.

48. Allen, *Black Awakening,* 171. For a discussion of the significance of Cruse's study, see Hortense J. Spillers, "The Crisis of the Negro Intellectual: A Post-Date," *Boundary 2: An International Journal of Literature and Culture* 21 (Fall 1994): 64–116.

Chapter 4: Black Women, Woodson, and the ASNLH, 1915–50

1. W. E. B. Du Bois, "A Portrait of Carter G. Woodson," *Masses and Mainstream* 3 (June 1950), 25.

2. Patricia Morton, *Disfigured Images: The Historical Assault on Afro-American Women* (New York: Praeger, 1991), 48–49.

3. For provocative discussions of black leaders' and scholars' conventional views of black women during the first half of the twentieth century, see Deborah Gray White, *Too Heavy a Load: Black Women in Defense of Themselves, 1894–1994* (New York: W. W. Norton and Co., 1999), 21–175; and Morton, *Disfigured Images,* 17–85.

4. Carter G. Woodson, *The Negro in Our History* (Washington, D.C.: Associated, 1922).

5. Carter G. Woodson, *The Story of the Negro Retold* (Washington, D.C.: Associated, 1935), 29, 209–11; and Carter G. Woodson, *Negro Makers of History* (Washington, D.C.: Associated, 1928).

6. Carter G. Woodson, *The Negro Professional Man and the Community* (New York: Negro Universities Press, 1969), xviii.

7. Woodson, *Negro Professional,* 140. For a discussion of black male leaders' views of black nurses' conventional roles, see Darlene Clark Hine, *Black Women in White: Racial Conflict and Cooperation in the Nursing Profession, 1890–1950* (Bloomington: Indiana University Press, 1989), 13–14.

8. Woodson, *Negro Professional,* 325.

9. Carter G. Woodson, "The Negro Washerwoman: A Vanishing Figure," *JNH* 15 (July 1930): 270, 272.

10. Woodson, "Negro Washerwoman," 274–75, 270.

11. Woodson, "Negro Washerwoman," 276–77.

12. Carter G. Woodson, "Women Should Have More Voice in Our Affairs," *Pittsburgh Courier,* December 17, 1932, sec. 2.

13. Woodson, "Women."

14. Woodson, "Women."

15. See Alice Dunbar-Nelson, "People of Color in Louisiana, Part I," *JNH* 1 (October 1916): 359–74; Alice Dunbar-Nelson, "People of Color in Louisiana, Part II," *JNH* 2 (January 1917): 51–78; and Mary Church Terrell, "The History of the High School for Negroes in Washington," *JNH* 2 (July 1917): 252–66.

16. W. B. Hartgrove, "The Story of Marie Louise Moore and Fannie M. Richards," *JNH* 1 (January 1916), 32.

17. Benjamin Brawley, "Three Negro Poets: Horton, Mrs. Harper, and Whitman," *JNH* 2 (October 1917): 384, 386, 391.

18. Ruth Bogin, "Elizabeth Ross Haynes," in *Notable American Women, The Modern Period: A Biographical Dictionary,* eds. Barbara Sicherman and Ilene Kantrov, 324–25 (Cambridge: Harvard University Press, 1980).

19. Elizabeth Ross Haynes, "Negroes in Domestic Services in the U.S.," *JNH* 8 (October 1923): 384–442. A year before her thesis appeared, Haynes published an article focusing on black working women: "Two Million Negro Women at Work," *Southern Workman* 51 (February 1922): 64–72.

20. E. Franklin Frazier, "The Negro Slave Family," *JNH* 15 (April 1930): 198–259.

21. "Notes," *JNH* 18 (July 1933): 351–54.

22. Dorothy B. Porter, "Sarah Parker Remond, Abolitionist and Physician," *JNH* 20 (July 1935): 293.

23. Edward D. Seeber, "Phillis Wheatley," *JNH* 24 (July 1939): 259–62. Seeber's article provides no real analysis of Wheatley; he simply notes how people such as Thomas Jefferson and other scholars treated her.

24. Morton, *Disfigured Images,* 1–53.

25. Jessie W. Parkhurst, "The Role of the Black Mammy in the Plantation Household," *JNH* 23 (July 1938): 349–69.

26. Lorenzo Johnston Greene, "Dr. Carter G. Woodson: The Man as I Knew Him," Papers of LJG, Container 92, Folder 1.

27. "Notes," *JNH* 8 (July 1923): 351.

28. Harvey C. Jackson Jr., "Summary of the Detroit Branch of the Association for the Study of Negro Life and History," *NHB* 26 (October 1962): 84; and "Harvey C. Jackson, a Friend to His Fellowman," *NHB* 7 (June 1944): 201, 214.

29. "Proceedings of the Spring Conference of the Association for the Study of Negro Life and History Held in Baltimore, April 5th and 6th, 1923," *JNH* 8 (July 1923): 355. Bethune's paper, "A Better Understanding Essential to Genuine Co-operation," was delivered at the annual meeting in Atlanta, Georgia, in late October 1923. See "Proceedings of the Eighth Annual Meeting of the Association for the Study of Negro Life and History Held in Atlanta, Georgia, October 24, 25, and 26, 1923," *JNH* 9

(January 1924): 105. For a discussion of Burrough's paper, see "Proceedings of the Spring Conference of the Association for the Study of Negro Life and History Held in Philadelphia, April 3 and 4, 1924," *JNH* 9 (July 1924): 275–380.

30. For a discussion of the curriculum at Nannie Burrough's school and her relationship with Woodson, see Traki L. Taylor, "'Womanhood Glorified': Nannie Helen Burroughs and the National Training School for Women and Girls, Inc., 1909–1945," *Journal of African American History* 87 (Fall 2002): 390–402.

31. "Proceedings of the Annual Meeting of the Association for the Study of Negro Life and History, Held in St. Louis, Missouri, October 21 to 25, 1928," *JNH* 14 (January 1929): 1–11.

32. "Proceedings of the Association for the Study of Negro Life and History Held in Washington, D.C., October 27–31, 1929," *JNH* 15 (January 1930): 1–13.

33. "Proceedings of the Thirty-Second Annual Meeting of the Association for the Study of Negro Life and History, Held in Oklahoma City, October 24–26, 1947," *JNH* 33 (January 1948): 1–6.

34. Audrey Thomas McCluskey, "In Pursuit of Unalienable Rights: Mary McLeod Bethune in Historical Perspective (1875–1955)," in *Mary McLeod Bethune: Building a Better World,* ed. Audrey Thomas McCluskey and Elaine M. Smith, 6 (Bloomington: Indiana University Press, 1999); Sadie Iola Daniel, *Women Builders* (Washington, D.C.: Associated, 1970), 109; and Rackham Holt, *Mary McLeod Bethune: A Biography* (New York: Doubleday, 1964), 266.

35. Elaine M. Smith, "Bethune, Mary McLeod," in *Black Women in America: An Historical Encyclopedia, Volume I: A-L,* ed. Darlene Clark Hine, Elsa Barkley-Brown, and Rosalyn Terborg-Penn, 121 (Bloomington: Indiana University Press, 1993).

36. McCluskey, "In Pursuit," 13; Mary McLeod Bethune, "The Association for the Study of Negro Life and History: Its Contributions to Our Modern Life," *JNH* 20 (October 1935): 409; Bethune, "Clarifying Our Vision with Facts," *JNH* 23 (January 1938): 10–15; Emma Gelders Sterne, *Mary McLeod Bethune* (New York: Knopf, 1957), 234; and Mary McLeod Bethune, "The Adaptation of the History of the Negro to the Capacity of the Child," *JNH* 24 (January 1939): 9–13.

37. Mary McLeod Bethune Papers, The Bethune Foundation Collection, Part 1: Writings, Diaries, Scrapbooks, Biographical Materials, and Files on the National Youth Administration and Women's Organizations, 1918–1955 (Bethesda, Md.: University Publications of America), reel 2.

38. Mary McLeod Bethune, "My Last Will and Testament," in McCluskey and Smith, *Mary McLeod Bethune,* 58–59.

39. Mary McLeod Bethune, "True Leadership is Timeless," *NHB* 13 (May 1950): 173.

40. The Papers of Carter G. Woodson and the Association for the Study of Negro Life and History, 1915–1950 (Bethesda, Md.: University Publications of America), reel 10.

41. Carter G. Woodson, "What's Behind 'The Negro History Bulletin,'" *NHB* 7 (October 1943): 18.

42. Carter G. Woodson, "Negro Historians of Our Times," *NHB* 8 (April 1945), 155–59, 166.

43. "Wilhelmina M. Crosson in Mexico," *NHB* 9 (June 1946): 206, 213; and "Wil-

helmina M. Crosson Reports on Intercultural Education in Mexico," *NHB* 10 (December 1946): 55–60, 68–71.

44. See Carter G. Woodson, "Supplying Children's Literature," *NHB* 9 (May 1946): 181.

45. "Always Aim Higher," *NHB* 8 (January 1945): 85; and "Lesson Plan Grade III–VI," *NHB* 12 (December 1948): 61.

46. Mary L. Williams, "'For My People,' A Re-Examination," *NHB* 7 (March 1944): 129–30.

47. Dorothy B. Porter, "Negro Women in Our Wars," *NHB* 7 (June 1944): 195–96, 215.

48. Jessie P. Guzman, "The Social Contributions of the Negro Woman Since 1940," *NHB* 11 (January 1948): 86–94.

49. "The Saturday Morning Art Class," *NHB* 5 (April 1942): 158. For a discussion of Jones's life and work, see Romare Bearden and Harry Henderson, *A History of African-American Artists* (New York: Pantheon Books, 1993), 381–88.

50. "Book of the Month," *NHB* 8 (January 1945): 85–86.

51. "Books," *NHB* 2 (October 1938): 6.

52. "Jane D. Shackelford and Her Book," *NHB* 2 (November 1938): 16.

53. "Jane Dabney Shackelford Receives Nation-Wide Praise," *NHB* 8 (February 1945): 107, 118.

54. "A Tribute to Jane Dabney Shackelford and Her Book, 'My Happy Days,'" *NHB* 9 (April 1946): 166.

55. "School News," *NHB* 1 (October 1937): 7; and "School News," *NHB* 2 (November 1937): 3.

56. Jessie H. Roy, "Some Personal Recollections of Dr. Woodson," *NHB* 28 (Summer 1965): 186.

57. Woodson, "Negro Historians," 19, 16–20.

58. "The Passing of Miss Lillian A. Duckett," *NHB* 12 (June 1949): 202–3; Carter G. Woodson, "Negro Women Eligible to Be Daughters of the American Revolution," *NHB* 7 (November 1943): 36, 39; "Chicago Goes Forward with Madeline R. Morgan," *NHB* 6 (February 1943): 112, 118; "Rachel C. McNeill, a Resourceful Teacher," *NHB* 6 (February 1943): 113, 119; "Mrs. Helen A. Whiting and the Children," *NHB* 2 (November 1938): 16; and "Miss L. A. Duckett and Her Pupils," *NHB* 2 (October 1938): 5.

59. Stephanie Shaw, *What a Woman Ought to Be and Do: Black Professional Women Workers During the Jim Crow Era* (Chicago: University of Chicago Press, 1996), 2.

60. Gloria T. Hull, *Color, Sex, and Poetry: Three Women Writers of the Harlem Renaissance* (Bloomington: Indiana University Press, 1987), 7.

61. Bettina Aptheker, *Woman's Legacy: Essays on Race, Sex, and Class in American History* (Amherst: University of Massachusetts Press, 1982); Jean Fagan Yellin, "Du Bois' *Crisis* and Woman's Suffrage," *Massachusetts Review* 14 (Spring 1973): 365–75; and Morton, *Disfigured Images,* 55–66.

Chapter 5: The Origins of a Creative Scholar and Historian, 1899–1928

1. The Progressive era meant different things to different people. As Glenda Elizabeth Gilmore recently noted, "One group's attempts to introduce order into society might depend on controlling another group's behavior." See Glenda Elizabeth

Gilmore, "An Overview of the Progressive Era," in *Who Were the Progressives?* ed. Glenda Elizabeth Gilmore, 3 (Boston: Bedford, 2002).

2. Rayford W. Logan, *The Negro in American Life and Thought: The Nadir, 1877–1901* (New York: Dial, 1954); and Rayford W. Logan, *The Betrayal of the Negro from Rutherford B. Hayes to Woodrow Wilson,* enlarged ed. (New York: Collier, 1968), 11.

3. Kenneth Goings, *Mammy and Uncle Mose: Black Collectibles and American Stereotyping* (Bloomington: Indiana University Press, 1994), 4.

4. James Allen et al., *Without Sanctuary: Lynching Photography in America* (Sante Fe: Twin Palms Publishers, 2000), 12; and Philip Dray, *At the Hands of Persons Unknown: The Lynching of Black America* (New York: Random House, 2002), 49.

5. National Association for the Advancement of Colored People, *Thirty Years of Lynching in the United States, 1889–1918* (New York: NAACP National Office, 1919), 13. For a detailed account of the lynching of Hose, see Dray, *At the Hands,* 4–16.

6. Allen et al., *Without Sanctuary,* 10.

7. August Meier and Elliott Rudwick, *Black History and the Historical Profession, 1915–1980* (Urbana: University of Illinois Press, 1986), 4.

8. For a discussion of academic racism that addresses the Progressive Era, see Michael R. Winston, "Through the Back Door: Academic Racism and the Negro Scholar in Historical Perspective," *Daedalus* 100 (Summer 1971): 678–719; and I. A. Newby, ed., *The Development of Segregationist Thought* (Homewood, Ill.: Dorsey, 1968).

9. Albert Bushnell Hart, *The Southern South* (New York: Appleton, 1910), 105.

10. Earl Lewis, "To Turn As on a Pivot: Writing African Americans into a History of Overlapping Diasporas," *The American Historical Review* 100 (June 1995): 765–87.

11. Ellen Fitzpatrick, *History's Memory: Writing America's Past, 1880–1980* (Cambridge, Mass.: Harvard University Press, 2002), 91.

12. Peter Novick, *That Noble Dream: The "Objectivity Question" and the American Historical Profession* (Cambridge: Cambridge University Press, 1998), 74–84.

13. Ernst A. Breisach, *American Progressive History: An Experiment in Modernization* (Chicago: University of Chicago Press, 1993), 79–80.

14. For a discussion of Marable's "corrective" principle of African American studies, see Manning Marable, "Black Studies and the Black Intellectual Tradition," *Race and Reason* 4 (1997–1998): 3. For Phillips's ideas, see Ulrich Bonnell Phillips, *American Negro Slavery: A Survey of the Supply, Employment and Control of Negro Labor as Determined by the Plantation Regime* (Baton Rouge: Louisiana State University Press, 1989); and John David Smith and John C. Inscoe, eds., *Ulrich Bonnell Phillips: A Southern Historian and His Critics* (New York: Greenwood Press, 1990), 2. For Du Bois's and Woodson's responses to Phillips, see W. E. B. Du Bois, "Book Review of *American Negro Slavery,*" *American Political Science Review* 12 (November 1918): 722–26; and Carter G. Woodson, "Book Review of *American Negro Slavery,*" *Mississippi Valley Historical Review* 5 (March 1919): 480–82. According to Meier and Rudwick, the first systematic scholarly critique of Phillips came in 1944 with Richard Hofstadter's essay, "U. B. Phillips and the Plantation Legend," published in *Journal of Negro History.* See Meier and Rudwick, *Black History,* 241.

15. Winston, "Through the Back Door," 684–87.

16. William M. Banks, *Black Intellectuals: Race and Responsibility in American Life* (New York: Norton, 1996), 33.

17. V. P. Franklin, *Living Our Stories, Telling Our Truths: Autobiography and the*

Making of the African-American Intellectual Tradition (New York: Scribner's, 1995), 15; V. P. Franklin and Bettye Collier-Thomas, "Biography, Race Vindication, and African-American Intellectuals: Introductory Essay," *JNH* 81 (Winter-Autumn 1996): 1, 14. For other discussions of "race vindication," see articles in "Vindicating the Race: Contributions to African-American Intellectual History," 80th Anniversary Year, *JNH* 81 (Winter–Autumn 1996).

18. Kevin K. Gaines, *Uplifting the Race: Black Leadership, Politics, and Culture in the Twentieth Century* (Chapel Hill: University of North Carolina Press, 1996), 75.

19. John Hope Franklin, *From Slavery to Freedom: A History of Negro Americans* (New York: Vintage, 1969), 397.

20. Goings, *Mammy and Uncle Mose,* xiii, 40, 48.

21. Adam Hochschild, *King Leopold's Ghost: A Story of Greed, Terror, and Heroism in Colonial Africa* (New York: Houghton, 1998), 233; and Annie E. Coombes, *Reinventing Africa: Museums, Material Culture and Popular Culture* (New Haven, Conn.: Yale University Press, 1994). For further discussions of the detrimental impact of colonialism on Africa and the violent nature of the colonial conquest, see A. Adu Boahen, *African Perspectives on Colonialism* (Baltimore: Johns Hopkins University Press, 1987); Festus Ugboaja Ohaegbulam, *Towards an Understanding of the African Experience from Historical and Contemporary Perspectives* (New York: University Press of America, 1990); Walter Rodney, *How Europe Underdeveloped Africa* (Washington, D.C.: Howard University Press, 1981); and Sven Lindqvist, *"Exterminate All the Brutes": One Man's Odyssey into the Heart of Darkness and the Origins of European Genocide* (New York: New Press, 1996).

22. Anthony M. Platt, *E. Franklin Frazier Reconsidered* (New Brunswick, N.J.: Rutgers University Press, 1991), 11.

23. The biographical information on Greene's early life, before he began working closely with Woodson, is limited. There are several sources on his life through the 1920s. In 1987, Arvarh E. Strickland edited *Working with Carter G. Woodson,* Greene's diary covering several years of when he worked with Woodson. Based upon personal interviews, Strickland briefly outlined Greene's life from 1899 until 1988. In the Papers of Lorenzo Johnston Greene, there are several documents shedding light on Greene's early life. In various letters to his close friends, he shares stories from his childhood. His extensive curriculum vitae, revised in 1988, helps fill in some of the gaps in reconstructing his long life. Most important, there exists in his papers an undated, ten-and-a-half page biographical sketch of Greene that succinctly chronicles his life and thought until the late 1940s. This document is very informative and will be cited in the remaining text as Lorenzo Johnston Greene, unpublished biographical sketch, The Papers of LJG, container 1, folder 8.

24. Greene, unpublished biographical sketch.

25. Greene, unpublished biographical sketch.

26. Arvarh E. Strickland, ed., introduction to *Working with Carter G. Woodson, the Father of Black History: A Diary, 1928–1930, Lorenzo J. Greene,* (Baton Rouge: Louisiana State University Press, 1989), xviii; and Greene, unpublished biographical sketch. For a provocative discussion of working-class resistance and consciousness, see Robin D. G. Kelley, *Race Rebels: Culture, Politics, and the Black Working Class* (New York: Free Press, 1994).

27. Greene, unpublished biographical sketch; and Robert S. Lynd and Helen Merrell Lynd, *Middletown: A Study in American Culture* (New York: Harcourt, 1956), 163–64.

28. Strickland, introduction to *Working,* xix.

29. Greene, unpublished biographical sketch; Strickland, introduction to *Working,* xix–xx.

30. Greene, unpublished biographical sketch.

31. For early biographical information on Du Bois, see David Levering Lewis, *W. E. B. Du Bois: Biography of a Race* (New York: Holt, 1993).

32. Rayford W. Logan, *Howard University: The First One Hundred Years, 1867–1967* (New York: New York University Press, 1969), 160; and Kelly Miller, "Historic Background of the Negro Physician," *JNH* 1 (April 1916): 108. Also see, Darlene Clark Hine, "To Heal the Race: African-American Health Care Professionals in Historical Perspective," in Darlene Clark Hine, *Speak Truth to Power: Black Professional Class in United States History* (New York: Carlson, 1996), 181–92.

33. Strickland, introduction to *Working,* xxi.

34. Logan, *Howard University,* 162, 223–24.

35. Mary Gibson Hundley, *The Dunbar Story* (New York: Vantage, 1965); and Kenneth Robert Janken, *Rayford W. Logan and the Dilemma of the African-American Intellectual* (Amherst: University of Massachusetts Press, 1993).

36. See Strickland, *Working,* 296, 336, 398.

37. Kwame Wes Alford, "A Prophet without Honor: William Leo Hansberry and the Origins of the Discipline of Black Studies" (PhD diss., University of Missouri–Columbia, 1998), 79–80; "The Passing of Alain Leroy Locke," *Phylon,* 15 (3rd Quarter 1954), 243. Also see Beth J. Singer, "Alain Locke Remembered," in *The Critical Pragmatism of Alain Locke: A Reader on Value Theory, Aesthetics, Community, Culture, Race, and Education,* ed. Leonard Harris, 327–33 (New York: Rowman, 1999).

38. Greene, unpublished biographical sketch; and Strickland, *Working,* 63.

39. Raymond Wolters, *The New Negro on Campus: Black College Rebellions of the 1920s* (New Jersey: Princeton University Press, 1975), 73, 76, 95.

40. Wolters, *New Negro on Campus,* 70–136.

41. Greene to Tolson, 28 July 1948, Papers of LJG, container 59, folder 12.

42. Lorenzo Johnston Greene, English 32, Part II notebook, 1924, Papers of LJG, container 40, folder 2.

43. Arvarh E. Strickland, ed., *Selling Black History for Carter G. Woodson: A Diary, 1930–1933, by Lorenzo J. Greene* (Columbia: University of Missouri Press, 1996), 290, 300, 383.

44. W. E. B. Du Bois, "The Negro Bourgeoisie," in *W. E. B. Du Bois: A Reader,* ed. Meyer Weinberg, 258 (New York: Harper, 1970).

45. Platt, *E. Franklin Frazier Reconsidered,* 11.

46. Greene, "To the Unknown Soldier," Papers of LJG, container 100, folder 7.

47. Greene, "The King's Jester," Papers of LJG, container 100, folder 7.

48. Greene, "To the Clouds," Papers of LJG, container 100, folder 7.

49. Greene, "To My Sister," Papers of LJG, container 100, folder 7.

50. Greene, "To Cynthia (The Moon)," Papers of LJG, container 100, folder 7.

51. Greene, "Class Poem to Howard," Papers of LJG, container 100, folder 7.

52. Greene, "Class Poem."

53. Strickland, *Working,* 398; and Greene, unpublished biographical sketch.

54. Harry Washington Greene, *Holders of Doctorates among American Negroes,* 23, 30, 34.

55. Strickland, *Working,* 295.

56. Lorenzo Johnston Greene, "Dr. Carter G. Woodson: The Man as I Knew Him," Papers of LJG, Container 92, Folder 1, 8–9.

57. Lorenzo Johnston Greene, "Love," Papers of LJG, container 100, folder, 7.

58. John S. Mbiti, *Introduction to African Religion,* 2nd rev. ed. (London: Heinemann, 1991), 75.

59. Lorenzo Johnston Greene, "To Beatrice," Papers of LJG, container 100, folder 7.

60. T. Willard Hunter, *The Spirit of Charles Lindbergh: Another Dimension* (Lanham, Md.: Madison Books, 1993); Susan M. Gray, *Charles A. Lindbergh and the American Dilemma: The Conflict of Technology and Human Values* (Bowling Green, Ohio: Bowling Green State University Popular Press, 1988), 14; Arthur Hooely, ed., *The Spirit of St. Louis: One Hundred Poems* (New York: Doran, 1927); L. Goldstein, "Lindbergh in 1927: The Response of Poets to the Poem of Fact," *Prospects* 5 (1980): 292–315; and Perry D. Luckett, *Charles A. Lindbergh: A Bio-Bibliography* (New York: Greenwood, 1986).

61. Lorenzo Johnston Greene, "To Lindberg," Papers of LJG, container 100, folder 7. Greene misspelled Linbergh's name, omitting the h. This does not appear to have been a typo, because he made the same mistake when sent a copy of this poem to the Missouri Historical Society in 1977.

62. Lorenzo Johnston Greene to the Missouri Historical Society, 19 May 1977, Papers of LJG, container 100, folder 7. According to evidence in Greene's papers, he shared only one other poem in this fashion.

63. Lorenzo Johnston Greene, "Man," Papers of LJG, container 100, folder 7.

64. Lorenzo Johnston Greene, "Exhortation," Papers of LJG, container 100, folder 7.

65. Scholarship on the Harlem Renaissance abounds. See, for instance, Nathan Irvin Huggins, *Harlem Renaissance* (New York: Oxford University Press, 1971); Arna Bontemps, ed., *The Harlem Renaissance Remembered: Essays* (New York: Dodd, 1972); Cary D. Wintz, *Black Culture and the Harlem Renaissance* (Houston, Tex.: Rice University Press, 1988); Victor A Kramer, ed., *The Harlem Renaissance Re-examined* (New York: AMS, 1988); George Hutchinson, *The Harlem Renaissance in Black and White* (Cambridge, Mass.: Belknap, 1995); Cary D. Wintz, ed., *The Emergence of the Harlem Renaissance* (New York: Garland, 1996); and Harold Bloom, ed., *Harlem Renaissance* (Philadelphia: Chelsea, 2004).

66. George S. Schuyler, "The Negro-Art Hokum," *Nation,* June 16, 1926, 662–63.

67. Langston Hughes, "The Negro Artist and the Racial Mountain," *Nation,* June 23, 1926, 692–94.

68. For a discussion of the "Genteel School" and other schools of thought during the Harlem Renaissance, see Arthur P. Davis and Michael W. Peplow, eds., *The New Negro Renaissance: An Anthology* (New York: Holt, 1975).

69. Lorenzo Johnston Greene, "The New Negro," Papers of LJG, container 100, folder 7.

70. Greene, "Of God," Papers of LJG, container 100, folder 7.

71. Greene, "Of God."

72. David Levering Lewis, *When Harlem Was in Vogue* (New York: Oxford University Press, 1989), 173; Davis and Peplow, *New Negro Renaissance,* 477; and J. A. Rogers, "Jazz At Home," in *The New Negro: An Interpretation,* ed. Alain Locke, 216–24 (New York: Boni, 1925).

73. Lorenzo Johnston Greene, "Jazz," Papers of LJG, container 100, folder 7.

74. Strickland, *Working,* 392.

Chapter 6: An Unselfish Worker for the ASNLH, 1928–33

1. Arvarh E. Strickland, ed., *Working with Carter G. Woodson, the Father of Black History: A Diary, 1928–1930, Lorenzo J. Greene* (Baton Rouge: Louisiana State University Press, 1989) 149; and Lorenzo Johnston Greene, "Dr. Carter G. Woodson: The Man as I Knew Him," Papers of LJG, Container 92, Folder 1, 9–12.

2. Greene, "Dr. Carter G. Woodson," 12; and Strickland, ed., *Working,* 31.

3. Strickland, *Working,* 11.

4. Strickland, *Working,* 20.

5. Strickland, *Working,* 35, 76.

6. Strickland, *Working,* 40.

7. Strickland, *Working,* 66.

8. Strickland, *Working,* 145.

9. Charlotte Forten, "Life on the Sea Islands," in *Slavery in the South,* ed. Harvey Wish, 95–96 (New York: Noonday, 1972).

10. W. E. B. Du Bois, *The Souls of Black Folk* (New York: Knopf, 1993), 2, 150–51.

11. Strickland, *Working,* 160.

12. Strickland, *Working,* 161–62.

13. Strickland, *Working,* 145.

14. Strickland, *Working,* 145, 124, 76.

15. Strickland, *Working,* 60.

16. Strickland, *Working,* 76–77.

17. Strickland, *Working,* 177–94.

18. Strickland, *Working,* 464.

19. Strickland, *Working,* 282, 325.

20. Strickland, *Working,* 421, 396.

21. John Higham, *History: The Development of Historical Studies in the United States* (New Jersey: Prentice, 1965), 94–96, 99–100.

22. See Lorenzo Johnston Greene, "Slaveholding New England and Its Awakening," *JNH* 13 (October 1928): 492–533.

23. Lorenzo Greene and Carter G. Woodson, *The Negro Wage Earner* (Washington: Association for the Study of Negro Life and History [ASNLH], 1930), vi; see also "Annual Report of the Director," *JNH* 16 (October 1931): 349–58.

24. Strickland, *Working,* 222.

25. Greene and Woodson, *Negro Wage Earner,* 35.

26. Greene and Woodson, *Negro Wage Earner,* 47.
27. Greene and Woodson, *Negro Wage Earner,* 67–70.
28. Greene and Woodson, *Negro Wage Earner,* 75–246.
29. "Book Reviews," *JNH* 16 (July 1931): 341.
30. Strickland, *Working,* 221.
31. Strickland, *Working,* 222, 384, 385.
32. Strickland, *Working,* 365–66.
33. Arvarh E. Strickland, ed., *Selling Black History for Carter G. Woodson: A Diary, 1930–1933, by Lorenzo J. Greene* (Columbia: University of Missouri Press, 1996),114.
34. Strickland, *Selling,* 199–200.
35. Strickland, *Selling,* 270, 368.
36. Lorenzo Johnston Greene, "Sidelight on Economic Conditions Among Negroes in the South During the Depression, 1930," Papers of LJG, container 93, folder 7, 7.
37. Greene, "Sidelight," 15–16.
38. Greene, "Sidelight."
39. Greene, "Sidelight," 18–19.
40. Greene, "Sidelight," 20.
41. Carter G. Woodson, *The Rural Negro* (New York: Russell, 1969), xv–xvi.
42. Jacqueline Goggin, *Carter G. Woodson: A Life in Black History* (Baton Rouge: Louisiana State University Press, 1993), 73–74; August Meier and Elliott Rudwick, *Black History and the Historical Profession, 1915–1980* (Urbana: University of Illinois Press, 1986), 82.
43. Myra Colson Callis is listed as the co-author, since she contributed the final chapter, "The Household Employment of Negroes." See Lorenzo Johnston Greene and Myra Colson Callis, *The Employment of Negroes in the District of Columbia* (Washington: ASNLH, 1932), 71–89.
44. Greene and Callis, *Employment of Negroes,* 69.
45. Strickland, *Selling,* 159.
46. Strickland, *Selling,* 281.
47. Strickland, *Selling,* 19–20.

Chapter 7: Discovering His Mission at Lincoln University, 1933–44

1. Greene to "Mildred," [fragment of a letter], circa 1973, Papers of LJG, container 65, folder 1.
2. Lorenzo Greene, Gary R. Kremer, and Antonio F. Holland, *Missouri's Black Heritage* (Columbia: University of Missouri Press, 1993), 2, 148–52.
3. William Sherman Savage, *The History of Lincoln University* (Jefferson City, Mo.: New Day, 1939).
4. Raymond Wolters, *The New Negro on Campus: Black College Rebellions of the 1920s* (New Jersey: Princeton University Press, 1975), 194.
5. Wolters, *New Negro,* 202–29.
6. Gary R. Kremer, "Lincoln University, Black Culture Mecca of the Midwest, 1921–1955," in *Black Heartland: African American Life, the Middle West, and the Meaning of American Regionalism,* ed. Gerald Early, 40–41 (St. Louis: Washington University, 1997).

7. Typed-out course evaluations, circa 1933–1943, Papers of LJG, container 21, folder 4.

8. Greene to "Mildred" [fragment of a letter], circa 1973, Papers of LJG, container 65, folder 1.

9. Michael R. Winston, "Through the Back Door: Academic Racism and the Negro Scholar in Historical Perspective," *Daedalus* 100 (Summer 1971): 702.

10. Savage, *History of Lincoln University,* 264–65.

11. Greene to Woodson, 21 February 1934, and Greene to Woodson, 7 January 1937, Papers of LJG, container 74, folder 7.

12. Greene to Woodson, 30 November 1937, Papers of LJG, container 74, folder 7.

13. Papers of LJG, container 100, folder 7.

14. "To a Brown Girl," Papers of LJG, container 100, folder 7.

15. Lorenzo Johnston Greene, "Lincoln University's Involvement in the Sharecropper Demonstration in Southeast Missouri, 1939–1940," *Missouri Historical Review* (October 1987): 26.

16. Greene, "Lincoln University's Involvement," 25; Arvarh Strickland, "The Plight of the People in the Sharecroppers' Demonstration in Southeast Missouri," *Missouri Historical Review* (July 1987): 403; and Lorenzo Johnston Greene, "Lincoln University's Involvement with the Sharecropper Demonstration in Southeast Missouri, 1939–1940," Papers of LJG, container 93, folder 4. For a detailed discussion of the demonstration, see Louis Cantor, *A Prologue to the Protest Movement: The Missouri Sharecropper Roadside Demonstration of 1939* (Durham, N.C.: Duke University Press, 1969).

17. Strickland, "Plight," 403–4.

18. Strickland, "Plight," 403–4. In the early 1970s, Greene said that she was one of the two students who stood out in his memory. He was impressed by this Boston native's devotion to social activism. At Greene's advice, she got master's degree in psychiatric social work at Boston University, then married a Jamaican and "became famous all over the island for her volunteer work." See a letter from Greene to "Mildred" [fragment of a letter], circa 1973, Papers of LJG, container 65, folder 1.

19. Greene to "Mildred" [fragment of a letter], circa 1973; and Strickland, "Plight," 413.

20. Greene to Wallace, 21 May 1939; and John Fischer to Greene, 6 June 1939, Papers of LJG, container 40, folder 10.

21. Greene, "Lincoln University's Involvement," 45, 50.

22. Papers of LJG, container 13, folder 10; container 33, folder 3.

23. Greene to the American Council of Learned Societies, 23 October 1941; Donald Goodchild to Greene, 16 December 1941, Papers of LJG, container 29, folder 1.

24. Greene to John E. Eubanks, 21 November 1941, Papers of LJG, container 28, folder 3.

25. Greene to George Braxton Pegram, 21 January 1942, Papers of LJG, container 33, folder 2.

26. Greene to Powell, 25 February 1942, Papers of LJG, container 33, folder 3.

27. Greene to James E. Shepard, 21 January 1942, Papers of LJG, container 34.

28. On June 20, 1942, Greene wrote a letter to Woodson informing him that Columbia University Press expected to publish his study "sometime between August

1–15." Whatever the case may have been, we know that the study appeared by the winter months of 1942 at the latest. See Papers of LJG, container 74, folder 8.

29. William M. Banks, *Black Intellectuals: Race and Responsibility in American Life* (New York: W. W. Norton, 1996), 130.

30. August Meier and Elliott Rudwick, *Black History and the Historical Profession, 1915–1980* (Urbana: University of Illinois Press, 1986), 105–6; Harvey Wish, *The American Historian: A Social-Intellectual History of the Writing of the American Past* (New York: Oxford University Press, 1960), 313–15; and Merle Curti, *The Social Ideas of American Educators* (New Jersey: Pageant, 1959).

31. Greene to Reddick, 17 February 1943, Papers of LJG, container 33, folder 5; and Greene, "Dr. Carter G. Woodson," 28, 29.

32. Lorenzo Johnston Greene, preface to *The Negro in Colonial New England, 1620–1776* (New York: Atheneum, 1968), 66.

33. Greene, *Negro in Colonial New England,* 99.

34. Greene, *Negro in Colonial New England,* 123.

35. Greene, *Negro in Colonial New England,* 213, 167, 191–92, 249.

36. Greene, *Negro in Colonial New England,* 299–300, 303, 312, 314.

37. Carter G. Woodson, "Book Review," *JNH* 28 (October 1943): 478–81; Greene to Reid, 12 April 1943, Papers of LJG, container 33, folder 6; and Clarence A. Bacote, "Black Merchandise in New England," *Phylon* 4 (2nd Quarter 1943): 185–87. Woodson also praised Greene's book in a less scholarly fashion in the *Bulletin,* February 1943. Horace Mann Bond, another black scholar, commented that he did "not recall ever having read a historical work with more satisfaction or pleasure."

38. Elizabeth Donnan, "Review of Books," *American Historical Review* 48 (July 1943): 797–98; Harvey Wish, "Book Reviews," *Journal of Southern History* 10 (February 1944): 96–97; Paul Lewinson, "Book Reviews," *Mississippi Valley Historical Review* 30 (September 1943): 276–77; Oscar Handlin, "Book Reviews," *New England Quarterly* 16 (June 1943): 346–47; and Harry J. Walker, "Book Reviews," *American Journal of Sociology* 49 (January 1944): 375–76. Other reviews written by white scholars appeared in Harvard University's *Isis,* as well as *American Sociological Review, Crozier Quarterly, Historical Bulletin, Journal of Economic History, Catholic Historical Review,* and *Essex Institute Historical Review.*

39. Papers of LJG, container 33, folder 5.

40. Meier to Greene, 28 August 1964; Meier to Arthur Wang, circa 1964; Greene to Meier, 12 October 1966; Meier to Greene, 11 March 1968; and Greene to Meier, 25 March 1968, Papers of LJG, container 31, folder 4. Benjamin Quarles, preface to *The Negro in Colonial New England* by Lorenzo Johnston Greene (New York: Atheneum, 1968).

41. William D. Piersen, *Black Yankees: The Development of an Afro-American Subculture in Eighteenth-Century New England* (Amherst: University of Massachusetts Press, 1988); and Joanne Pope Melish, *Disowning Slavery: Gradual Emancipation and "Race" in New England, 1780–1860* (Ithaca, N.Y.: Cornell University Press, 1998).

42. Woodson did not advertise Greene's study extensively in the *Bulletin.* He asked Greene to submit a simple article about his study to the magazine so that the nonprofessional scholar could develop an appreciation for his work. See Thomasina Talley, "Another Negro Historian—Lorenzo Johnston Greene," *NHB* 6 (November 1942): 38–40, 46.

43. Greene to Reddick, 20 January 1943, Papers of LJG, container 33, folder 5; and Greene to Elsie M. Mountain, 11 February 1943, Papers of LJG, container 31, folder 6.

44. Greene to Duffy, 12 March 1943, Papers of LJG, container 27, folder 1; and Greene to Duffy, 25 September 1943, Papers of LJG, container 9, folder 4.

45. "Thomasina Talley, Concert Pianist," n. d., Papers of LJG, container 2, folder 7; Arvarh E. Strickland, ed., *Selling Black History for Carter G. Woodson: A Diary, 1930–1933, by Lorenzo J. Greene* (Columbia: University of Missouri Press, 1996), 9; Greene to Reddick, 17 February 1943, Papers of LJG, container 33, folder 5.

46. Papers of LJG, container 74, folder 8; Greene to "Fellow Worker," 12 January 1942, container 42, folder 3.

47. Elsie M. Mountain to Greene, 2 January 1935; Greene to Mountain, 17 February 1944; Greene to Mountain, June 1944; Greene to Mountain, 23 September 1944; and Greene to Mountain, 28 November 1944, Papers of LJG, container 31, folder 6.

48. Woodson to Greene, 1 July 1942; and Greene to Woodson, 17 January 1944, Papers of LJG, container 74, folder 8.

49. Greene to William Hastie, 12 December 1941; Hastie to Greene, 15 December 1941; Greene to Hastie, 23 February 1942; Hastie to Greene, 26 February 1942; Greene to Hastie, 21 March 1942; Greene to Hastie, 18 June 1942; Greene to Hastie, 5 November 1942; and Greene to Hastie, 16 November 1942, Papers of LJG, container 29, folder 5.

50. Greene to Caliver, 27 January 1942; Caliver to Greene, 10 February 1942, Papers of LJG, container 26, folder 6; Greene to Berry, 5 March 1942; Greene to Berry, 14 March 1942; Greene to Berry, 21 March 1942; and Greene to Bethune, 5 November 1942, Papers of LJG, container 25, folder 7.

51. Greene to Barnes, 6 November 1942, Papers of LJG, container 25, folder 6.

52. Lorenzo Johnston Greene, "Jefferson City Negroes Share in the 'Food Fights for Freedom' Campaign," unpublished speech broadcasted over KWOS, Jefferson City, Missouri, 2 December 1943.

53. Lorenzo Johnston Greene, unpublished biographical sketch.

Chapter 8: Life at Lincoln University, 1944–50

1. Greene to Davis, 28 August 1944, Papers of LJG, container 27.

2. Greene to Dawson, 24 March 1944; Dawson to Greene, 7 April 1944; Greene to Dawson, 10 May 1944; and Scruggs to Greene, 15 September 1944, Papers of LJG, container 36, folder 2.

3. Greene to Scruggs, 2 March 1945, Papers of LJG, container 36, folder 2.

4. Scruggs to Greene, 7 March 1945, Papers of LJG, container 36, folder 2.

5. Scruggs to Special Committee Members, 7 March 1945, Papers of LJG, container 36, folder 2.

6. Greene to Scruggs, 10 March 1945, Papers of LJG, container 36, folder 2.

7. Greene to Dr. Walter R. Talbot, Chairman, Special Committee, 25 April 1945, Papers of LJG, container 9, folder 4.

8. Greene to Dr. Walter R. Talbot, Chairman, Special Committee, 25 April 1945.

9. Greene to Dr. Walter R. Talbot, Chairman, Special Committee, 25 April 1945.

10. Robert Cotton et al., "Preliminary Report of the Special Committee Appointed

by the President of the University to Consider the Salary Question Raised by Professor Lorenzo Johnston Greene," unpublished report, 7 December 1945, Papers of LJG, container 9, folder 4.

11. Cotton et al., "Preliminary Report," 28–29.

12. Cotton et al., "Preliminary Report," 46–47.

13. Cotton et al., "Preliminary Report," 39.

14. Greene to Dr. T. Thomas Fortune Fletcher, 24 April 1948, Papers of LJG, container 56, folder 12.

15. Lincoln University Faculty to the President and the Board of Curators, circa 1948, Papers of LJG, container 63, folder 5.

16. Greene to Fletcher, 24 April 1948, Papers of LJG, container 56, folder 12.

17. Lorenzo Johnston Greene, "The New England Negro as Seen in Advertisements for Runaway Slaves, *JNH* 29 (April 1944): 127, 131–32, 146.

18. Lorenzo Johnston Greene, "Mutiny on the Slave Ships," *Phylon* 5 (4th Quarter 1944): 346–54.

19. Greene, "Mutiny," 354; and Vincent A. Harding, *There Is a River: The Black Struggle for Freedom in America* (New York: Harcourt, 1981).

20. Review of John Hope Franklin's *From Slavery to Freedom* (1947), n.d., Papers of LJG, container 45, folder 4.

21. Greene to Scruggs, 7 November 1945, Papers of LJG, container 36, folder 2.

22. Greene to Scruggs, 11 October 1946, Papers of LJG, container 34, folder 1; and Scruggs to Greene, 14 January 1947, Papers of LJG, container 36, folder 2.

23. Minutes for a meeting held at Greene's home between Greene, Reedy, and Blue, 21 November 1947, Papers of LJG, container 50, folder 11.

24. Greene to Sterling Brown, 26 March 1948, Papers of LJG, container 55, folder 9; Greene to Benjamin Quarles, 26 March 1948, Papers of LJG, container 58, folder 12; and Greene to Luther Porter Jackson, 13 March 1948, Papers of LJG, container 57, folder 14.

25. Greene to colleagues at Lincoln University, 10 August 1948, Papers of LJG, container 28, folder 7.

26. Greene to Reddick, 26 March 1949, Papers of LJG, container 58, folder 13.

27. Greene to M.B. Tolson, 5 May 1949, Papers of LJG, container 59, folder 12; and Melvin B. Tolson, "The Negro Scholar," unpublished copy, Papers of LJG, container 51, folder 5.

28. Greene to colleagues at Lincoln University, 4 August 1949, Papers of LJG, container 50, folder 12.

29. For an overview of communism, see Ellen Schrecker, *The Age of McCarthyism: A Brief History with Documents* (Boston: Bedford, 1994). Also see Gerald Horne, *Communist Front? The Civil Rights Congress, 1946–1956* (London: Associated University Presses, 1988); Horne, *Black Liberation/Red Scare: Ben Chavis and the Communist Party* (Newark: University of Delaware Press, 1994).

30. Shu-yi Yang, "Role of Students in China's Struggle," *Midwest Journal* 1 (Summer 1949): 89–94; W. E. B. Du Bois, "The Freedom to Learn," *Midwest Journal* 1 (Winter 1949): 9–11; and Gary R. Kremer, "Lincoln University, Black Culture Mecca of the Midwest, 1921–1955," in *Black Heartland: African American Life, the Middle*

West, and the Meaning of American Regionalism (St. Louis: Washington University, 1997), 44–45.

31. Greene to Patricia W. Romero, 15 March 1984, Papers of LJG, container 70, folder 8; and William Brewer to Greene, 30 June 1950, Papers of LJG, container 72, folder 8.

32. Kenneth Robert Janken, *Rayford W. Logan and the Dilemma of the African-American Intellectual* (Amherst: University of Massachusetts Press, 1993), 215–18.

33. Greene to Reddick, 13 September 1950, Papers of LJG, container 73, folder 12; Greene to Brewer, 7 October 1950, Papers of LJG, container 72, folder 8; and Brewer to Greene, 12 October 1950, Papers of LJG, container 72, folder 8.

34. Greene to Brewer, 21 October 1950, Papers of LJG, container 72, folder 8.

35. Greene to Hine, 1 November 1985, Papers of LJG, container 29, folder 6.

36. Greene to Logan, 8 November 1950, Papers of LJG, container 73, folder 8; Reddick to Members of the Executive Council of the Association for the Study of Negro Life and History [ASNLH], 1 November 1950, Papers of LJG, container 73, folder 12.

37. Greene to Logan, 8 November 1950, Papers of LJG, container 73, folder 8; Greene to Reddick, 8 November 1950, Papers of LJG, container 73, folder 12; and Logan to Greene, 14 November 1950, Papers of LJG, container 73, folder 8.

38. Greene to President Scruggs, n.d.; and President Scruggs to Lincoln faculty and staff, 7 August 1952, Papers of LJG, container 48, folder 7.

39. Dawson to Greene, 9 June 1956 ; Scruggs to Greene, 30 June 1955; and Greene to Dawson, 18 June 1956, Papers of LJG, container 56, folder 6.

40. Lorenzo Johnston Greene, *Desegregation of Schools in Missouri, 1954–1959: Report to the United States Commission on Civil Rights on Desegregation of Schools in Missouri by the Missouri Advisory Committee,* July 1959, 33.

41. Greene, *Desegregation,* 16, 102.

42. Greene, *Desegregation,* 80–81, 158.

Conclusion

1. See Bakari Kitwana, *The Hip Hop Generation: Young Blacks and the Crisis in African-American Culture* (New York: Basic, 2002), xi–24.

2. Na'im Akbar, *Chains and Images of Psychological Slavery* (New Jersey: New Mind, 1992), 34.

3. Darlene Clark Hine, "The Black Studies Movement: Afrocentric—Traditionalist—Feminist Paradigms for the Next Stage," in Darlene Clark Hine, *HineSight: Black Women and the Re-Construction of American History,* 237 (New York: Carlson, 1994).

4. For refreshing discussions of black Southern culture during the era of segregation, see R. Douglas Hurt, ed., *African American Life in the Rural South, 1900–1950* (Columbia: University of Missouri Press, 2003).

5. Russell L. Adams, "African-American Studies and the State of the Art," in *The African-American Studies Reader,* ed., Nathaniel Norment Jr., 107 (Durham. N.C.: Carolina Academic Press, 2002).

6. Wilson J. Moses, "African American Historiography and the Works of Benjamin Quarles," *The History Teacher* 32 (November 1998), 77.

7. Franklin is the only black historian to write a major autobiography published by a popular press. See John Hope Franklin, *Mirror to America: The Autobiography of John Hope Franklin* (New York: Farrar, 2005).

8. August Meier, "Introduction: Benjamin Quarles and the Historiography of Black America," in Benjamin Quarles, *Black Mosaic: Essays in Afro-American History and Historiography,* 7 (Amherst: The University of Massachusetts Press, 1988).

9. Meier, "Introduction: Benjamin Quarles," 3.

10. Moses, "Historiography," 78.

11. See, for instance, Benjamin Quarles, *Frederick Douglass* (Washington: Associated, 1948); Quarles, *The Negro in the Civil War* (Boston: Little, 1953); Quarles, *The Negro in the American Revolution* (Chapel Hill: University of North Carolina Press, 1961); Quarles, *Lincoln and the Negro* (New York: Oxford University Press, 1962); Quarles, *The Negro in the Making of America* (New York: Collier, 1964); Quarles, *Black Abolitionists* (New York: Oxford University Press, 1969); Quarles, *Blacks on John Brown* (Urbana: University of Illinois Press, 1972); and Quarles, *Allies for Freedom: Blacks and John Brown* (New York: Oxford University Press, 1974).

12. Quarles, *Black Mosaic,* 203.

13. Quarles, *Black Mosaic,* 205.

14. Quarles, *Black Mosaic,* 207.

15. Quarles, *Black Mosaic,* 208.

16. Quarles, *Black Mosaic,* 209.

INDEX

PERO GAGLO DAGBOVIE is an assistant professor of African American history, American history, Comparative Black history, and African American and African studies at Michigan State University.

The New Black Studies Series

Beyond Bondage: Free Women of Color in the Americas *Edited by David Barry Gaspar and Darlene Clark Hine*

The Early Black History Movement, Carter G. Woodson, and Lorenzo Johnston Greene *Pero Gaglo Dagbovie*

The University of Illinois Press
is a founding member of the
Association of American University Presses.

University of Illinois Press
1325 South Oak Street
Champaign, IL 61820-6903
www.press.uillinois.edu